CRITICAL PERSPECTIVES ON POLICE LEADERSHIP

D1612499

KEY THEMES IN POLICING

Series summary: This textbook series is designed to fill a growing need for titles which reflect the importance of incorporating 'evidence-based policing' within Higher Education curriculums. It will reflect upon the changing landscape of contemporary policing as it becomes more politicised, professionalised and scrutinised, and draw out both changes and continuities in its themes.

Series Editors: Megan O'Neill, University of Dundee, Marisa Silvestri, University of Kent and Stephen Tong, Canterbury Christ Church University

Forthcoming

Practical Psychology for Policing – Jason Roach, January 2021

Towards Ethical Policing – Dominic Wood, April 2020

Police Occupational Culture: Research and Practice – Tom Cockcroft, March 2020

Published

Policing the Police: Challenges of Democracy and Accountability – Michael Rowe, February 2020

Miscarriages of Justice: Causes, Consequences and Remedies – Sam Poyser, Angus Nurse and Rebecca Milne, May 2018

Key Challenges in Criminal Investigation – Martin O'Neill, February 2018

Plural Policing: Theory and Practice – Colin Rogers, November 2016

Understanding Police Intelligence Work – Adrian James, April 2016

Editorial advisory board
Paul Quinton, College of Policing
Nick Fyfe, University of Dundee
Jennifer Brown, London School of Economics
Charlotte E. Gill, George Mason University

CRITICAL PERSPECTIVES ON POLICE LEADERSHIP

Claire Davis and Marisa Silvestri

First published in Great Britain in 2020 by

Policy Press
University of Bristol
1-9 Old Park Hill
Bristol
BS2 8BB
UK
t: +44 (0)117 954 5940
pp-info@bristol.ac.uk
www.policypress.co.uk

North America office:
Policy Press
c/o The University of Chicago Press
1427 East 60th Street
Chicago, IL 60637, USA
t: +1 773 702 7700
f: +1 773-702-9756
sales@press.uchicago.edu
www.press.uchicago.edu

British Library Cataloguing in Publication Data
A catalogue record for this book is available from the British Library

Library of Congress Cataloging-in-Publication Data
A catalog record for this book has been requested

978-1-4473-4963-1 hardback
978-1-4473-4964-8 paperback
978-1-4473-4966-2 ePub
978-1-4473-4965-5 ePDF

Cover design by Andrew Corbett
Front cover image: Getty

Contents

List of figures

List of abbreviations

ACPO	Association of Chief Police Officers
BME	black and minority ethnic
EBP	evidence-based policing
HMICFRS	Her Majesty's Inspectorate of Constabulary and Fire and Rescue Services
LGB(T)	lesbian, gay, bisexual (and trans)
NPM	New Public Management
PCC	Police and Crime Commissioner
PEQF	Police Education Qualification Framework

Series preface

Megan O'Neill, Marisa Silvestri and Stephen Tong

The *Key Themes in Policing* series aims to provide relevant and useful books to support the growing number of policing modules on both undergraduate and postgraduate programmes. The series also aims to support all those interested in policing – from criminology, law and policing students and policing professionals to those who wish to join policing services. It also seeks to respond to the call for evidence-based policing led by organisations such as the College of Policing in England and Wales. By producing a range of high-quality, research-informed texts on important areas in policing, contributions to the series support and inform both professional and academic policing curriculums.

Critical Perspectives on Police Leadership, by Claire Davis and Marisa Silvestri, is the seventh publication in the series and explores the important subject of police leadership. Police leadership has experienced significant reform, political criticism and a long period of austerity. Police leadership has sustained interest over a long period of time from the police, public, academics and politicians. The range of leadership styles and approaches used to respond to the continued changes in policing have been subject to much debate. This text provides a critical analysis and solid foundation in outlining key concepts, summarising leadership research and outlining the historical context in which policing and leadership have developed. The book explores the contemporary police leadership context acknowledging the introduction of a professional policing body before analysing theoretical explanations contributing to understandings of police leadership and issues relating to wellbeing and resilience. This book fills an important space in the series and policing curriculum more generally. The text will provide essential reading for students of policing and criminal justice.

Claire Davis is a Lecturer in Criminology at the University of Leicester. Her research interests lie in the sociology of policing, and in particular, the practice and experience of leadership, power and authority, in a policing context. She is an Associate Inspector for Leadership with Her Majesty's Inspectorate of Constabulary and Fire & Rescue Services and the Book Review Editor for *Policing and Society*. *Marisa Silvestri* is a Reader in Criminology at the University of Kent and is a member of the *Key Themes in Policing* series editorial board. Marisa's main research interests include the intersections of gender, crime, justice, policing and organisational cultures. More specifically, her research focuses on the gendered dimensions of policing and police leadership. Marisa has published widely including texts on gender and leadership.

1

Introduction

Contemporary police leadership operates in a highly scrutinised and ever-changing environment. This is particularly so since 2010 and the advent of the Comprehensive Spending Review's announcement of a 20 per cent reduction in central police funding, equating to a saving requirement of £2.4 billion for police constabularies in England and Wales. With an average of 70 per cent of police funding coming from central government, the scale and impact of the cuts to British policing are unprecedented. The increasing financial pressures have necessitated significant organisational and operational reform, and constabularies have had to make concerted moves to understand and reduce demand (Neyroud, 2011a; HMIC, 2014). Despite the political rhetoric of 'protecting the front line', from 2010 to 2018, police officer strength fell by over 21,330, reaching the lowest number of officers since comparable records began in 1996 (Hargreaves et al, 2018; Allen and Zayed, 2019). Police organisations have also had to make fundamental changes to how policing activity is organised and delivered. Police force amalgamation and regionalisation, privatisation, and partnership working are now normalised as 'business as usual' (Manning, 2014; O'Neill, 2014). Combined with other policy reforms, such as changes to police pay and pensions following the Winsor Review (Winsor, 2011), this means that increasing productivity within the context of diminishing resources and the management of low staff morale is an accepted feature of contemporary police leadership (Brogden and Ellison, 2013; De Maillard, 2015). These economic challenges are situated as the responsibility of police leadership, with HMIC (2013: 20) confirming that 'leaders will need to demand more of fewer people, ensuring they can work in different ways, against a backdrop of fewer opportunities to advance, and less advantageous conditions'.

Alongside the reduction in resources, contemporary demand on the police in Britain is also changing. Overall recorded crime has fallen, with the 2015 crime survey for England and Wales reporting the lowest estimate of incidents of crime since it began in 1981 (Office for National Statistics, 2015). However, the picture is complex. Recorded sexual offences have risen significantly, particularly historic cases, as has child sexual exploitation (College of Policing, 2015a; Ministry of Justice, 2015). There are also indications of rising rates of violence.

Recent figures from the Office for National Statistics (2019) show an increase in lower-volume but higher-harm violence: an 8 per cent increase in police-recorded offences involving knives or sharp instruments, a 16 per cent increase in admissions to hospital in England for assaults involving a sharp instrument, and a 14 per cent increase in the number of homicides. However, the data are situated within the context of changes in policing policy, such as the changes to crime recording standards (Home Office, 2018; Office for National Statistics, 2018), the introduction of new legislation and changing rates of reporting practices in domestic abuse (TNS BMRB, 2016; Barlow and Walklate, 2018), and changing policing practices, such as rates of stop and search (Bowling and Weber, 2011; Lennon and Murray, 2018). Therefore, within this context, responding effectively to complex social issues and 'wicked problems' has become a routinised aspect of contemporary police leadership (Grint, 2005a). The global nature of crime and the increasingly complex global security climate, the expanding role of the police in statutory protective arrangements, the role of technology in policing, and the increasing role of the police in the public health field have created 'new' and more 'costly' demands on the police, with a need for specialist expertise (College of Policing, 2015a; Van Dijk and Crofts, 2017). The role of the police in responding to crime and disorder is expanding, and, consequently, police leadership is positioned as a mechanism to achieve this.

In Britain, austerity has centralised the principles of economy and efficiency in the management and organisation of policing; the rhetoric of 'value for money' has, once again, achieved political prominence. Policing in the 21st century, it appears, is increasingly conceptualised in economic terms. Contemporary complexities continue to expose the inadequacies of traditional, top-down, bureaucratic organisational processes (Bayley, 2016; Loveday, 2017). The expansion of the policing task is also under considerable challenge (Millie, 2013; Innes, 2014). The model of 43 police constabularies in England and Wales is under heightened scrutiny and there is a shift towards greater regionalisation and collaboration regarding policing practices. This exposes the tensions between the localisation and centralisation of policing activity. All in all, the demands of the contemporary landscape have intensified the debate about what the role and task of the police are, and has encouraged a re-imagining of policing and of police leadership in a post-austerity context. In this book, we explore the changeful environment within which the police and its leaders operate, and critically assess the usefulness of traditional and yet dominant conceptualisations of police leadership. Underpinned by literature from sociology, criminology, policing and leadership studies, the book aims to problematise conventional discourse about the nature and practice of police leadership. In doing so, it challenges traditional discourse on police leadership and offers a more critical and alternative reading. While the arguments that we make throughout the book have much international resonance, the primary focus of the book is on police leadership in the UK. In this chapter, we begin with an examination of the complexities involved in defining leadership, and through an analysis of the interplay between leadership and management, the prioritisation of leadership over management in dominant discourse will become apparent. The extent to which police leadership represents a distinctive form of leadership will also be explored to reveal the competing narratives of leadership, both inside and outside of the police. In order to make sense of the present, this chapter also provides a critical examination of how police leadership has been imagined over time. Through situating contemporary debates in a historical context, we demonstrate the extent to which contemporary understandings of police leadership reflect a range of historical legacies. We argue that police leadership cannot be separated from the wider social, political and economic context of its time. Rather, we encourage readers to recognise the importance of conceptualising police leadership as a socially constructed process in which leadership is conceived of as a product of historical, cultural and institutional norms, values and processes, as well as institutionally defined power and authorities. Our aim in conceptualising leadership as socially constructed is to challenge the essentialist and deterministic assumptions of dominant ideologies, thereby enabling alternative practices in leadership in the police to emerge.

Defining police leadership

The literature on leadership is vast, incorporating a range of academic disciplines, including management and organisational studies, public administration, politics, economics, psychology, sociology, and education. As an expanding industry, leadership development is a top priority of UK-based organisations in the public and private sector (Gagnon and Collinson, 2014; Ford and Harding, 2007). There is an increasing market among those in leadership positions to understand 'what works' in leadership, as well as a plethora of research that presents various theories, models, typologies, dichotomies, dimensions and classifications of leadership. Despite such attention, there is little consensus about how leadership should be defined within the scholarship (Rost, 1993; Alvesson and Sveningsson, 2003). Encapsulating a broad range of assumptions, leadership remains an essentially 'contested concept', a 'semantic sponge' of different, often conflicting, meanings (Grint, 2005b; Van Dijk et al, 2015). The concept can be substituted for administration, culture, headship, organisation, power, strategy or supervision, and leaders are simultaneously referred to as 'administrators' or 'executives' (Washbush, 2005; Alvesson, 2011). Almost all individual, relational or organisational activity, it seems, can be understood as leadership.

However, the way in which leadership is defined has important consequences for organisational practices. Definitions of leadership offer organisations a mechanism to give order and predictability to leadership, and function to simplify the ambiguity and uncertainty of 'who' is selected in leadership positions (Bolden and Gosling, 2006). It provides a framework for how police organisations select and promote leaders, as Grint (2005b: 17) explains: 'If organisations promote individuals on the basis of one particular interpretation of leadership then that approach will be encouraged and others discouraged.' Theorists have attempted to define the term through traits, behaviours, relationships and interactions, and organisational position and seniority (Stogdill, 1997). As Burns (1978: 2) observes, leadership is 'one of the most observed and least understood phenomena on earth'. Typically, scholars define leadership as a process of influence (Antonakis et al, 2004). As an attempt to summarise the competing accounts, Yukl (2013: 23) provides a working definition of leadership: 'Leadership is the process of influencing others to understand and agree about what needs to be done and how to do it, and the process of facilitating individual and collective efforts to accomplish shared objectives.' Therefore, despite a long history of empirical and theoretical work, academic understanding of leadership remains incomplete. There is a lack of clarity about what leadership is and inconsistent evidence about what effectiveness in leadership means (Alvesson and Svenningsson, 2003; Wright et al, 2008). As Alvesson and Spicer (2012: 369) conclude: 'our impression is that this has not changed much in recent years and that the increasing popularity of using the idea of leadership has reinforced conceptual confusion and endemic vagueness'.

Mainstream leadership literature has attempted to define leadership through distinguishing it from management. This is a particular area of contention in the literature, where there has been a long-standing debate about the interplay between leadership and management. Zaleznik (1977) provides one of the first attempts to differentiate between leadership and management. According to Zaleznik, management seeks rationality, stability and control, and places emphasis on processes to identify risk and avoid problems. In contrast, leadership tolerates chaos and instability in order to foster innovation, vision and entrepreneurial activity. Zaleznik explains that managers focus on process – 'how' things get done – while leaders emphasise 'what' the activity means to individuals and organisations. Bennis's (1989: 45) work on becoming a leader provides the most commonly cited definition of the differences between leaders and managers, as follows:

- The manager administers; the leader innovates.
- The manager is a copy; the leader is an original.
- The manager maintains; the leader develops.
- The manager focuses on systems and structure; the leader focuses on people.
- The manager relies on control; the leader inspires trust.
- The manager has a short-range view; the leader has a long-range perspective.
- The manager asks how and when; the leader asks what and why.
- The manager has his eye always on the bottom line; the leader has his eye on the horizon.
- The manager imitates; the leader originates.
- The manager accepts the status quo; the leader challenges it.
- The manager is the classic good soldier; the leader is his own person.
- The manager does things right; the leader does the right thing.

'Management' is therefore used to describe practices that focus on structure and processes – control, monitoring and regulation – in order to produce stability, order and consistency. Management is an authority relationship focused on coping with complexity. In contrast, leadership is an influence relationship that emphasises coping with change (Yukl, 1989; Mintzberg, 1998).

There are two problems with the conventional differentiations of leadership and management. Much of the mainstream literature assumes a compatibility between the two activities: leadership is assumed to complement management. As Kent (2005: 1013) explains: 'the two processes, while distinct, cannot effectively work without each other working in tandem'. The emphasis is placed on the interdependence between leadership and management, and the value and necessity of both activities for organisations. In a policing context, it is largely accepted that police leaders need to display expertise in both leadership and management (Casey and Mitchell, 2007; Wright et al, 2008). However, this position neglects to consider the tension between leadership and management. As Long (2003: 641) explains, police leaders are faced with 'two competing, and in some ways incompatible, sets of expectations'. The focus on process, scrutiny and status quo in management, and the associated bureaucratic requirements, conflict with the entrepreneurial and 'risk-taking' activity of leadership (Golding and Savage, 2011). The qualities of reform and innovation in leadership are likely to challenge managerialist objectives and practices. Therefore, in contrast to conventional assumptions, the skills and aptitudes of leadership and management are understood as opposing, rather than complementary. Villiers and Adlam (2003: xii) conclude that 'the cautious, artful, consensus-seeking manager – who knows the cost of everything, who is determined to please everyone and upset no one, and whose quota is always fulfilled – may be quite incapable of swift and dynamic leadership when the situation requires it'.

In distinguishing between leadership and management, the mainstream literature also privileges leadership over management, where leadership is positioned as superior. In Bennis's (1989) list, the leader is described as an 'original', an 'innovator', inspiring trust and someone who 'does the right thing', as compared with the 'classic good soldier' characteristic of the manager. It appears that compared with management, leadership is synonymous with 'better' or 'more important'. Leaders are 'born' while management is a practice that can be learnt. As a result, leadership is reserved for the 'elite few' at the top of organisational hierarchies while management occurs more readily at junior levels. In the context of the increasing development of leadership courses and initiatives, Ford and Harding (2007) emphasise that leadership, rather than management, is endorsed in mainstream management and organisational literature as fundamental to the effectiveness of organisations. The role of management is undervalued and excluded, as compared with leadership, which is celebrated as essential for success. Gardner (1990: 3) observes that 'leaders generally end up looking like a cross between Napoleon and the Pied Piper, and managers like unimaginative clods'. While it is important to differentiate between the activities of leadership and management, the prioritisation of leadership further reinforces the idealisation and romanticisation of leadership in dominant discourse (Meindl, 1995; Mastrofski, 2002).

Such debates have considerable resonance for the study of police leadership. For the most part, police leadership has been conceptualised in managerial terms. Historically, police officers have been more familiar with the practice of management and supervision rather than leadership. In Reiner's (1991) study, chief constables conceptualised their role in managerial rather than operational or leadership terms. There has been a shift towards 'better management' and an emphasis on performance management, with an underinvestment in leadership (Cope et al, 1997; Loveday, 2008). Consequently, the skills of management, such as the management of processes, systems and risk, are an established and accepted feature of contemporary police leadership (Davies and Thomas, 2003; Butterfield et al, 2004).

The advent of New Public Management (NPM), in the late 20th century more specifically, placed emphasis on the skills of management rather than leadership in the police. There was an emerging willingness from senior policing ranks to experiment with different managerial practices prior to the NPM reforms. Parts of the police service, for example, had voluntarily adopted 'policing by objectives' and a Home Office circular in 1983 had a significant impact in pushing forward the 'value for money' agenda. However, NPM accelerated the transfer of managerial practices from industry into public service and formalised the managerial function of contemporary police leadership (Leishman et al, 1995; Savage et al, 2000). Set against a backdrop of a 'crisis' of public expenditure, where the police service was seen to have failed to deliver an economically viable service to the public, NPM represented a philosophical, ideological and cultural movement, and one of the most fundamental transformations to public administration (McLaughlin and Murji, 1995; Savage and Charman, 1996). A principal feature of NPM was the reform programme in the 1980s, which situated the private sector principles of 'economy', 'efficiency' and 'effectiveness' into public service management (Boyne, 2002). In policing, the doctrine of 'value for money' was evident in key publications, such as that by the Audit Commission (1990), which furthered the managerialist agenda in the police service. Hood (1991: 5), in one of the most well-known commentaries on the rise of NPM, refers to the phenomenon as 'a marriage of two streams', namely, 'new institutional economics', as reflected in the administrative ideals of contestability, user choice, transparency and incentive structures, and 'business-type managerialism', which generated reforms associated with centralisation and the measurement of organisational outputs.

Designed to deliver both structural and cultural change by incorporating businesslike managerial practices into all aspects of policing activity, the principles of managerialism and 'getting results' have become integral and accepted features of police leadership (McLaughlin and Murji, 1995; Cope et al, 1997; Fleming and Lafferty, 2000). An empirical study of the impact of NPM on a UK police constabulary found that police leadership had incorporated more strategic and managerial responsibilities (Butterfield et al, 2005). According to the study, the changes to leadership were particularly noticeable at the rank of sergeant, with emerging new managerial responsibilities, devolved from inspectors, for performance appraisals, planning, supervision, communication and administration. The study concluded that the middle-management ranks in the police had incorporated more managerial responsibility following the NPM reforms but, importantly, this was not accompanied with greater autonomy. In part, this reveals the tensions between leadership and management practices. Butterfield et al (2005: 338) explain that 'there was a shift towards more managerial and strategic responsibilities, but this did not imply greater autonomy for the sergeants, nor a closer identification with senior management. Rather, it entailed less personal contact with superiors, but tighter central control and scrutiny by means of organisational performance management systems.'

Today, the managerial philosophies of NPM are visible in much of the taken-for-granted activity of police leadership. Competitive tendering and outsourcing, decentralisation, performance indicators and league tables, inspection and audit regimes, staff appraisal systems and performance reviews, performance-related pay, customer charters, and feedback mechanisms can all be traced back to the NPM reforms (Cockcroft and Beattie, 2009; Golding and Savage, 2011). The principles of efficiency, effectiveness and economy form a 'guiding rationality' that shapes beliefs about what leadership means and how it should be performed (O'Malley and Hutchinson, 2007; Loveday, 2008). The monitoring of police activity against performance criteria functions to 'concentrate their minds and activities on doing well on these figures' and, consequently, 'what gets measured, gets done' (Reiner, 1998: 65). Therefore, such managerial processes have pedagogic functions and reinforce the need for top-down organisational control (Diefenbach, 2009). NPM represented a shift towards managerial practices emphasising monitoring and regulation; one legacy of NPM is therefore the primacy of management over leadership in the public service. There is therefore a well-established managerial culture in police organisations, with an emphasis on the stability of process and structure, while an entrepreneurial and learning culture of leadership remains less developed (Smith, 2008).

The debate surrounding NPM in policing reveals the competing narratives of police leadership. Underpinning much of the academic and policy literature on the topic is the question of whether leadership in the police represents a distinctive form of leadership. Adlam (2003), for example, calls for a systematic analysis of the ways in which police leadership is similar to, and distinct from, other forms of leadership. On the one hand, leadership in the police is conceptualised as a unique activity performed in a distinctive environment where the emphasis is placed on the operational uniqueness of the police leadership role. On the other hand, police leadership is understood as a universal, transferable practice, not dissimilar to leadership in industry or other public sector agencies, where emphasis is placed on the generic leadership competencies of the senior leadership role. Over 30 years ago, Reiner (1991: 347) asked: 'How far is the police organisation unique and how far is the job of chief executive in it essentially like being the managing director of any complex bureaucracy?' Therefore, in defining police leadership, the 'distinctiveness debate' is a further area of contention.

The NPM reforms set in motion a readiness within policing to accept leadership principles and processes from 'outside'. The assumption is that leadership in the police is not fundamentally different from leadership in other contexts and, indeed, external, particularly private sector, practices are deemed to be 'better'; as such, practices from outside industry can be successfully replicated to 'improve' leadership within the police. The normalisation of the managerial rather than operational emphasis of the police leadership role has been recognised in empirical work in Britain (Davies and Thomas, 2003; Butterfield et al, 2005). Early chief constables in Reiner's (1991) study defined their role in generic, businesslike terms. As Reiner (1991: 247) explains: 'they had evolved into professional managers. As the directors of complex organisations their role had more in common with senior administrators in any large modern bureaucracy than with the policemen they managed.' Wall (1998) similarly documents the rise of 'the executive director' chief constable, and those in Manning's (2007: 71) 'top command' describe themselves as 'police CEOs [chief executive officers]', their speech and manner mirroring that of the business world, placing greater emphasis on 'management' rather than 'the job'. Likewise, Savage et al (2000) capture the changing nature of police leadership from a command team towards 'directive' or 'executive' models reflective of other public sector and private sector organisations. More recently, Caless and Tong (2015: 62), in a study of police leadership in Europe, note that competencies exhibited by police leaders 'would be unremarkable in any boardroom, top team or cabinet anywhere in the world'. In other words, the emphasis is placed on the universality of leadership skills rather than the distinctive nature of the police environment.

Police leadership has therefore become conceptualised through universal managerial discourse and primacy is placed on the value of leadership from 'outside'. The recent move to develop the Direct Entry scheme in England and Wales reveals the value of transferring leadership skills from 'outside' into the police service and has accelerated the trend towards rewarding less police-specific forms of leadership (Kernaghan, 2013; Smith, 2015). Similarly, the endorsement of transformational leadership, which emerged from the private sector, highlights assumptions about the transferability of leadership practices (Cockcroft, 2014). The College of Policing (2015b: 30) confirms the managerial emphasis from business in formal policy rhetoric:

> Senior police leaders manage complex organisations, and the ability to do so successfully will be enhanced by encouraging positive aspects of a more commercial mindset. This does not imply a profit-motivated attitude but alludes to specific attributes, such as: creating opportunity rather than waiting for it; being able to 'pitch' new ideas convincingly; valuing positive relationships with peers, teams, and customers; adapting quickly to new circumstances.

In contrast, police leadership is also conceptualised as a distinctive enterprise, requiring specialist leadership skills. Research has captured the attachment to the necessity of operational experience for police leaders (Wall, 1994; Silvestri, 2003; Rowe, 2006). Police leadership is positioned as a 'special case', performed in a unique operational, political and cultural environment. There is an exclusivity here in relation to police leadership, developed through police leaders 'having done the job' of street police work (Caless, 2011). In this context, rapid promotion or direct entry schemes, which are commonplace in private sector practice, are met with suspicion in the police (Rowe, 2006). A key area of resistance to the Direct Entry scheme in England and Wales is the perceived lack of policing experience among candidates. This lack of operational credentials is associated with concerns about poor decision-making and not 'earning' rank (Hoggett et al, 2019). These assumptions underpin beliefs about the necessity of street policing for legitimatising leadership status in the police (see Chapter 2). Police leadership and management have therefore acquired a 'special status' that challenges the adoption of private sector managerial practices and principles. As Bradley et al (1986: 58) explain:

> Any discussion of police management which throws all of its emphasis upon 'management' and none upon 'police' is liable to be a waste of time. Any attempt to import 'theory

of managing' or an administrative technique into policing which is not based upon an understanding and grasp of the particularities of policing and the ways in which police work is structured in terms of its context and relationship with wider society is liable to have unintended and unwelcome consequences.

The debate about whether leadership in the police represents a distinctive form of leadership remains unresolved. Reflecting on the leadership landscape in Europe, Caless and Tong (2015) confirm that there appears to be no consensus on the distinctive nature of leadership skills within policing. Indeed, its distinctive status and the 'exceptional skills' required do little to challenge the normative assumptions of heroism of police leadership (see Chapter 6). However, while distinctive features of police leadership may be difficult to identify, what can be said is that leadership occurs in a distinctive occupational and political terrain. Policing has a unique status as a state institution with legitimacy to use lethal force against citizens (Waddington, 1991). Likewise, as Reiner (1998) explains, the police service performs a diverse range of activities, from controlling traffic to responding to terrorism, and is accountable to diverse audiences. While the distinctive skills required of police leaders appear contested, what is clear is that this environment places the police leader in a uniquely complex position. As Van Dijk et al (2015: 20) explain:

> This makes policing an irreducibly complex business with multiple functions that are defined by law, regulations and custom, that are implemented with diverse publics, that attract constant scrutiny and that – crucially – require the routine giving of accounts in a number of arenas, including the courts, government, oversight agencies and media, as well as to a bevy of stakeholders. The sensitive nature of many of the issues to be dealt with implies that the nature of leadership within the policing enterprise has an intrinsic 'moral' or values component.

Leadership is a complex theoretical concept and its relationship to other social activities, such as management or supervision, remains contested. Critical leadership scholars conceptualise leadership as a social process where the meanings of leadership are produced and reproduced by social agents within social, cultural and historical contexts (Meindl, 1995; Collinson, 2005a). From a social–constructionist perspective, the way in which leadership is defined forms a powerful framework to regulate the meanings and understandings of leadership (Barker, 2001; Kort, 2008). The debate about the distinctiveness of police leadership reveals the way in which understandings of leadership draw on established knowledge about the nature of power and authority, social hierarchy, and command structures (Washbush, 2005; Gordon, 2011). Therefore, definitions of leadership reveal the taken-for-granted beliefs about what is valued and legitimate in leadership in the police.

Studies of police leadership

Historically, leadership in the police has been a neglected area of academic study. Reiner (1991) explains this, in part, in terms of research access and funding, which has typically privileged studies of front-line policing. Much of the contemporary academic understanding of police occupational culture has, for example, evolved from the classic ethnographies of the rank and file (see, for example, Banton, 1964; Cain, 1973; Holdaway, 1983). Similarly, the evidence-based policing agenda in Britain has largely focused on the effectiveness of front-line policing practices. There is less empirical evidence about the experiences, perceptions and practices of senior policing ranks. Reiner (1991: 6) persuasively argued that 'virtually nothing is known about the life of the men at the top', and, more recently, Caless (2011: 1) describes the senior police leader as a 'quite unknown and elusive factor in criminology and in the analysis of policing'. However, within the context of heightened political scrutiny, police leadership has attracted academic interest and has been the focus of edited collections by Adlam and Villiers (2003), Fleming (2015) and Ramshaw et al (2019). In order to better contextualise the arguments made in this book, we explore a number of key studies that have made a significant contribution to the scholarship on police leadership.

Reuss-Ianni (1983) provided an early insight into the senior policing role. Based on an ethnographic study of the New York Police Department, Reuss-Ianni depicted the police organisation in terms of two cultures of 'street cops' and 'management cops'. According to Reuss-Ianni, management cops placed emphasis on public administration, productivity and planning processes. While the two cultures broadly shared the same goal to combat crime, the perspectives and practices to achieve these goals differed. In contrast to street cops, management cops have a wider strategic overview of crime and balance priorities against political, social and economic considerations. This study was the first to consider 'difference' in the experiences and practices of junior and senior ranks in the police. The work captures the distance and conflict between street cops and management cops, as well as the capacity of street cops to negotiate and resist decisions from above. Such findings continue to have ongoing relevance, with recent research highlighting the division between junior and senior ranks, and resistance in the police to external or top-down reform (Chan, 2007a; Sklansky and Marks, 2008). Therefore, the contemporary policing landscape and the pressures for change in leadership practice demand that divisions within the police organisation be scrutinised by academics and policymakers.

Reiner (1991) provided the first empirical study of police leadership in Britain. Prior to this, much of the insight into police leadership came from autobiographies of former chief constables. Based on interviews with 40 chief constables in the late 1980s, Reiner's study documented the origins, experiences and philosophies of chief constables, depicting four ideal types: the baron, the bobby, the boss and the bureaucrat. The study captures the shift in the chief constable role from the operational 'bobby', traditionally of working-class origin and a 'man of the people', towards the managerial 'bureaucrat', who combined 'a mastery of modern managerial approaches with the characteristic image of a traditional bobby or detective' (Reiner, 1991: 308). Reiner's work made a number of important contributions to the understanding of police leadership. The study not only emphasised the authority of chief constables in shaping policing practices, but also drew attention to the lack of research on the role of the police leader in the academic literature. Consequently, Reiner positioned police leadership as an important source of academic study. He also provided an insight into the shared understandings and commonality of leadership pressures and practices, and, in doing so, made a persuasive argument for the presence of a 'dominant culture' among chief constables. Finally, he highlighted the managerial nature of police leadership and the tensions between the management and operational aspects of the chief constable role. Chief constables, Reiner (1991: 225) explains, 'recognise the pressures driving them in the bureaucratic direction but hanker after the policing role as well and try to distance themselves from a purely managerial conception of their function'.

Wall (1998) provides further empirical insight into the chief constable role in an analysis of the social and professional histories of the chief constables who held the position in England and Wales between 1835 and 1995. Wall captures the changing role of chief constables into 'professionally trained managers' by documenting police organisational history through periods of standardisation, centralisation, unification and corporatisation. Providing a historical context to Reiner's earlier observations, Wall (1998: 84) charts the changing nature of the chief constable role: 'As the growth in size and administrative complexity of police forces gradually removed chief constables from operational police work, their managerial role changed from being warrior/leader to being administrator/leader to becoming a chief executive.' Through the ideology of internal recruitment, Wall considers the two traditions of external and internal selection procedures, and documents the historical shift from externally to internally recruited police managers. Again, much of this discussion is pertinent to the contemporary context, particularly the recent Direct Entry proposals in England and Wales. Wall's analysis further demonstrates the difficulties in the acceptance of 'difference' at senior levels of the police organisation and the enduring prestige of operational experience in police leadership, despite the reality that there is no practical need for this at chief constable level.

Savage et al (2000), in their empirical analysis of the role of the Association of Chief Police Officers (ACPO), provide a further contribution to the understanding of police leadership. Savage and colleagues interviewed 41 ACPO members, which included 23 assistant chief constables, eight deputy chief constables and ten chief constables, and documented the changing role of ACPO from a secretive and fragmented body in the 1980s to a more coherent, corporate and persuasive body in the 1990s. In the context of the professionalisation of ACPO, the research captures the greater integration of managerialist philosophies and practices in police leadership. Extending Reiner's and Wall's arguments about the commonality of experiences of senior officers, Savage et al's research documents the career path to senior rank and reinforces the challenges associated with a reliance on a single-entry system of recruitment for police leaders.

In contrast to previous empirical research, Silvestri (2003) considers the gendered nature of police leadership in the first empirical study of senior policewomen in Britain. Based on 30 interviews with senior policewomen, from inspector to chief officer rank, Silvestri documents the barriers to the advancement of women in the police and reveals the construction of police leadership as highly masculine. This work provides an important contribution to empirical evidence on diversity and leadership, and the challenges experienced by women as police leaders. As Silvestri (2003: 22) explains: 'police organisational cultures are powerful sites where symbols, images, and forms of consciousness that explicate and justify gender divisions are created and sustained'.

Caless (2011) provides a more recent contribution to the understanding of the selection, promotion and development processes to chief officer rank, echoing the findings of Savage et al's earlier work. Based on 85 interviews with chief officers in England and Wales, Caless documents the route to senior rank and highlights the challenging nature of the process. Caless considers the required competencies of police leaders, noting that many of these competencies can be applied to command roles in other organisations, consequently challenging the idea of police leadership as a distinctive enterprise. Caless (2011: 117; original emphasis) confirms that 'research is needed into whether or not there is a specifically *police* leader, or whether leaders from any sphere would translate successfully into the upper echelons of the police'.

Caless and Tong's (2015) study of strategic police leadership in Europe provides a comparative contribution to the field. Based on a combination of 59 questionnaires and 49 interviews, Caless and Tong explored the leadership selection experiences, perceptions of accountability, networks of relationships and future challenges of senior leadership in Europe. Many of the findings resonate with the previously cited research. Caless and Tong, for example, identify the prevalence of patronage and nepotism in leadership selection, which echoes Savage et al's (2000) and Caless's (2011) earlier observations. The study also notes the predominance of men in strategic leadership positions, which is illustrative of Silvestri's (2003) gendered account of leadership in the police, and further emphasises the generic nature of leadership competencies in the police. However, the authors argue that a shift is needed away from the universalised conception of police leadership to consider its distinctive features. As Caless and Tong (2015: 231) conclude: 'we need to get away from thinking only about generic leadership skills and begin to elaborate those skills that are necessary to be able to perform excellently at the strategic level of policing'.

The research cited in this section highlights an established interest in police leadership and engagement with the complexity of leadership as a theoretical concept. The studies reveal the socially constructed nature of police leadership and that leadership is managerial and highly gendered. An overview of the research also illustrates the relative stability and consistency of knowledge about the nature of police leadership over time.

History of police leadership

Police leadership is not performed independently of its social, political and historical context. Wright Mills (1959: 3) reminds us that 'neither the life of an individual nor the history of a society can be understood without understanding both'. Contemporary debates surrounding professionalisation, corporatisation and politicisation in police leadership all have historical foundations. Wall (1998: 315) confirms that the 'social history of the chief constable has demonstrated that debates in the history of the police do have the habit of repeating themselves and that many contemporary debates find a resonance in the past'.

The history of the police leadership literature captures the recurring nature of debates and their link with contemporary debates about professionalisation and accountability, diversity, and representation. The Peelian principles of the police as 'citizens in uniform' – that 'the police are the public and that the public are the police' – situate the notion of representation as a celebrated feature of the British policing model. These principles underpin a history of legal, political and moral debate about the role of the police and contemporary understanding of police legitimacy. Police leadership similarly embodies these idealised notions, as Reiner (1991: 10) explains, 'if the British police in general have been invested with a sacred character, then the chief constable is *primus inter deos* [a first among equals]'.

The histories of police leaders – their social origins, philosophies and experiences – reveal how credibility and legitimacy in leadership is constructed over time. Ireland (2018: 110) notes that 'the importance of social background in underlying character cannot be understated'. The 19th century saw the gradual recognition that the origins of chief constables should reflect those in their command and the people they policed, rather than their elite employers (Wall, 1998). Prior to this point, recruitment into leadership positions functioned on the basis of 'direct entry'; early chief constables achieved their position through the demonstration of their similar social standing to the local or military elite, rather than through their operational policing expertise or by representing the police workforce (Cox, 2018; Stevenson, 2018). As a result, the appointment of these chief constables is best understood in terms of symmetry with the elite, being heavily influenced by social networks, patronage and 'social standing'.

A shift towards internal recruitment in the police created the opportunity for greater representation and the possibility that junior officers could achieve senior rank (Wall, 1998). In other words, senior office was no longer reserved for elite 'outsiders'. Towards the end of the 19th century, the police as an occupation became a recognised route of social mobility and status for working-class men (Reiner, 1978; Steedman, 1984; Emsley, 1996). However, the emphasis on internal recruitment was set against growing public scepticism about the respectability of the police as a 'profession', which continued into the 20th century. As Lee and Punch (2004: 234) confirm: 'historically the image of the police was of amateur, untrained, unskilled, part-time and often venal thief-catchers'. During this period, the police institution was perceived as rigidly conservative and promotion in the hierarchy was particularly slow (Critchley, 1978; Rawlings, 2002). As Punch (2007: 109) observes: 'the image looking up must have been not of a pyramid but rather of the Eiffel Tower, with its pinnacle shrouded in mist'.

In response, scholars have documented a history of continued emphasis on the professionalisation of the police through the education and training of police officers, external appointments into the police and 'fast-track' promotion schemes (Holdaway, 1977; Klein, 2012; Silvestri, 2018a). Initiatives such as the Trenchard Scheme in the early 1930s and Bramshill Scholarships, introduced in 1966, aimed to present the police as an attractive employer for the highly educated and to establish a supply of educated officers of 'the right calibre' into senior ranks. As a result, by the 1980s, it was an accepted norm that chief constables should hold at least one university degree (Punch, 2007). However, direct entry continued to be met with strong opposition. The 'ideology of internal recruitment' – the notion of joining the police at the most junior rank of police constable and working upwards through the police hierarchy – became a powerful framework to assess the credibility and legitimacy of police leaders (Wall, 1994). Education was firmly established as indicative of leadership capability and meritocratic and democratic ideals as inherent features of the internal processes of police recruitment and promotion.

This literature on the history of police leadership demonstrates the long-standing relationship between the social origin of chief constables, the nature of their leadership and broader understandings of a 'professional police service'. Such literature captures the extent to which taken-for-granted assumptions about policing and leadership practices, and contemporary debates believed to be 'new', have powerful historical legacies. The characteristic features of contemporary police leadership, such as diversity and professionalisation, have a long history; many of the challenges facing modern-day police leadership are not unique to the contemporary landscape. Wall's (1994) ideology of internal recruitment, in particular, challenges the long-standing belief that police officers have always been promoted from 'within' and reveals that the resistance to direct entry initiatives is not isolated as a 'contemporary problem'.

The literature also reveals how credibility and legitimacy in leadership in the police has been constructed over time. Reforms to recruitment and selection processes have altered the character of police leadership, the nature of leadership practices and assumptions about credibility for senior office. As Wall (1998: 203) explains: 'Over the past 160 years the selection and appointment process has changed dramatically. Qualities once revered are now reviled.' The level of education attained by contemporary chief constables is in marked contrast to the early appointments based on patronage and social standing, yet similarities are also obvious. Contemporary scholars have, for example, highlighted the continued importance of mentoring and social networks for prospective chief officers (Charman et al, 1999; Caless, 2011). Therefore, an analysis of the history of police leadership captures the changes and continuities in police leadership, which is best viewed through a lens of simultaneous reform and resistance, progression and regression (Silvestri, 2018a).

Structure of the book

Thus far, we have outlined some of the key ideas and knowledge bases that have shaped the understandings of contemporary police leadership. In the remainder of the book, we provide a comprehensive analysis of the broad range of perspectives and debates in police leadership, and challenge dominant discourses underpinning the nature and practice of leadership. The book considers two main areas. Firstly, it critically analyses the theoretical context as the foundation of understanding police leadership as socially constructed. Chapter 2 examines the contemporary policing landscape in England and Wales, and documents the key developments most relevant to police leadership practice. Chapter 3 provides a critical analysis of conventional leadership theory and explores how leadership has been conceptualised in trait, behavioural, situational and transformational theories. This chapter demonstrates that conventional theory, as the dominant discourse of police leadership, perpetuates deterministic and reductionist assumptions about the nature of leadership in the police. Drawing on literature from critical leadership studies, Chapter 4 examines emerging perspectives on police leadership, including followership and shared and distributed leadership, which forms the theoretical basis for re-imagining police leadership as socially constructed.

The book then shifts to theorise police leadership as socially constructed and explores the implications of the dominant narratives for current and future leadership practice. Chapter 5 foregrounds the concept of police occupational culture(s) to explore the taken-for-granted assumptions about police leadership and the challenges of creating 'difference'. This chapter demonstrates that diversity in the police workforce does not necessarily create diverse practice in police leadership. Chapter 6 examines the contemporary emphasis on well-being and resilience within the context of police occupational culture, drawing on the concept of 'heroism' in leadership. Chapter 7 draws together the main arguments of the book and considers the implications for the future of police leadership practice. This chapter concludes with a call to re-imagine the nature and practice of police leadership as a socially constructed and power-laden activity.

Further reading

Adlam, R. and Villiers, P. (2003) *Police Leadership in the Twenty-First Century: Philosophy, Doctrine and Developments*. Hampshire: Waterside Press.

Fleming, J. (2015) *Police Leadership: Rising to the Top*. Oxford: Oxford University Press.

Stevenson, K., Cox, D.J. and Channing, I. (2018) *Leading the Police: A History of Chief Constables 1835–2017*. London: Routledge.

2

The contemporary context
of police leadership

Policing in England and Wales is undergoing significant and relentless change across a range of domains. The last decade has witnessed unprecedented reforms to police governance and accountability, education and recruitment, and pay and conditions – all of which challenge traditional working practices in the police. This chapter situates the understanding and practice of police leadership within such a context. Set against a backdrop of concerns over leadership standards and integrity, the chapter begins by critically exploring the meanings of professionalisation. It provides an examination of changes to police education and training, evidence-based policing (EBP), ethics, and recruitment practices as illustrative of the contemporary narrative of police professionalisation. The chapter then outlines the radically altered landscape within which contemporary police leaders now operate through an appreciation of the arrival of the police and crime commissioner and the attendant changes in the governance of policing. Through a consideration of such reforms, this chapter demonstrates that the contemporary professionalisation agenda is celebrated as a solution to the 'problem' of police leadership.

Professionalisation

A series of high-profile leadership failings in recent years has increased the scrutiny of leadership in the police in England and Wales. The inquest into the 96 deaths at Hillsborough Football Stadium, Sheffield in 1989 signalled the most significant exposure of the systematic failings of the police system for a generation. The standards and ethics of police practices have been exposed in the Leveson Inquiry and the Inquiry into Undercover Policing, and the priorities of and decision-making in the police have been criticised following the failure of the police to adequately investigate child sexual abuse allegations. This has sparked the unprecedented scrutiny of the standards and integrity of leadership at the operational and institutional levels. In response to such failures, professionalisation has been heralded as the solution. Police leaders are now being held to account to ensure that ethics are inherent in police working practices. In other words, professionalism, ethics and integrity have been positioned as a leadership problem.

The establishment of the College of Policing in 2012 marks the most obvious declaration that professionalisation is central to the contemporary police leadership agenda. While there is a heightened emphasis on professionalisation, the rhetoric of professionalisation in the police is not a new phenomenon. On the contrary, the police service in Britain has a long history of attempting to achieve professional status. In the first empirical study of police work, Banton (1964) placed emphasis on shared experience and social status as indicative of the police as a profession. Police officers at all ranks, Banton (1964: 107) explains, 'exercise the obligations and enjoy the privileges of the constable's office'. However, the meaning of 'a profession' is contested. In the police, professional status has typically been understood in terms of high standards of conduct or expertise, the assumption being that professionalisation describes the professional behaviour of police officers (Sklansky, 2014). However, the professional status of an occupation should not be confused with individuals within that occupation being 'professional' or acting 'professionally'. In contrast, sociologists have explored the process by which occupations claim professional status, and have theorised about the organisational structure, working practices, occupational ideologies and identities of the professions. This body of work differentiates the professions from other occupations through characteristics such as: public service rather than economic gain; the possession of an extensive body of knowledge and expertise, where competence develops over time; considerable autonomy over working practices; shared experience and occupational identity; and the legitimacy to inform public opinion on issues affecting them (Davies, 1983; Dingwall, 1983; Friedson, 1983). Sociologists have also drawn attention to the acquired status and prestige of the professions. As Dingwall (1976: 340), in the well-cited article 'Accomplishing Profession', explains:

> A 'profession' involves its members being certain kinds of people who carry out tasks in particular kinds of ways within a particular work setting. But to claim a professional status involves more than this. It is also the assertion of a claim to a particular kind of social location in relation to other social groups.

As such, sociologists call for a study of how occupations construct or 'accomplish' professional status and, specifically, the occupational characteristics that are emphasised (or, importantly, de-emphasised) to legitimatise professional standing (Dingwall, 1976; Holdaway, 2017). Therefore, this sociological literature provides an important contribution to understanding how the contemporary professionalisation of the police service is constructed within particular social, economic and political contexts.

Neyroud's (2011b) *Review of Police Leadership and Training* signalled an acceleration towards the professionalisation of the police service in England and Wales. The establishment of a new professional body in policing, particularly in terms of police legitimacy and public confidence, was the central focus of the report. As Neyroud (2011b: 2) explains: 'The cornerstone of my report is the creation of a new Professional Body for policing, embracing the whole of the police service and responsible for leadership, learning and standards. It should be transparent, accountable and act as the public's guardian of excellence in policing.' In setting out the vision of the new professional body, Neyroud draws on medicine, teaching, law, engineering and other professions to define key features, such as a depository of research, accredited educational qualifications and a code of ethics. The report made 14 substantial recommendations, including the appointment of independent non-executives as directors, the consolidation of guidance and strategy, and the development of policing, management and senior management qualifications. In making his case for the professionalisation of policing, Neyroud (2011b: 45) concludes that:

> The police service has now reached a position where the developing nature of the knowledge requirement and skills development within the occupation, mean that formal professionalisation has potentially significant benefits for policing and the public it serves. In particular a professional body, in the right form, would provide the opportunity to provide clearer standards, a service-owned qualification framework, greater focus on professional development across all roles and, as a result, a new more productive relationship with other providers such as Further and Higher Education.

In 2012, the College of Policing replaced the National Police Improvement Agency as the professional body for the police service in England and Wales. Professionalisation, public trust and confidence, and developing professional practices are inherent in the activities of the College of Policing. The vision of the College of Policing (2014a:

8) is 'to be a world-class professional body, equipping our members with skills and knowledge to prevent crime, protect the public and secure public trust'. The transformation of education and training in the police is therefore as an essential feature of the contemporary professionalisation agenda.

Police education and training

Unlike most other professions, there has traditionally been no expectation of degree-level education to join the police service. Set against a backdrop of growing concerns about the standards of police training, the reforms to education represent one of the most significant moves towards professional status (White, 2006; Wood and Tong, 2009). Higher education, as seen in medicine, is commonly utilised to legitimatise an occupation's professional status: nurses 'become' professional through higher education (White and Heslop, 2012). As Paterson (2011: 292) observes, the integration of higher education into policing 'provides a significant progression towards the professionalization of police learning through a shift from a technical focus on competencies towards a more reflexive appreciation of the complexity of the police role and the importance of lifelong learning'.

Alongside the establishment of a new professional body, Neyroud's review also provided a framework of professional development in policing. The review recommended that the professional body 'owns and develops a police initial qualification (PIQ) for entry into the profession' (Neyroud, 2011b: 86). According to the review, this approach would 'reinforce the perception of policing as a profession' (Neyroud, 2011b: 85). In 2016, the College of Policing published the initial proposals for the Police Education Qualification Framework (PEQF) to address the lack of consistency in the educational requirements for policing roles. The PEQF sets out minimum educational standards for entry and promotion in the police service in England and Wales. According to the College of Policing (2017a), an entry-level qualification was 'commensurate with that of a profession'. While there has been a history of graduate entry and fast-track schemes in the police, for the first time, the PEQF formalised the expectation that all new police officers joining the service would have, or be working towards, a degree-level qualification. The PEQF situates higher education as fundamental to the claim of professional status. As Bryant et al (2014: 388) confirm: 'the notion of a profession in the UK is intimately linked with that of qualification'.

The role of higher education in policing has long attracted scholarly interest. Lee and Punch (2004) argue that higher education can be powerful in disrupting 'groupthink' processes and embedding practices of reflexivity and critical challenge. Empirical studies have also explored the beneficial impact of higher education on police attitudes and socialisation (Christie et al, 1996; Scott et al, 2009), police occupational culture (Heslop, 2011; Cox and Kirby, 2018), occupational attitudes (Paoline et al, 2015), authority and misconduct (Manis et al, 2008; Telep, 2011), police use of force (Paoline and Terrill, 2007; Chapman, 2012; Lim and Lee, 2015), and diversity (Decker and Huckabee, 2002). This body of work reveals the role of higher education in transforming the characteristics of police occupational culture, embedding criticality in police decision-making and challenging 'groupthink' processes. Traditionally, however, the police and university education have been viewed as occupying separate and often conflicting worlds (Punch, 2007). Indeed, 'value' in police leadership has typically been attached to operational experience or 'tradecraft' and 'time served', rather than educational qualifications (Rowe, 2006; Silvestri, 2006; Roberts et al, 2016). In placing primacy on knowledge-based expertise, reforms to police education and training therefore challenge the status of police occupational 'craft' and the importance of experiential knowledge.

University education in other public sectors, such as nursing and teaching, is more established; however, the relevance of higher education to the 'craft' of policing is a particularly contentious area (White and Heslop, 2012). Empirical research on the positive impact of higher education on policing practices is mixed and critics have highlighted the unintended consequences of academic study for police officers (Hough and Stanko, 2019). Early studies found negative effects of higher education on police officers, such as less job satisfaction (Hudzik, 1978) and more cynical occupational attitudes (Lotz and Regoli, 1977). Reflecting on his experience of academic study, Young (1991: 62) describes the 'total change in perspective and new semantic outlook' gained through higher education, and highlights the tensions in the 'reintegration' back into the disciplined and structured nature of the police. There appears to be a 'process of readjustment' for police officers returning to operational work after academic study (Lee and Punch, 2004). Paoline et al (2015: 67) found few benefits of higher education on police officers' job satisfaction, views of top management and role orientation, concluding that 'college educated patrol officers' negative views of top management (whom they may perceive as intellectual equals) and low job satisfaction could very well be a function of resentment and frustration with one's current position in the police food chain'. While revealing the complexities in demonstrating the positive impact of education in policing, this body of work also captures the challenges for police leaders in supporting the transition from higher education to the police, and effectively engaging and empowering an increasingly educated workforce.

Scholars have also problematised the assumption that higher education is a mechanism to disrupt police occupational culture. Heslop (2011) observes the 'reproduction' of the negative aspects of police occupational culture in the university environment, which appears to show a transference and strengthening, rather than transformation, of dominant occupational values and behaviours. Likewise, Hallenberg and Cockcroft (2017) document the indifference and hostility towards police officers undertaking higher education. The structure, content and process of police education is central to ensuring that university education is 'different' from police training (Lee and Punch, 2004). Writing critically about police reforms, Chan (2007a: 342) observes that 'instead of challenging officers' identity and purpose, reforms had in fact reinforced certain accepted wisdom about who they are, what they are doing, what matters and why'. The role of higher education in challenging dominant occupational ideologies is therefore more complex. As Hallenberg and Cockcroft (2017: 285) confirm: 'the shift from a paradigm based on experience (often denoted through "years served") to one based on knowledge is likely to meet with cultural resistance'. That said, the value of higher education in disrupting the uniformity of police occupational culture and encouraging greater criticality in the police is a central feature of the contemporary reform rhetoric.

Therefore, despite the complexities of the PEQF, contemporary police leaders are required to embrace higher education and effectively manage an increasingly educated workforce. The introduction of the PEQF accelerates the need for police leaders to embed a culture of learning in constabularies, and an important precursor to this is an organisational infrastructure to support learning and development (Kilgallon et al, 2015; Hallenberg and Cockcroft, 2017; Wood, 2018). As Lee and Punch (2004: 235) observe: 'the receiving police organisation did not always tend to see the practical relevance of university training, and often did not know how to exploit the benefits gained by the individual officer'. This organisational 'readiness' of the police represents an acute challenge for contemporary leadership, which requires a transformation of the way in which police officers and staff are managed and developed. Therefore, for the PEQF to have a meaningful change in the police, it is necessary for police leaders to engage and address the challenges and complexities associated with managing new graduates. Within this context, it appears that traditional approaches to leadership in the police are likely to be increasingly outdated.

Evidence-based policing

In addition to the reforms to police education and training, evidence-based policing (EBP) forms another pronounced feature of the contemporary professionalisation agenda. Sociologists remind us that a body of knowledge is indicative of 'accomplishing' professional status (Dingwall, 1976). However, the dissemination of research to police practice is not a new phenomenon. Research-informed practice in the police is evident in problem-oriented policing (Goldstein, 1990), intelligence-led policing (Tilley, 2008; Ratcliffe, 2016) and the Compstat approach in New York (Willis et al, 2007). Academic research into the police in Britain has a rich history, beginning with Michael Banton's seminal sociological study in 1964, which paved the way for ethnographic work on the police and policing practices into the 1980s (for example, Cain, 1973; Holdaway, 1983; Foster, 1989). The 1980s also saw the increasing involvement of central and local government departments in commissioning and conducting policing research and the emergence of 'in-house' research capacity within police organisations. Therefore, for the first time, there was a body of empirical evidence about the role of the police, the demographic characteristics of police officers, police occupational culture and public perceptions of the police.

Contemporary EBP practices have been heavily influenced by the work of Lawrence Sherman, who introduced the concept in the series of papers *Ideas in American Policing*, published by the Police Foundation in the United States. According to Sherman (1998: 2), EBP represents 'the most powerful force for change', with police practice shaped by 'scientific evidence' of 'what works'. As Sherman (1998: 3) explains: 'Evidence-based policing uses research to guide practice and evaluate practitioners. It uses the best evidence to shape the best practice.' EBP situates scientific evidence as indicative of police 'effectiveness'. In other words, policing activities should be guided by systematic research and evidence (Bullock and Tilley, 2009). Therefore, like the changes to police education, EBP further challenges conventional wisdom in the police, or 'the police know best', by centralising research in policing practice (Kalyal, 2019).

Under the College of Policing's professionalisation remit, the contemporary evidence-based movement has a renewed drive. As set out in Neyroud's (2011b) review, the vision for the College of Policing was to act as the central body that defined and communicated evidence of 'what works' and 'best practice' in policing. In September 2013, the College of Policing, in collaboration with universities, launched the What Works Centre for Crime Reduction. The aim of the What Works Centre is to support the development, dissemination and use of research evidence in policing, the key driver being that police practices are informed by the 'best available evidence'. This trend is supported by an expansion in regional collaborations between universities and police constabularies in a shift to further embed research into contemporary police leadership and management (Fyfe and Wilson, 2012; Bryant et al, 2014). These factors therefore demonstrate a formalisation of the relationship between research and practice as part of the professional development of the police service.

Within this context, there is increasing emphasis on police leadership to demonstrate their understanding and commitment to EBP practices and principles. There is emerging evidence of receptivity to EBP among senior leaders. A US study by Telep and Winegar (2016) found that only a minority, less than 9 per cent, of police executives were not familiar with EBP. Senior police officers in a Canadian study expressed a belief in the importance of EBP for leadership decision-making (Huey et al, 2018), and a study by Rojek et al (2012) likewise found the established use of EBP practice, with 90 per cent of police organisations in the study reporting using research to inform decision-making. Evidence-based principles have also been incorporated into the promotion and assessment processes in police organisations (Lum et al, 2010). Research also indicates a relationship between educational attainment and engagement with EBP (Telep, 2017; Huey et al, 2018), so it follows, perhaps, that this trend may continue as the PEQF is further embedded in police constabularies. Therefore, there appears to be increasing understanding of and commitment to EBP among police leaders for leadership and organisational practices.

Evidence-based principles appear more embedded in other areas of the public sector, such as social work, nursing and probation (Gambrill, 1999; Dobrow et al, 2004; Behague et al, 2009). However, there are distinctive features to the emergence of the evidence-based discourse in policing and the resistance to its implementation. A long history of sociological studies of policing has demonstrated the significance of understanding police officers as knowledgeable agents (Manning, 1977; Van Maanen, 1978a; Punch, 1979). Scholars have challenged the contemporary EBP agenda as being externally imposed on the police, which neglects to engage with police officers as 'co-producers' and lacks appreciation of the occupational culture environment (Bradley and Nixon, 2009; Fyfe and Wilson, 2012). In particular, the hierarchical structure in the police and the traditional militaristic and conservative culture have been identified as key barriers to the acceptance of evidence-based principles (Lum, 2009; Kalyal, 2019). Without meaningful engagement with the lived experiences of and working realities in the police, the contemporary EBP trend risks exacerbating historical tensions between the police and academia, and, contrary to intention, furthering the divide between research and practice. As Willis and Mastrofski (2018: 28) explain: 'Evidence-based policing, similar to evidence-based medicine, has tried to persuade others through the strength and consistency of its arguments on the benefits of scientific research, yet in doing so the needs, habits, and interests of practitioners have been mostly overlooked, underrepresented, or devalued.'

While the emergence of EBP represents an important trend in recognising the relevance of academic research to policing, there are a number of criticisms of the contemporary EBP agenda. First, the rhetoric of 'best available evidence' is a particular source of contention. Critics have argued that the basic assumptions underpinning EBP reinforce a hierarchy of research evidence, with quantitative methods, particularly randomised control trials and systematic reviews, understood as the 'gold standard' of research evidence (Bullock and Tilley, 2009; Tilley, 2009). Traditional conceptualisations of EBP advocate science-based processes and principles, such as the concepts of targeting, testing and tracking, known as the 'triple T approach', as central to establishing 'what works' (Sherman, 2013). Yet, these positivistic and context-free assumptions of EBP conflict with qualitative approaches to social research that emphasise the importance of understanding social interaction and processes as inseparable from the social, cultural, historical and political context (Berger and Luckmann, 1967; Blumer, 1969). The emphasis on the positivistic determinants of 'proof' discredits the value of ethnography, in particular (Jackson, 2019; Souhami, 2019). Indeed, much of our understanding of policing and police occupational culture has been built on the ethnographic studies of the 1980s. This body of work has been fundamental in developing scholarly knowledge of, for example, the nature of police relations with minority communities (such as Holdaway, 1983) and police misconduct and corruption (Punch, 1985). Policing and police leadership are context dependent, highly complex and ambiguous. It is notoriously difficult to measure the 'effectiveness' or outcome of policing activity (Bayley and Bittner, 1984; Reiner, 1998). Critics therefore argue that the contemporary EBP trend, and its emphasis on positivistic definitions of 'evidence', is removed from the realities of routine police work. Policing, and consequently the study of policing, cannot be separated from its political and cultural context (Manning, 2005; Wood et al, 2017).

The emphasis on 'what works' and 'policy relevance', as inherent features of the dominant discourse of EBP, has also been critiqued. The emphasis on 'what works' risks neglecting topics of study that do not appear immediately transferable to policy (Wood et al, 2017). For studies of police leadership, Van Dijk et al (2015) call for a greater focus on 'what is important' in addition to 'what works'. As Punch (2010: 158) confirms: 'In policing I believe that there has certainly been research that has influenced policy but that more important has been the stream of research that has opened up policing to external scrutiny, has made policing an object of study, and has altered the thinking of police elites.'

Evidence-based principles are firmly entrenched in the discourse of professionalisation, and positivist notions of testing, measurement and generalisation are now commonplace in official rhetoric. The activities of the College of Policing have accelerated the shift towards the police as 'knowledge driven' (Hallenberg and Cockcroft, 2017). Embedding research-informed practice into policing is understood and accepted as a demonstration of the professional status of the police (Brown et al, 2018); as Fleming et al (2015: 237) confirm, 'a profession's research base is its foundation'. Therefore, despite the challenges to the adoption and acceptance of EBP, police leaders are required to act as ambassadors of evidence-based principles and practices. However, as Huey et al (2018) note, the 'institutionalisation' of EBP has been slow. It is necessary that the value of research in a policing context is clearly communicated to support and develop EBP practices, and police leaders have an important role here. It appears that the legitimacy of EBP rests on the credibility of research 'making sense' in the context of police work and police occupational culture.

The Code of Ethics

In line with other professions that are governed by codes of ethical conduct, the College of Policing introduced the Code of Ethics in 2014 as 'one step towards obtaining full professional status for policing' (College of Policing, 2014b). The literature on police occupational culture has captured the significant amount of discretion and autonomy afforded to front-line police officers. Police work is complex and there is a variety of contextual and subjective factors that influence police officers' decision-making (Bayley and Bittner, 1984; Reiner, 1998). The strength of solidarity within the police, the 'them and us' division between police and outsiders, and the 'blue code of silence' form a powerful shield to protect members from external scrutiny and 'muckraking' (Van Maanen, 1978b; Punch, 1985; Westmarland, 2005). These features of police occupational culture, combined with the discretionary nature of police work, create ethical dilemmas and present challenges for police leaders (Van Maanen, 1974; Neyroud and Beckley, 2001). There has been a history of frameworks of ethical conduct for the police service in England and Wales; for example, the Police Act introduced the Code of Conduct in 1996. However, the newly created Code of Ethics was introduced as a pivotal feature of the contemporary professionalisation agenda and a mechanism to restore public trust and confidence in the police (MacVean and Spindler, 2015). Ethics and ethical practice are constructed as indicative of what it means to be a profession.

The Code of Ethics sets out the standards of behaviour expected of those who work in the police and positions the principle of 'doing the right thing in the right way' as fundamental to informing policing practice. There are nine policing principles and ten standards of professional behaviour in the Code of Ethics (see Box 1); consequently, 'the combination of principles and standards of behaviour encourages consistency between what people believe in and aspire to, and what they do' (College of Policing, 2014b: 3).

Box 1: College of Policing (2014b) *Code of Ethics*

Policing principles
1. Accountability
2. Fairness
3. Honesty
4. Integrity
5. Leadership
6. Objectivity
7. Openness
8. Respect
9. Selflessness

Standards of professional behaviour

1. Honesty and integrity
2. Authority, respect and courtesy
3. Equality and diversity
4. Use of force
5. Orders and instructions
6. Duties and responsibilities
7. Confidentiality
8. Fitness for work
9. Conduct
10. Challenging and reporting improper behaviour

Ethics in leadership, in particular, designating police leaders as role models of ethical practice, are key features of the Code of Ethics. The Code of Ethics both sets out the expected standards of leadership and also positions the promotion and embedding of ethical practice as a leadership responsibility, situating the principles of integrity, conduct and fairness in the discourse of good and effective leadership. However, as MacVean and Spindler (2015: 117) explain, 'codes of ethics do not have an impact by simply existing; they require motivational leadership to create high standards'. Similarly, Westmarland (2014) challenges the credibility of codes of ethics, which are typically ambiguous and imposed from the top down on junior police officers and staff. The practical application of such formal codes, Westmarland (2014: 465) continues, 'render[s] them useless if not damaging'. Establishing an ethical culture in the police is more than the production of formal codes and rules; rather, it requires the critical understanding of police occupational culture as a powerful framework for shaping police practice. In their study of misconduct, Hough et al (2018) recommend that this requires a meaningful combination of training and recruitment, performance management, and organisational justice. As Westmarland and Rowe (2018: 868) conclude: 'we do question how the new College of Policing's Code of Ethics will overcome the much stronger and long established "cop code" especially as the new code seems to take no account of existing police culture or notions of within-group or partner loyalty'. Despite these challenges, ethics in policing is understood in policy as the responsibility and obligation of police leadership.

In sum, the establishment of the College of Policing and its subsequent activities mark a fundamental shift towards the professionalisation of the police service in England and Wales. The claim of professional status in the police service is being achieved through the systematic emphasis of particular characteristics. The current trend, Holdaway (2017: 589) observes, represents a 'public declaration in which particular attributes of a profession are emphasized and related, implicitly or explicitly, to the social context within which they are articulated'. A certain form of professionalisation is being constructed. Sociologists remind us that the way in which 'the profession' is constructed – in other words, how an occupation acquires a 'special status' – is an important scholarly focus. As Larson (1977: xvi; original emphasis) explains:

> I see professionalization as the process by which producers of special services sought to constitute *and control* a market for their expertise. Because marketable expertise is a crucial element in the structure of modern inequality, professionalization appears also as a collective assertion of special social status and as a collective process of upward social mobility.

As central features of the process of professionalisation, EBP, the PEQF and the Code of Ethics play a significant role in shifting the emphasis from policing as an occupational 'craft' and integrating the concepts of education, evidence and accountability into police leadership discourse. The claim of police as a profession is underpinned by assumptions about specialist occupational knowledge in policing and control and autonomy over the practice of police work (Holdaway, 1977). The 'process of upward social mobility' of the police is demonstrated through the development of the policing-specific body of knowledge, and the acquisition, demonstration and evaluation of police knowledge. The contemporary discourse draws heavily on medicine and science; the importance of evidence, education and ethics in policing has been strengthened as a defining characteristic of becoming 'a profession', and legitimacy in leadership is increasingly framed in these terms (Fleming, 2014).

Direct entry

The representation of the police service in Britain has a long-standing presence in public discourse, interconnected with the fiercely protected tradition of policing by consent: a belief that the police should represent the communities they serve, and a driver to improve relations between police and minority communities (Rowe, 2002). Within the context of highly publicised leadership failings, workforce modernisation and the professionalisation agenda, and an expanding equalities agenda within policing, the homogeneity of police leadership is facing considerable challenge. The Direct Entry scheme in England and Wales has been heralded as a mechanism to diversify the experiences, perspectives and practices within senior ranks, and to challenge the chronic lack of representation at senior levels of the police organisation (Leishman and Savage, 1993; Smith, 2015; Silvestri, 2018b). As a Home Office (2013: 14) consultation confirms: 'improving the diversity of officers at senior ranks goes to the very nature of what the direct entry schemes are trying to achieve – an open culture'.

In November 2014, on recommendation of the Winsor Review (Winsor, 2012), nine Direct Entry superintendents began their training as the first cohort of direct entrants (Smith, 2016). Prior to this, the police service in England and Wales functioned based on a single-entry system of recruitment: all police officers entered the organisation at the rank of police constable (Savage et al, 2000). In most cases, therefore, all chief constables have achieved their position by progressing through each rank from police constable level; consequently, all police officers, regardless of rank, share a common experience of street policing (Van Maanen, 1997; Savage, 2003). Therefore, chief officers are typically 'cut from the same cultural cloth as lower-ranking officers' (Cockcroft, 2013: 138). While there have been recurring attempts to reform police recruitment – the Trenchard Scheme in the 1930s is a well-known example of the recruitment of educated officers directly into the Metropolitan Police above constable rank – the Direct Entry proposals set out in the Winsor Review signalled a watershed moment in leadership recruitment (Wall, 1994; Smith, 2015). In recommending direct entry at inspector, superintendent and chief officer ranks, Winsor formalised the inclusion of less police-specific experience among senior police leaders in the policy.

The single-entry system of recruitment in the police has long been recognised as presenting distinct challenges for the police service. The limited number of senior leadership ranks combined with the length of time it takes to reach senior office risk a 'leadership skills deficit' at the top of the organisation (Leishman and Savage, 1993; Roberts et al, 2016). The single-entry system necessitates the provision of 'fast-track' talent management schemes to identify and develop leadership potential. Unlike multiple-entry systems of recruitment, a single-entry system places considerable pressure on the internal processes of leadership development and succession planning (Savage et al, 2000). Since the identification of leadership potential occurs from within the police, it allows the organisation to prioritise particular experiences and skills, and to construct and reconstruct the type of leadership that is most valuable (Wall, 1994; Rowe, 2006). Notions of 'good' police leadership are therefore intertwined with the norms and values of police occupational culture; as Manning (2007: 53) argues, 'as one rises in rank, rewards are attached to new mini and situated rhetorics'. Particular forms of leadership are legitimatised and other forms are excluded; in other words, the single-entry system risks the promotion of 'more of the same' leaders. Therefore, the Direct Entry scheme represents an attempt to embed greater flexibility in recruitment and promotion as a mechanism to equip police organisations to respond effectively to the changing and complex contemporary landscape. Consequently, the scheme represents an attempt to disrupt the conventional narratives underpinning legitimacy and credibility in police leadership. As Silvestri (2018b: 319) explains: 'Direct Entry can be considered as a transformative intervention strategy with the capacity to challenge core organisational values, beliefs about work, and the way in which work is organised and valued'.

By disrupting the single-entry recruitment system, the Direct Entry scheme aimed to introduce 'difference' directly at leadership positions within the police. The reforms are based on the principle that direct entry recruitment is transformative. Diversifying the understandings, experiences and backgrounds of senior police officers aims to transform how leadership is practised, thereby maximising the possibility of successful organisational change; as Smith (2016: 312) explains, 'transformational change can only occur by injecting new ideas directly into more senior ranks, thereby delivering much more fundamental change at a much quicker pace'. The relationship between direct entry and diversity has global appeal. Emphasising that direct or prolonged operational experience is not a condition for the acquisition of rank among senior police leaders in Europe, Caless and Tong (2015: 10) draw attention to the variety of mechanisms of recruitment and for promotion within European police organisations. The Swedish police, with a celebrated reputation for gender equality, provide policies for work–family reconciliation to support the recruitment and progression of women, and the Netherlands has a special programme to promote women to managerial roles in the police, the only country to have this system (Van der Lippe et al, 2004; Osterlind and Haake, 2010; Haake et al, 2017; Silvestri, 2018b). Although such initiatives have supported an increase of women in leadership roles, the body of research continues to emphasise the reality that leadership credibility continues to be strongly associated with operational policing backgrounds.

The proposals for direct entry into British policing were met with highly publicised opposition from the police service, illustrative perhaps in the low take-up of the scheme; only seven police constabularies initially elected to be involved (Smith, 2016). A national survey of 12,549 police officers in England and Wales found that over 80 per cent reported that they strongly disagreed or disagreed that the scheme 'was a good idea' (Hoggett et al, 2019). The Police Superintendents Association and Police Federation criticised the lack of policing experience of candidates, and there were indications of a lack of support among chief officers for the scheme (Smith, 2016). Direct entrants in the police therefore face symbolic 'credibility contests' through which they are required to demonstrate their contribution and value to the police organisation (Silvestri, 2018b). Despite the intention to diversify the experience and backgrounds of senior management in the police, the resistance to it reveals the strong attachment to the 'craft' of street policing as legitimatising those in police leadership roles.

The symbolic necessity of operational experience is an accepted and fiercely protected principle in British policing, the tradition of the police as an 'egalitarian meritocracy' in which 'all officers start at the bottom' and have the opportunity to work towards senior office has acquired an almost sacred status (Wall, 1994; Savage, 2003). A long history of police research has captured the cultural capital assigned to front-line operational experiences (Holdaway, 1977; Reuss-Ianni, 1983; Van Maanen, 1997). Credibility in police leadership is understood through the demonstration of expertise in police 'street' work and a commitment to the police service ethos. According to Wall (1994: 336), this forms a powerful part of the ideology of internal recruitment: 'More of a symbolic act than a practical necessity, the operational experience of chief officers tends to be closely scrutinised by police officers at all levels.' In the Direct Entry proposals, Winsor (2012) signalled a fundamental challenge to the symbolic character of police leadership and the dominance of operational experience in leadership credibility and legitimacy.

The resistance to the Direct Entry proposals reveals tensions between the generic nature of the type of leadership required in a policing environment and the protection of the unique status of the police leadership role. In placing less emphasis on operational police experience in police leadership, the introduction of Direct Entry represents a critical moment in accelerating the trend towards the police leader as the 'police executive', removing the police leader from 'street cops', which furthers the divide between senior leadership and front-line staff in the police (Reuss-Ianni, 1983; Reiner and O'Connor,

2015). It also signals the normalisation of the police leadership role as comparable with the public service executive rather than the front-line police officer. The legitimacy of the Direct Entry programme, it appears, requires police leaders to carefully negotiate these competing narratives. As Wall (1994: 336) argues: 'In any organisation, the success of managerial policies literally depends upon the confidence that the managed have in the managers and an essential part of the common police psyche is the confidence that senior officers have experience of operational police-work and understand the pressures of "the job".'

While the Direct Entry proposals are a welcome attempt to create 'difference' in police leadership, the work of Loftus (2009) and Chan (1997) on police culture reminds us that, in isolation, reform policies do little to transform beliefs about how to establish credibility in leadership. Rather, the continual resistance may instead strengthen the primacy of 'street work' in police leadership and perpetuate a divide between those 'with' and those 'without' the operational credentials. A cultural shift is required within the police to ensure that the principles of direct entry move from 'supplement' or 'add-on' to dominant recruitment and promotion systems towards the acceptance of 'difference' as 'the norm'. Therefore, more is needed to challenge the fundamental assumptions of 'the ideal police leader' and to decouple this from the necessity of operational experience. As Silvestri (2018b: 322) explains: 'The Direct Entry scheme therefore should be acknowledged for its inherent transformative power to challenge the very essence and core organisational beliefs about "ideal" officers and the "heroic male" more specifically. Its power is enhanced when placed alongside other reforming strategies that call into question the core police identity.'

The professionalisation of the police service in England and Wales is constructed to place emphasis on particular occupational characteristics of the professions. As this chapter has demonstrated, the claim of professional status draws heavily on the narratives of education, evidence and ethics as symbols of the professional status of the police. The framing of 'becoming' a profession through these narratives represents an attempt to disrupt the taken-for-granted assumptions underpinning legitimacy in police leadership. The discourse of professionalisation represents a 'clash of knowledge' between the value placed on practical, operational knowledge and evidence, education or 'theoretical knowledge' (Adlam, 2002). Within the landscape of professionalisation, holding police leaders to account is an increasingly complex area. The final part of this chapter considers these tensions within the context of contemporary reforms to governance and accountability.

Governance and accountability

In 2012, in the most fundamental constitutional reform of police governance since the Police Act 1964, locally elected police and crime commissioners (PCCs) replaced police authorities in 41 police force areas in England and Wales under the Police Reform and Social Responsibility Act. This ended the traditional tripartite governance arrangement shared between the chief constable, the Home Office and the police authority (Loveday, 2013). PCCs have responsibility for ensuring the effective delivery of criminal justice and community safety, with authority to appoint and dismiss chief constables, set the budget for the police force, and determine local priorities through the Police and Crime Plan. The significance of the introduction of PCCs to police leadership cannot be overestimated. As Caless and Owens (2016: 4) further confirm: 'for the very first time in policing history, a person elected by the people and representing their views and concerns has formal oversight of policing, with wide ranging powers vested in statute'.

Democratic governance is at the heart of the PCC reforms by altering the conditions of police accountability through placing the public as decision-makers (Loader, 2000). Under the police authorities, the public lacked engagement and understanding of the structure of accountability (Myhill et al, 2003). In the context of concerns over leadership standards in the police, the introduction of PCCs aimed to demonstrate a commitment to local accountability and the increased visibility of police governance as a mechanism to improve relationships between the police and the communities they serve (Jones et al, 2012; Mawby and Smith, 2017). The appointment of a full-time elected official was considered 'self evidentially more rigorous than that provided in the past by a police authority' (Caless and Owens, 2016: 74). Therefore, not only would PCCs build stronger relationships with communities, but the intention was also to transform perceptions of the inefficiency and unresponsiveness of police constabularies (Lister and Rowe, 2015). The reforms therefore associate 'electoral answerability' with public connectedness and responsiveness as central features of police leadership legitimacy.

However, the PCC reforms sparked considerable controversy. The report of the Independent Police Commission (2013) was highly critical of the reforms, describing the PCC model as an 'experiment' that was 'riddled with failings'. As the report explained: 'the Commission concludes that the PCC model is systematically flawed as a method of democratic governance and should be discontinued in its present form at the end of the term of office of the 41 serving PCCs' (Independent Police Commission, 2013: 5). Unsurprisingly, perhaps, the introduction of PCCs was met with considerable unease among chief officers. Caless and Owens' (2016: 78) study, for example, noted 'the aggressive reception' from chief officers. A number of chief constable posts became vacant in the run-up and aftermath of the 2012 elections. A total of 22 chief constable appointments were made between the elections and July 2013, the highest chief officer turnover since the 1974 amalgamations (Brain, 2013). Public support for the initiative was also questioned, with only 14.7 per cent of registered voters participating in the 2012 PCC elections, the lowest recorded level of voter turnout in a UK local election during peacetime (Electoral Commission, 2013). The elections were branded 'a shambles' and the low voter turnout and spoilt ballet papers were considered an indication of public resentment to the concept of PCCs (Loader, 2014). The election process itself therefore raised questions about the legitimacy of the initiative (Mawby and Smith, 2017). In May 2016, PCC candidates stood for re-election in a less contentious atmosphere and with an improved voter turnout.

The introduction of PCCs shifts the dynamics of power in police governance. Indeed, the authority afforded to the PCCs is perhaps the most significant area of contention. Powers that had previously been held by local police authorities have shifted to a single individual, creating, Lister (2013: 243) argues, 'too powerful an office holder'. The authority of PCCs to 'hire and fire' chief constables, seemingly with limited scrutiny, was an especially contentious issue. Concerns over the 'unfettered authority' of PCCs were clearly expressed by the Independent Police Commission (2013: 82): 'The Commission has deep concerns about the dismissal of chief officers and the (uneven and lightly scrutinized) processes that have been used to appoint new ones ... the Commission believes that the new powers of dismissal risk exerting a damaging chilling effect over the leadership of the police service.' This authority to 'hire and fire' underpinned well-publicised examples of turbulent relationships between chief constables and PCCs. The dismissal of the chief constable of Gwent amid allegations of bullying caused particular concern and was the subject of a Home Affairs Select Committee inquiry launched that same year. The Home Affairs Select Committee (2013) concluded that 'It is very easy for a police and crime commissioner to remove a chief constable, even when the stated concerns of a PCC are about operational policing matters or are of an insubstantial nature. The statutory process provides little safeguard.'

Much of the resistance to PCCs is centred on concerns of the 'politicisation' or 'Americanisation' of police governance in England and Wales (Newburn, 2012; Sampson, 2012). The police service in Britain has long prided itself on its 'apolitical' status. The PCC embodies 'the direct insertion of electoral politics in local police affairs' (Lister and Rowe, 2015: 361), which is in stark contrast to the deeply entrenched sentiment of constabulary independence. Most of the PCC candidates are sponsored by political parties. In the 2016 elections, the 188 candidates comprised of 40 Conservative, 40 Labour and 30 Liberal Democrat nominees, and 37 of the 40 newly elected PCCs were representatives of political parties (Mawby and Smith, 2017). The politics of PCCs is particularly relevant, considering the statutory authorities assigned to the PCC. Questions were therefore raised as to whether the decision-making of PCCs would be influenced by political allegiance and financial considerations rather than public interest. The influence of the Mayor of London in the departures of the former Metropolitan Police Commissioners Sir Ian Blair in 2008 and Sir Paul Stephenson in 2011 illustrates the significance of tensions between elected officials and senior police leaders (Loveday, 2013). The introduction of PCCs represents a shift towards the greater integration of politics into policing and police governance. Again, this represents a new and complex challenge for senior police leadership.

With the advent of the PCC, chief constables now have to negotiate a fundamentally different governance relationship. While the PCCs' duty is to define the strategic focus of the police force and the chief constable defines the operational direction, in practice, the responsibilities of the two roles are unclear. The PCC role, in particular, was ill-defined from its inception; consequently, the lack of clarity risks PCCs engaging in operational decision-making more than intended (Caless and Owens, 2016). A fifth of PCCs in the 2012 elections were former police officers, with occupational knowledge of policing, which furthers the potential for local political interference in operational decisions (Lister and Rowe, 2015). It appears that the boundaries between the strategic and operational remit of the PCCs and chief constables are perhaps not as strictly defined as envisaged. As Lister (2013: 244) explains: 'the quality of the working relations between PCCs and chief constables is likely to be determined, at least partly, by how each understands, interprets, and acts out this slippery distinction'.

Conclusion

The contemporary landscape has accelerated the demand for change in police leadership. There are distinct challenges for the contemporary chief constable, who needs to effectively respond to these complexities in an environment of heightened scrutiny and risk. Police leaders are now required to manage an increasingly educated workforce and navigate a fundamentally different governance relationship. In this context, traditional approaches to police leadership are increasingly outdated. This chapter has critically examined the construction of the contemporary professionalisation agenda in the police within a broader historical and political context. The professionalisation reforms, justified as equipping police organisations to respond effectively to future demand, have situated education, evidence and ethics as central to desirable police leadership and effective policing practice. However, as this chapter demonstrates, establishing the credibility of policies of reform represents an acute leadership challenge. The resistance to the reforms from all parts of the police service reminds us of the power of police occupational 'craft' knowledge and the agency of the police to evade outside intrusion. While there is evidence of emerging change in the police service, the reforms may act to strengthen, rather than transform, the traditional assumptions about the nature and practice of police leadership. It appears that the contemporary policing landscape is one of both continuity and change (Chan, 2007a; Silvestri, 2018a).

Further reading

Herrington, V. and Colvin, A. (2016) 'Police Leadership for Complex Times', *Policing* 10(1): 7–16.

Holdaway, S. (2017) 'The Re-Professionalization of the Police in England and Wales', *Criminology & Criminal Justice* 17(5): 588–604.

Silvestri, M. (2018) 'Disrupting the "Heroic" Male within Policing: A Case of Direct Entry', *Feminist Criminology* 13(3): 309–28.

3

Conventional leadership theories

Leadership theory has long been critiqued for its lack of relevance to policy and practice, and the gap between the lived experience of leaders, the concerns and priorities of organisations, and leadership theorists. However, leadership theory has made a significant contribution to informing the understanding of what leadership is and how it ought to be performed. Empirical studies of police leadership in particular have typically conceptualised leadership through conventional theory. This chapter provides a critical insight into the conventional theories of trait, behavioural, situational and transformational theories. Through a consideration of these theories, we demonstrate how leadership has been conceptualised and studied over time. In doing so, we argue that conventional theory has a powerful legacy in relation to dominant discourses of police leadership, which perpetuate the person–centred assumptions about the nature and practice of police leadership.

Trait theory

As the first attempt to define and study leadership, many reviews of leadership theory begin with the trait approach. Popular in the 1920s and 1930s, the central premise of trait theory is that leadership is a product of individual characteristics or qualities. Leader traits refer to the 'relatively stable and coherent integrations of personal characteristics that foster a consistent pattern of leadership performance across a variety of group and organisational situations' (Zaccaro et al, 2004: 104). Traits are therefore understood as stable or consistent individual psychological or biological characteristics; these characteristics are measurable, temporally and situationally stable, and predict behaviours and outcomes (Antonakis, 2011). As such, trait-based leadership research focuses on the identification of the traits that predict an individual's capacity for leadership. As Bass (2008: 103) explains: 'traits of leadership are competencies. They are needed if someone is to emerge, succeed, or be effective as a leader.' Research on leadership traits emerged in the early 20th century from 'Great Man' theories and was prominent from the 1920s to the 1950s (Antonakis et al, 2004). Drawing on the fields of psychology and biology, studies of leadership during this period explored the key characteristics that differentiated leaders from non-leaders. Investigations examined the relevance of a diverse range of characteristics, from gender, height, age and appearance, to authoritarianism and the need for power (see Mann, 1959). Leaders were assumed as possessing distinctive intellectual, personal and physical qualities. Gibb (1949: 262), for example, noted that leaders seem to 'give more human movement responses which are supposed to suggest mature intellect and cultural interests'. In a well-cited review of the evidence on personal factors in leadership, Stogdill (1948) identified the traits most relevant to leadership as:

- capacity (intelligence, alertness, verbal facility, originality, judgement)
- achievement (scholarship, knowledge, athletic accomplishments)
- responsibilities (dependability, initiative, persistence, aggressiveness, self-confidence, desire to excel)
- participation (activity, sociability, cooperation, adaptability, humour)
- status (socio-economic position, popularity).

However, early trait research produced unconvincing results, mostly due to methodological errors and possible bias. In particular, the measurement instruments used in this early work lacked validity and few of the studies were replicable (Zaccaro et al, 2004). Many of the characteristics investigated were also both positively and negatively associated with leadership (Stogdill, 1948). As Jenkins (1947: 74) confirmed: 'The record of accomplishment is not a brilliant one. No single trait or group of characteristics has been isolated which sets off the leader from the members of the group.' Paying insufficient attention to the complex and dynamic nature of leadership, the study of traits consequently lost momentum towards the middle of the 20th century in favour of greater consideration of the influence of the social, cultural or organisational context.

Despite the criticism, the principles of trait theory have proven to be incredibly resilient. With more sophisticated research methods, the 1980s saw a revival in the study of traits in leadership. During this period, two bodies of research were evident: first, studies that attempted to isolate specific leadership traits; and, second, studies that examined the stability of leadership traits in different situations (Kenny and Zaccaro, 1983). Lord et al (1986), for example, conducted a meta-analysis of leadership perceptions and effectiveness, and confirmed the importance of personality traits. The study found significant correlations between leadership and intelligence, dominance and masculinity/femininity, concluding that 'personality traits are associated with leadership perceptions to a higher degree and more consistently than the popular literature indicates' (Lord et al, 1986: 407). The significance afforded to intelligence and personality remains a characteristic feature of contemporary interest in leadership. General intelligence appears as the strongest predictor of leadership potential (Gottfredson, 2002; Antonakis, 2011). Schmidt and Hunter's (2004) review found that general intelligence is a more important indicator of the occupational level attained, training performance and job performance than any other personality trait.

More recently, there has been a revival in the study of leader personality (Zaccaro et al, 2004). Personality has typically been understood in terms of the 'Big Five': neuroticism, extroversion, openness, agreeableness and conscientiousness (Digman, 1990; Goldberg, 1990). A review of trait-based studies by Judge et al (2002) points to strong, multiple correlations between leadership and the Big Five personality traits, with extroversion identified as the strongest predictor of effective leadership. The authors conclude that 'the Big Five typology is a fruitful basis for examining the dispositional predictors of leadership' (Judge et al, 2002: 773). Personality traits are similarly inherent in popular leadership discourse. Despite criticism of the validity of the typologies, the Myers-Briggs Type Indicator (MBTI) remains particularly popular with practitioners and leadership consultants (Antonakis, 2011). Leadership research has examined the link between the MBTI types and leadership, with contradictory results (Zaccaro et al, 2004). As McCauley (1990) cautions, there is evidence that associates all 16 MBTI types with leadership. Emotional intelligence is similarly popular in the mainstream management literature (see, for example, Goleman, 1995), although empirical studies are limited. Van Rooy and Viswesvaran (2004) conducted a meta-analysis of the relationship between emotional intelligence and performance outcomes which indicated that general intelligence was a stronger predictor of outcomes than emotional intelligence. Yet, the limited number of empirical studies of emotional intelligence have been criticised for the lack of validity and reliability of the measures and methods used (Antonakis et al, 2009). Although having a somewhat contentious history, trait theory formalised the belief in the significance of the personal qualities and characteristics of the leader in leadership. A key implication of the trait approach is that leaders are 'born' rather than 'made'.

Leadership scholars have continued to pursue the idea that personal characteristics improve leader performance. Contemporary leadership research has begun to consider the application of cognitive neuroscience to the study of leadership. This area of leadership research incorporates theories and research methods from biology, life sciences and experimental psychology to identify the distinguishing cognitive traits of leaders. Boyatzis et al's (2012) study, for example, monitored brain scans of neural activity when participants discussed their leadership experiences. The authors argued that understanding the neurological processes involved in leader behaviour and follower response could support leaders to develop more effective working relationships. Chaturvedi et al (2012) explored the 'heritability' of leadership in a study using a database of over 12,000 twins in Sweden. The study found 'a significant genetic component in self-reported ratings of emergent leadership', noting that 'genetic research on leadership emergence can inform interpretations of the effectiveness of efforts to encourage people to try and attain leadership and otherwise managerial roles' (Chaturvedi et al, 2012: 228). However, researchers are critical of the implications of using neuroscience to identify effective and 'authentic' leadership, particularly on ethical grounds. As Lindebaum (2012: 298, emphasis in original) argues: 'it raises important philosophical questions in terms of whether it undermines our appreciation of equity at work, personal accomplishment, autonomy and effort, as well as the value of *individuals* as opposed to mere *objects*'.

Empirical investigation of leader biography is perhaps a less controversial application of trait theory in the contemporary field. Adopting a narrative approach, this body of research examines the life stories of leaders, such as oral and written autobiographies, to explore the relationship between leader traits or behaviours and the leadership experience. As Shamir et al (2016: 13) explain:

> We argue that the leader's biography is an important source of information from which followers and potential followers learn about the leader's traits and behaviours, that the leader's life story provides the leader with a self-concept from which he or she can lead, and that telling the biography is an important leadership behaviour.

In trait theory, leadership is therefore understood as an observable, measurable and identifiable property of the individual. There is a powerful legacy of trait principles in contemporary leadership theory and practice. Dominant discourse draws heavily on populist management ideas or 'fads', central to which is a reliance on leadership traits (Zaccaro and Horn, 2003; Van Rooy and Viswesvaran, 2004).

Many of the leadership development courses delivered by management consultants are influenced by trait principles, and the emphasis on MBTI and emotional intelligence is illustrative of the power of leadership traits (Antonakis, 2011). Therefore, despite the lack of convincing empirical evidence, trait theory continues to influence mainstream thinking and contemporary leadership research. It seems that the person-centred principles of trait theory have acquired the status of accepted and unquestioned 'truth'. As Grint (2011: 9) concludes: 'coupled with concerns about the importance of emotional intelligence, identity leadership and the development of inspiring visions and missions, this seems to have ensured the return of the original normative trait approaches: we seem to have gone forward to the past'.

Behavioural theory

In a continued pursuit of the universal characteristics of effective leadership, behavioural theory emerged in the late 1940s in response to the criticisms levied at the trait approach. This approach dominated the leadership field until the 1980s, during which time, studies focused on the observation and measurement of leader behaviour (House and Aditya, 1997; Ayman, 2004). Behavioural theorists have been strongly influenced by the contributions of the Ohio State Leadership Centre, formed in 1945 (Schriesheim and Bird, 1979; Shartle, 1979). The centre bought together psychologists, sociologists and economists to study leadership in business, government and education from a behavioural perspective. As Shartle (1979: 132) explains: 'leader behaviour variables were the core, with lines showing relationships to other variables such as group behaviour and structure, organisational characteristics and environmental situations'.

The Ohio State researchers developed the Leader Behaviour Description Questionnaire, which provides scales for various different leadership activities and remains one of the most commonly used instruments in leadership research (Bryman, 2011). Researchers at the University of Michigan are also particularly associated with the behavioural school. Likert (1961), for example, developed the popular attitudinal scale based on behavioural principles. Behavioural theorists were therefore known for the development of various taxonomies, typologies and dichotomies to conceptualise effective leadership behaviour. These behavioural categorisations, Yukl (2013: 63) explains, 'are derived from observed behaviour in order to organise perceptions of the world and make them meaningful'. There has been a proliferation of behavioural models; Fleishman et al (1991) identified 65 different classifications of leadership behaviour. Leader behaviours have, for example, been described in terms of clarifying, developing or organising. Many of the behavioural typologies are featured in contemporary leadership and management training (Hunt, 2004; Dinh et al, 2014).

A central premise of behavioural theory is that leadership behaviours reflect either a 'task orientation', that is, a concern for the production and achievement of objectives, or a 'relations orientation', that is, a concern for the needs and interests of followers. A range of behavioural models were hypothesised using the task and relations principles, beginning first with Lewin et al's (1939) authoritarian–democratic dichotomy. The principles of the authoritarian–democratic dichotomy were further developed by Tannenbaum and Schmidt (1958) in their continuum of boss-centred to subordinate-centred leadership styles. Tannenbaum and Schmidt's continuum (see Figure 1) depicts behaviours that emphasise the use of authority by the manager at one end, and behaviours that provide freedom for staff at the other.

Blake and Mouton (1978) provided one of the most well-cited leadership behaviour models. The Managerial Grid (see Figure 2), first published in 1964, integrates both task and relations orientations in leadership. The central concept of the model is that leaders demonstrate varying levels of concern for people, that is, relations orientation, and concern for production or task orientation.

Figure 1: Tannenbaum and Schmidt continuum of leadership behaviour

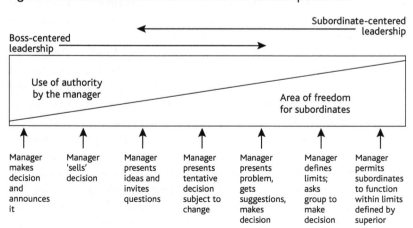

Source: Tannenbaum and Schmid (1958: 96)

Figure 2: Blake and Mouton's Managerial Grid

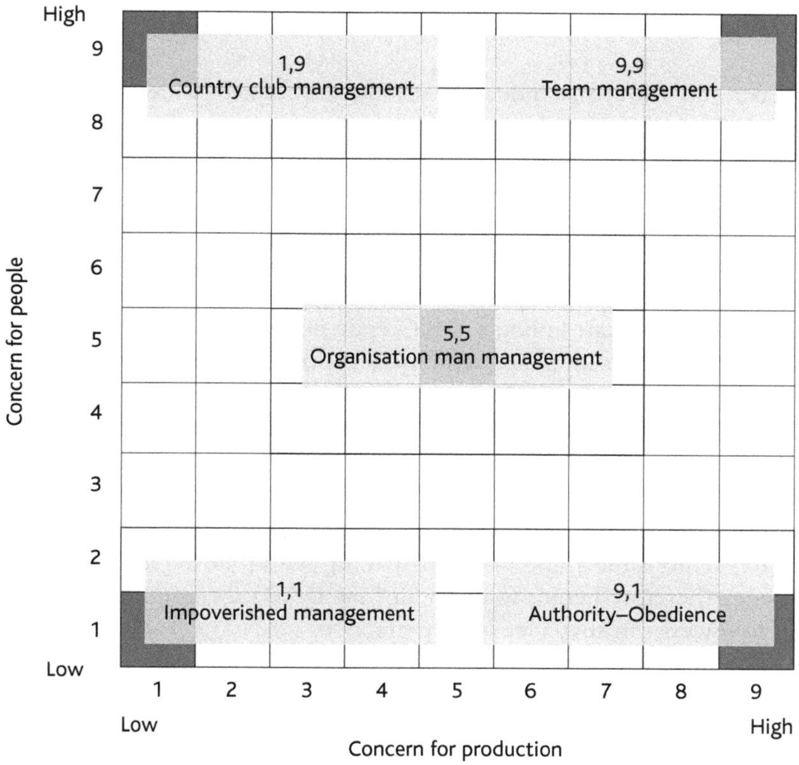

Source: Blake and Mouton (1978: 11)

The model depicts the varying emphasis on task and relations in five main leadership styles, as follows:

- *Authority-Obedience:* efficiency in operations results from arranging conditions of work in such a way that human elements interfere to a minimum degree.
- *Country Club Management:* thoughtful attention to the needs of people for satisfying relationships leads to a comfortable and friendly organisational atmosphere and work tempo.
- *Impoverished Management:* exertion of minimum effort to get required work done is appropriate to sustain organisation membership.
- *Organisation Man Management:* adequate organisation performance is possible through balancing the necessity to get out work with maintaining the morale of people at a satisfactory level.

- *Team Management:* work accomplishment is from committed people – interdependence through a 'common stake' in the purpose of the organisation leads to relationships of trust and respect.

Blake and Mouton argue that the most effective leadership occurs when leaders are highly concerned with both task and relations. The Managerial Grid depicts 'team management' as the ideal leadership style, reflecting a strong emphasis on both task and relationships.

Despite being one of the lesser known of the behavioural theorists, McGregor (1989), in 'The Human Side of Enterprise', made an important contribution to understanding how leader behaviour motivates people. McGregor proposed that there are two approaches to leadership, which he captures in his description of Theory X and Theory Y. According to McGregor, the Theory X manager assumes that people have a fundamental dislike of work, and consequently adopts an autocratic, carrot-and-stick approach to management. Conversely, the Theory Y manager, who assumes that people are fundamentally motivated to work, is democratic and shares responsibility and decision-making with followers. McGregor's theory therefore begins to consider how beliefs about the motivation of followers can shape leadership practice.

The study of effective leader behaviour is evident in police leadership research, particularly American studies. Much of this research focuses on the identification of leadership styles or typologies to describe leadership behaviour. Kuykendall (1985), for example, applied Blake and Mouton's Managerial Grid to police managers across 165 law enforcement organisations in America and found that a 'team' style was the most common primary managerial style. More recently, Engel's (2001) study of 85 patrol supervisors identified four supervisory styles: traditional, innovative, supportive and active. Andreescu and Vito (2010) applied the Leader Behaviour Description Questionnaire to 126 American police managers who identified ideal leadership behaviours. The study found that individual characteristics influenced preferences for a task-oriented or relations-oriented style of leadership. Schafer (2010) surveyed over 1,000 police supervisors to identify desirable behaviours; integrity, work ethic, communication and care for personnel featured strongly in the descriptions of effective leaders. In the UK, a central focus of the Scottish Police Service Leadership Study in 2008 was the relationship between leadership style and leader performance (see Hawkins and Dulewicz, 2007, 2009). The study identified three distinct leadership styles as 'engaging leadership', 'involving leadership' and 'goal-oriented leadership', and found that engaging leadership was the most common leadership style in the police.

Overall, therefore, the conceptualisation of leadership in task and relations terms was a fundamental contribution of behavioural theory. The interaction between the task and relations dimensions in leadership also helps to understand the complex, and at times contradictory, demands faced by police leaders. Relations orientation considers the importance of the follower; this approach typically emphasises practices such as open communication, delegating and the enabling of staff (Yukl, 2013). Behavioural theorists also furthered understanding of the positive and negative impact of leader behaviours. Autocratic or authoritarian behaviours, which have been a feature of many of the behavioural models, may produce obedience and rule compliance, which is particularly useful in organisations in crisis (Bass, 2008). However, these behaviours can also be disempowering and create an environment of fear and distrust. Therefore, from a behavioural perspective, effective leadership is largely understood as a combination of task and relations orientation, and this assumption is inherent in more contemporary leadership theories.

Over the last two decades, interest in behavioural theory among leadership scholars has reduced dramatically (Lowe and Gardner, 2001). Like trait theory, the validity of the measurements used have been heavily criticised (House and Aditya, 1997). Much of behavioural research is based on the self-assessment of behaviour, or follower assessment of leadership behaviour, so critics question the reliability of this work. As Podsakoff et al (2003: 881) explain:

> It is generally viewed as the tendency on the part of individuals to present themselves in a favourable light, regardless of their true feelings about an issue or topic. This tendency is problematic, not only because of its potential to bias the answers of respondents (i.e., to change the mean levels of the response) but also because it may mask the true relationships between two or more variables.

Likewise, behavioural theory assumes a linear relationship between behaviour and performance; this assumption has been criticised as oversimplified and reductionist (Yukl, 2013). Scholars have also challenged the assumption that certain behaviours will be universally desirable, and instead draw attention to the way in which effective behaviours may vary across different organisational contexts (Pfeffer, 1977; Biggart and Hamilton, 1987). Lieberson and O'Connor's

(1972) study of the sales, earnings and profit margin data of 167 large corporations highlights the internal and external constraints on leadership. The authors argue that experimental design, which is adopted by behavioural theorists, does not reflect the social reality of leadership (Lieberson and O'Connor, 1972). In other words, leadership in contemporary organisations is much more complex than leader behaviour. They conclude that 'these results suggest that in emphasizing the effect of leadership, we may be over-looking far more powerful environmental influences. Unless leadership is studied as part of a total set of forces, one cannot gauge its impact' (Lieberson and O'Connor, 1972: 129).

Despite the limited support for behavioural theory, the principle of task–oriented and relations–oriented styles has gathered momentum in subsequent theories of leadership (Yukl, 2011). DeRue et al (2011), for example, produced an integrative model of leadership using trait and behavioural theories. Transactional and transformational leadership, which is currently one of the most researched areas of leadership, similarly incorporates task and relations orientations (Bass, 2008; Antonakis, 2011). The assumption that leader behaviour is an important predictor of leadership effectiveness therefore remains a central feature of dominant discourse.

Situational theory

Preoccupied with leader traits or behaviours, early leadership studies failed to provide strong empirical support for universal indicators of effective leadership. Context, it appears, had been overlooked. Situational or contingency theory was the first attempt to consider the importance of the social context in leadership. The premise of situational theory is that there is no universal 'best' way to influence people; rather, effective leadership involves adapting the approach to leadership relative to the circumstances (Hersey et al, 2008). Situational theories attempt to explain the different leadership styles that are required in different situations. From the 1960s to the 1980s, models of leadership were developed that aimed to capture the interaction between leader behaviours/characteristics and the situation (Ayman, 2004). Situational theories develop the principles of behavioural theory in that leader behaviour is understood as the independent variable relative to the conditions of the situation (Yukl, 2011). Situational theorists therefore recognise the dynamic nature of the organisational environment, which requires leaders to adapt their practices.

Fiedler developed the first situational leadership model, the 'Least Preferred Coworker' (LPC) Contingency Model, in 1964. Fiedler's theory proposes that leadership effectiveness depends upon the interaction between the personality of the leader and the leadership situation. Here, the leader's personality is defined in terms of 'relationship motivated' and 'task motivated', which are measured by the LPC score. Fiedler emphasises the 'match' between personality and situation; effective leadership occurs when the leader's personality is matched to the demands of the situation, which Fiedler conceptualises in terms of low, moderate or high control. Relationship-motivated leadership is said to be more effective in moderate control situations, whereas task-motivated leadership is suited to high and low control situations. As Fielder (1997: 133) explains:

> The effectiveness of the group or organisation depends on leader personality (leadership style) as well as situational control. For this reason, we cannot really talk about a 'good' leader or 'poor' leader. Rather leaders may be good in situations which match their leadership style and poor in situations in which leadership style [and] situational control are mismatched.

In the late 1960s, Paul Hersey and Kenneth Blanchard developed the Situational Leadership model, which is one of the most widely known of the situational theories. Since its inception, Hersey and colleagues have made a number of revisions to the model, but it remains one of the most popular leadership models among practitioners (Graeff, 1997). The Situational Leadership model proposes the most effective leadership style relative to the needs and capabilities of the follower, referring to follower 'maturity' or follower 'readiness' (Hersey et al, 2008). According to the theory, follower readiness reveals how an individual is likely to perform in a task and includes two components: ability, that is, knowledge, experience and skills; and willingness, that is, confidence, commitment and motivation (Hersey, 1997). Like other situational theorists, the model includes task behaviours and relationship behaviours, with leadership style described as a pattern of both behaviours. According to the model, task behaviour is defined as the extent to which the leader 'spells out' and tells people what to do. This is compared with relationship behaviour, which is defined as engaging in a more communicative approach of listening, encouraging, facilitating and providing socio-emotional support. Relations and task behaviours are considered against 'follower maturity', which is the willingness and ability of followers. These concepts are incorporated in the Situational Leadership model in four leadership styles: telling, selling, participating and delegating. First, 'telling' describes a directive approach, with a focus on task rather than the relationship and support of the individual. Second, 'selling' is both directive and supportive, and describes a coaching approach to leadership. Third, 'participating' is a highly supportive style, demonstrating a high level of trust in followers, with less emphasis on the leader providing the direction. Finally, 'delegating' involves low support and direction, and assumes that followers are highly competent and trusted. According to the model, as a follower's maturity increases, a less directive approach to leadership is needed. The leadership style is therefore most effective when it corresponds to the needs of the follower.

These theoretical models have been applied to police leadership. Kuykendall and Unsinger (1982) used Hersey and Blanchard's model to assess the leadership style of 155 police managers in America, and found that police managers were more likely to adopt the selling approach and exhibited a strong aversion to the delegating style. Kuykendall and Roberg (1988) also used Hersey and Blanchard's model with 410 American police managers to explore the leadership style appropriate for different types of police employee. The authors identified six different employee types based on different attitudes to work, competence and motivation: rookie, worker, star, cynic, retiree and depleted. According to the authors, each employee type requires a different combination of the telling, selling, participating and delegating styles. For example, on the basis of their lack of experience, 'rookies' are best managed through a telling approach, gradually using the selling style as their competency in work improves. In contrast, 'stars' are considered highly motivated and experienced, and consequently respond best to the delegating style. Situational leadership theory has therefore informed the development of police leadership in terms of the differential responses relative to the needs of the follower and the demands of the situation.

Situational theorists have largely focused on contextual factors, such as the level of leader control in Fiedler's LPC Contingency Model or follower need in Hersey and Blanchard's Situational Leadership model. Other situational contingencies, such as gender, also influence perceptions of leadership effectiveness. Eagly and Carli (2003) note the extent to which leaders are evaluated in the context of conventional beliefs about gender and gender roles. Followers are more critical of women leaders, rather than male leaders, who display traditionally masculine approaches to leadership, such as directive or autocratic practices.

In contrast to earlier theoretical approaches, situational leadership theory emphasises the context or situation in leadership practices, which is a move away from understanding leadership solely in terms of the personality or behaviours of the leader. That said, situational theory is not a fundamental departure from earlier theoretical interpretations, with principles from trait and behavioural theories, particularly the conceptualisation of leadership in terms of task and relations, incorporated into situational leadership models. Through contextualising the nature of leadership, situational leadership theory was pivotal in emphasising the complexity of leadership as a social process.

However, situational theory has also attracted much criticism. Conceptual ambiguity, particularly the lack of a clear, theoretically robust rationale for the proposed relationships depicted in situational models, is among the most common criticisms levied at situational models (Yukl, 2013). There is also an overreliance on behavioural categories; situational theorists, like behavioural theorists, assume a linear relationship between the situation, leader behaviour and follower response, which fails to capture the dynamic nature of leadership (Podsakoff et al, 2003). Similarly, the behaviour description questionnaires used in situational leadership studies have also been critiqued for producing a halo effect of desirable leadership behaviours and reinforcing leadership stereotypes (Yukl, 2011).

Despite these criticisms, situational leadership theory has intuitive appeal. In policing, Whitfield et al (2008) emphasised that leadership in critical incidents was highly adaptive to the dynamic and fast-paced nature of the situation. While the prominence of situational theory has receded somewhat in recent years, its theory of the influence of the organisational context on leadership remains an important consideration in police leadership discourse. Set against a complex policing landscape, the influence of the situation on contemporary police leadership is likely to become increasingly pertinent.

Transformational theory

Transformational leadership is currently the most utilised theory in leadership research (Antonakis, 2011). Leadership is conceptualised as either transformational or transactional. Transactional leadership assumes an exchange between the leader and the follower, in which the follower is rewarded or sanctioned depending on their performance (Bass, 2008). In other words, leadership is conceptualised as a contractual relationship between the leader and the follower

(Sashkin, 2004). In contrast, transformational leadership considers the capacity of leaders to transform the values and attitudes of followers in order to motivate them to perform at a higher level. Transformational leadership encourages followers to prioritise the interests of the organisation over their personal interests (Podsakoff et al, 1990). As Diaz-Saenz (2011: 299) explains: 'transformational leadership is the process by which a leader fosters group or organisational performance beyond expectation by virtue of the strong emotional attachment with his or her followers combined with the collective commitment to a higher moral cause'.

Unlike previous theories, transformational leadership considers the role of emotions in leadership. James MacGregor Burns made a significant contribution to the understanding of transformational leadership. In *Leadership*, Burns (1978) compares transactional leadership with what he termed 'transforming leadership'. For Burns, transactional leadership is considered as an exchange or a bargain, such as goods, services or money, but with no fundamental transformation of purpose. As Burns (1978: 20) explains: 'The bargainers have no enduring purpose that holds them together; hence they may go their separate ways. A leadership act took place, but it was not one that binds leader and follower together in a mutual and continuing pursuit of a higher purpose.' In contrast, transforming leadership describes the process whereby leaders and followers form a strong attachment to produce higher levels of motivation among followers in the pursuit of shared goals. In transforming leadership, Burns (1978: 20) explains, the purposes of the leader and follower become 'fused'. There is an inherent mutuality and interdependency between the needs and motivations of the follower and the organisation; therefore, both strive towards a common or joint purpose.

In his book *Leadership and Performance beyond Expectations*, Bass (1985) draws on Burns' work to develop a new paradigm based on the assumption that transformational and transactional leadership are distinct and independent dimensions. Bass conceptualised leadership through seven factors that combined transformational and transactional approaches with 'laissez-faire' leadership, which describes the absence of leadership. Transactional leadership is understood as having two factors: contingent reward and management-by-exception. Transformational leadership includes four factors, also referred to as the 'Four I's' (Bass, 1990; Avolio et al, 1991):

- *individualised consideration* describes the concern for followers, such as treating employees as individuals;

- *intellectual stimulation* describes promoting intelligence and supporting followers to solve problems;
- *inspirational motivation* describes providing vision, communicating high expectations and displaying optimism and confidence that these will be achieved; and
- *idealised influence* describes attributes and behaviours that communicate confidence, ethics and values, and provide a sense of mission.

Empirical research on transformational leadership has been positive and generally supports the impact of transformational behaviours on employee attitudes, motivation and performance (Podsakoff et al, 1990). Transformational leaders, it appears, establish stronger relationships with staff and contribute more effectively to organisational performance compared with transactional leaders (Bass, 1990). Encouraging participation, collective activity and collaboration in leadership, transformational leadership has been hailed for its capacity to bring about positive organisational change. In the context of increasing demands and pressures to reform, there is high level of support for transformational leadership practices in the police across the globe. In a New Zealand study, Singer and Jonas (1987) applied the Multifactor Leadership Questionnaire to assess follower perceptions of police leadership behaviours and found that transformational behaviours were the favourable option. Densten (2003) surveyed 480 senior police officers in an Australian police organisation to explore the variation of transformational behaviours by rank. The study found that senior sergeants considered individualised consideration, idealised influence and management-by-exception as predictors of leadership effectiveness, while executives valued inspirational motivation. Sarver and Miller (2014) examined the leadership styles of 161 police chiefs in Texas and found that transformational leadership was perceived as most effective. According to the study, transformational leaders were considered to be confident, energetic and open-minded. Murphy and Drodge's (2004) qualitative study in a Royal Canadian Mounted Police Department found that transformational leadership was associated with improved levels of work commitment, satisfaction and motivation. More recently, Swid (2014) surveyed 154 police members in two Middle Eastern countries and found a positive relationship between transformational and transactional leadership with job satisfaction. In Britain, Dobby et al (2004) found that of the 53 leadership behaviours that were identified by police officers as effective, 50 behaviours closely matched the transformational leadership style. According to the study, these behaviours had a positive impact on job satisfaction and commitment to the organisation. Transformational practices have been endorsed as a mechanism to challenge the quasi–militaristic culture and outdated, command–oriented approaches to leadership in the police (Foster, 2003; Villiers, 2003). Therefore, unlike transactional approaches, transformational leadership has the potential to challenge traditional command-based, militaristic leadership practices and promote a more approachable, supportive and empowering workplace.

However, drawing on the dominance of transformational leadership in the private sector, scholars have raised doubts about the relevance and applicability of transformational approaches in public sector leadership. Currie and Lockett's (2007) study of secondary schools in England found considerable political constraint on transformational leadership in education. The authors therefore challenge the assumption that leaders within public sector organisations have the power to 'transform' practices, arguing that leadership in public services is heavily constrained by political and governmental pressures. The same is true in police leadership. Cockcroft (2014) argues that the operational context of police work conflicts with the transformational approaches of participation, collaboration and innovation, and Silvestri's (2003) study of senior policewomen shows that the rank-oriented culture acts as a barrier to embedding transformational leadership. Resistance to transformational leadership in the police is therefore underpinned by a 'mismatch' between the working environments of the private and public sectors (Cockcroft, 2014).

Critics have also drawn attention to the premise that transformational leaders 'transform' the attitudes of employees towards organisational goals (Grint, 2010a). Tourish (2013) argues that transformational leadership has corrupting and coercive consequences that have been overlooked by transformational theorists. According to Tourish, followers are disempowered and leaders are encouraged to engage in unethical and risky behaviours. As Tourish (2013: 7) explains: 'theories that seek to entrench leader power without considering the downsides of doing so need to be challenged'.

Transformational leadership theory furthered understanding of the role of emotions and change in leadership, which had not previously been captured in situational, behavioural or trait theories. However, studies of transformational leadership have neglected to adequately explain the influence of situational variables on the effectiveness of transformational practices. Therefore, not unlike its predecessors, transformational theory assumes leadership as context-free rather than context-dependent. Indeed, the universality of desirable leadership behaviour is reminiscent of the criticisms first levied at trait theory. In other words, leadership is too complex to reduce to a prescription of universal, desirable behaviours.

A critique of conventional theory

Despite the prevalence of conventional theory in police leadership discourse, there are fundamental criticisms of these perspectives. First, conventional theories define and study leadership as an individualistic phenomenon. Leadership is assumed to be the property of the individual, an inherent quality of the leader (Grint, 2005b). In other words, leadership is synonymous with the leader. As Hosking (1997: 300) explains:

> The bulk of research claiming to be concerned with leadership has, in fact, largely been top-down, attention being directed to those role occupants who are either assumed or active in leadership, or assumed to meet some conceptual requirement. As a result, a considerable portion of research has investigated leaders' characteristics, leadership being treated as though it were one.

Understanding leadership in person-centred terms prioritises the leader as superior; leaders are positioned as idealised and heroic figures (Meindl, 1995; Mastrofski, 2002). As the initiators of action, followers are reduced to passive, inferior recipients, assumed as powerless in leadership (Grint, 2010a). However, police officers have significant discretion and autonomy to adapt managerial policy so that it 'makes sense' in the context of their work (Holdaway, 1977; Skogan, 2008). Likewise, police officers have long demonstrated the capacity to resist and negotiate leadership. Therefore, conventional accounts of leadership overlook the ability of followers to contribute to, adapt or resist leadership.

The second criticism of conventional theory is the overemphasis on leaders as those occupying formal positions of authority. Leadership in the police has strong associations with the rank-based hierarchy (Silvestri, 2003; Herrington and Colvin, 2016). Police leadership has traditionally drawn on militaristic and positional connotations, such as 'leading from the front' (Davis and Bailey, 2018). This reveals leadership as understood in positional terms, equivalent to senior hierarchical rank, and associated with vertical authority (Bennis, 1999; Grint, 2005a). This neglects to consider how peers of the same organisational position have leadership influence (Charman, 2018). Panzarella (2003) explains that police officers are more likely to follow the leadership of peers rather than senior management. In this way, leadership is better understood as a relational, negotiated and collaborative process.

Third, conventional theory presumes that leadership is instrumental to organisational, team or individual performance. Problems and performance in organisations are simplified by situating them in one location, the leader, rather than dispersed across an organisation or the result of external social or economic influences (Gemmill and Oakley, 1997). The notion of causality is inherent in the rhetoric of transformational leadership in the police; transformational leadership has been celebrated as 'a vital component for changing police cultures' (Foster, 2003: 220). Police leaders are charged with transforming complex crime and social problems; the response to such complexity is typically the call for 'better leadership' (Wilson, 1968; Herrington and Colvin, 2016). It is virtually impossible to isolate the actions of leaders from the multitude of external social, economic or political factors, and to associate them with improved organisational performance. The functioning of an organisation cannot be reduced to the actions of a single individual (Lieberson and O'Connor, 1972; Grint, 2005a). Pfeffer (1977) criticised the 'personification of social causality' in leadership and argued that there are many factors that influence organisational performance that are beyond leadership control. According to Pfeffer (1977), the observable effects of leaders on organisational outcomes are likely to be small. It is therefore a myth that leaders are in complete control of complex social, economic or political events. Moreover, the performance of an organisation is simply too complex to understand solely in terms of leadership.

Finally, in conventional theory, leadership is removed from its social, cultural or historical context, and is assumed as power-neutral and value-free. Scholars describe leadership as 'reach and influence' (Gardner, 1990: 4), the 'business of persuasion' (Barnard, 1997: 97) and 'a special form of power' (Burns, 1978: 12). Therefore, in conventional theory, power appears as an accepted but uncomplicated and unproblematic component of leadership. There is an assumed mutuality and coherence between the needs and interests of leaders and followers. Follower compliance is understood as positive and desirable, and resistance as abnormal (Collinson, 2011). Police organisations have long been criticised for 'closing ranks', with occupational secrecy and police solidarity being problematic features of police occupational culture (Westmarland, 2005). Junior officers therefore have considerable power to resist leadership. However, follower compliance is not always positive and desirable. Tourish (2013) argues that compliance in organisations can inadvertently support unethical and dysfunctional business practices, which was similarly identified in Hough et al's (2018) study of chief officer misconduct. The pressure of compliance can, as Collinson (2012) argues, have 'silencing effects'.

Conventional theory assumes leadership to be an objective, identifiable entity, observable in the traits or behaviours of the leader, for example. However, to fully understand leadership, there needs to be greater recognition of leadership as a highly contextual, power-centric and value-laden process. Greater appreciation of the nature of power and the dynamics of rank in leadership practice in the police is essential (Gordon, 2002; Davis, 2019). In contrast to conventional theory, leadership is not a product 'out there', separate from social, cultural, historical and organisational influences, but rather situated in political and social context.

Conclusion

For almost a century, leadership scholars have grappled with what leadership means, and how it should be studied. We have outlined the ways in which leadership has been defined in a plethora of models, typologies and dichotomies, in traits and behaviours, relative to the situation, and in transformational or transactional terms. Dominant understandings of leadership draw heavily on the principles of early leadership theory; the concepts of task and relations orientations are evident in contemporary theoretical models. Conventional theory forms the premise of powerful normative assumptions about the nature and practice of leadership in the police. Contemporary theorists remain preoccupied with the study of leader characteristics and capabilities, and the identification of effective leadership, improving organisational performance and 'getting results'. However, the basic assumptions of conventional theory fail to capture the complexity of leadership as a dynamic, social process, and constrain alternative understandings of leadership. In Chapter 4, we provide a critical consideration of leadership as a socially constructed and power-centric activity.

Further reading

Grint, K. (2005) *Leadership: Limits and Possibilities*. Hampshire: Palgrave Macmillan.

Pearson-Goff, M. and Herrington, V. (2013) 'Police Leadership: A Systematic Review of the Literature', *Policing: A Journal of Policy and Practice* 8(1): 14–26.

Van Maurik, J. (2001) *Writers on Leadership*. London: Penguin Books.

4

Alternative theories of police leadership

Conventional theory, which dominates current understanding of leadership in the police, neglects to consider leadership as a complex and dynamic social process. This chapter explores the key principles of critical leadership studies and the theories of followership and shared and distributed leadership as alternative perspectives, and considers their relevance to police leadership. We argue that a social-constructionist approach to leadership, where leadership is considered as a product of historical, cultural and institutional processes, has an important contribution to the understanding of leadership in the police.

Critical leadership studies

Influenced by the principles of critical management studies, critical leadership studies, as an emerging strand of leadership research, represents a body of work that 'denaturalises' the basic assumptions of conventional theory (Collinson, 2005a; Grint, 2005b; Ford, 2010). Rather than being concerned with effectiveness or efficiency in leadership, critical leadership scholars consider leadership as a dynamic, negotiated, emergent and contested process. As Hosking (1997: 293) explains:

> We need to understand leadership, and, for this, it is not enough to understand what leaders do. Rather, it is essential to focus on leadership processes: processes in which influential acts of organising contribute to the structuring of interactions and relationships, activities and sentiments; processes in which definitions of social order are negotiated, found acceptable, implemented and renegotiated; processes in which interdependencies are organised in ways which, to a greater or lesser degree, promote the values and interests of social order.

Leadership as socially constructed

The work of critical leadership scholars is influenced by Meindl et al's (1985) concept of the 'romance of leadership', which refers to the 'false assumption making' of the exaggerated importance of leadership in mainstream discourse and a leader-centric understanding in which leadership is romanticised, idealised and understood as essential (Meindl, 1995). Here, the term 'romance' is used to capture how leadership is glorified beyond reality, with a strong emphasis placed on the causal attributions of leadership, where the capacities of leaders are celebrated. As Meindl and Ehrlich (1987: 92) explain:

> The romanticized conception of leadership denotes a strong belief – a faith – in the importance of leadership factors to the functioning and dysfunctioning of organized systems. It implies that leadership is the premier force in the scheme of organizational events and occurrences. It can be construed as an assumption, preconception, or bias that interested observers and participants bring to bear when they must find an intellectually compelling and emotionally satisfying comprehension of the causes, nature, and consequences of organizational activities.

Much of critical leadership studies is based on the premise that leadership is socially constructed. With its roots in symbolic interactionism (Mead, 1934), social constructionism is commonly associated with *The Social Construction of Reality* by Berger and Luckmann (1967). The basic premise of social constructionism is that social reality is produced, or constructed, through social interactions. Through social interaction, individuals learn social norms, values, rules and expectations, as well as the appropriate standards of behaviour in different social and cultural contexts. As Fairhurst and Grant (2010: 173) explain: 'people make their social and cultural worlds at the same time these worlds make them'. Perceptions, experiences and understandings are viewed as part of the social world, rather than objective and independent entities, and individuals participate in their construction and reconstruction as social actors. Multiple social 'realities', 'truths' and meanings are possible (Uhl-Bien and Pillai, 2007; Fairhurst and Grant, 2010). The focus of social constructionism is therefore the way in which social phenomena are produced and reproduced. As Berger and Luckmann (1967: 33) note: 'If the reality of everyday life is to be understood, account must be taken of its intrinsic character before we can proceed with sociological analysis proper. Everyday life presents itself as a reality interpreted by men and subjectively meaningful to them as a coherent world.'

The social-constructionist approach to leadership challenges the person-centred assumptions of conventional theory. Leadership is not attributed solely to the leader. Rather, followers are conceived of as active participants and co-producers in leadership (Shamir, 2007; Bligh, 2011). A socially constructed perspective contends that learned assumptions about the nature of leadership influence who is defined as leaders, and where we 'see' leadership emerging (Bligh, 2011). The focus therefore shifts to understanding leadership not in the activities or actions of leaders, but in followers' perceptions, interpretations and experiences. In other words, leadership is understood as 'in the eyes of the beholder' (Meindl, 1995: 331). Critical leadership scholars are therefore interested in the constructions of leadership – how leadership is imagined and legitimatised – rather than specific leader attributes or behaviours. As Meindl (1995: 330) explains:

> It assumes that followers react to, and are more influenced by, their constructions of the leader's personality than they are by the 'true' personality of the leader. It is the personalities of leaders as imagined or constructed by followers that become the object of study, not 'actual' or 'clinical' personalities per se.

Leadership is therefore understood as a social construct and followers are positioned as active participants. Lord et al's (1984) leadership categorisation theory suggests that learned 'leadership prototypes' are accessed by followers to construct an image of effectiveness in leadership. According to this theory, having identified a number of characteristics, these act as a trigger for the follower to construct the complete leadership image (Lord et al, 1984). In other words, a 'halo effect' influences the understanding and experience of leadership (Carsten and Bligh, 2007). Therefore, rather than considering leader traits as objective entities, particular attributes, such as charisma, confidence or decisiveness, are learned as indicators of legitimacy in leadership. This has implications for how followers understand their role and participate in leadership. As Uhl-Bien and Pillai (2007: 188) explain: 'the images we create of leaders not only influence attributions about leadership but also attributions followers make about themselves and their own roles and participation in the leadership process'. In conceiving leadership as socially constructed, the process by which followers perceive, construct and define leadership can be critically examined. Leadership is not an objective and observable entity separated from the social world, but, rather, highly contextual and highly subjective (Alvesson and Spicer, 2012). Therefore, critical leadership studies shift the focus from 'natural leadership ability' to the critical examination of how leadership is constructed, and the processes by which leadership is considered legitimate and credible.

There is an emerging recognition of the value of understanding police leadership from a social–constructionist position. Applying the romance of leadership concept, Mastrofski (2002) argues that much of the police leadership and management literature is underpinned by assumptions of romanticism, idealism and heroism. This leads to unrealistic expectations of and unsustainable pressures on police leadership. Police leaders are required to respond effectively to the outcomes of poverty, unemployment, drugs or alcohol; complex social and crime problems are positioned as a police leadership problem to resolve. As Mastrofski (2002: 154) explains:

> Those who study police organisations, those who attempt to reform them, and those who make policy about them labour too often under the assumption that the chief is the principal mover and shaker, someone who makes things happen. This is a romance that leads them to expect things of chiefs that are not within their capacity to deliver, it encourages them to assume a breadth, depth and immediacy of impact that is not supported by the evidence, and it diverts attention from contributions that chiefs can and do make to public police organisations.

Police leadership is therefore understood as 'getting results'; the expectation is that leadership is able to get results (Davis, 2018). Drawing attention to the complex internal and external influences on police leadership, Mastrofski (2002: 169) challenges the assumptions of causality, that is, that police leaders are able to transform organisational or team performance single-handedly, noting that:

> The metropolitan police chief is not powerless to effect substantive results, but he is not as powerful as the romance of leadership suggests.... He is one of many actors or forces who influence what the members of the organisation do and accomplish. His authority is limited, and that authority

is seldom translated directly into power that can realistically be exercised unilaterally.

In a study of senior policewomen in the UK, Silvestri (2003) captures the gendered nature of the social construction of the police leader identity. Drawing on notions of masculinity and heroism, legitimacy in police leadership is understood in highly gendered terms. As Silvestri (2003: 68) explains:

> To suggest that the career ladder is being climbed by a universal and disembodied worker is a myth. Progression within policing is premised on an 'ideal' type worker. Through women's own narratives of their journeys to the job, the characteristics of this 'ideal' worker become clearly visible. Reflecting on their careers through temporal (time) and spatial (place) dimensions, senior policewomen emphasise the importance of achieving credibility and commitment.

Understanding police leadership as socially constructed therefore challenges the person-centred and results-oriented assumptions of conventional understanding. Despite emerging work in this area, the criticality of social constructionism is not yet embedded in dominant discourse of police leadership.

Leadership, context and sensemaking

From a social-constructionist perspective, critical leadership scholars also consider how situations are constructed to legitimatise forms of leadership. In contrast to situational theory, which contends that the demands of the situation determine the effective leadership style, this perspective considers how the situation is interpreted and understood. Grint (2010b) argues that problems faced by organisations are constructed as tame, wicked and critical. According to Grint, each type of problem requires a different form of authority. Wicked problems require leadership, tame problems require management and problems defined as critical require command. However, the definition of the problem as tame, wicked or critical is highly subjective; consequently, a leader with a preference to adopt a particular form of authority is able to provide a 'persuasive account' of the situation to justify their approach to leadership. Grint (2010b) argues that individuals are 'addicted to command' and consequently frame situations as critical in order to legitimise a command approach to leadership. This has particularly resonance with policing as police leadership has typically been understood in terms of command and control (Herrington and Colvin, 2016; Davis and Bailey, 2018). In other words, how the situation is constructed, or 'framed', is important (Grint, 2005a). Critical leadership scholars are therefore influenced by the concept of 'sensemaking': the process of 'framing', or the management of meanings, realities and context (Weick, 1995; Fairhurst, 2005). This body of work is typically associated with Smircich and Morgan (1982) and their conceptualisation of leadership as the 'management of meaning', which captures leadership as a process of negotiation to define situations in order to influence behaviour. As Smircich and Morgan (1982: 261) explain: 'in understanding the way leadership actions attempt to shape and interpret situations to guide organisation members into a common interpretation of reality, we are able to understand how leadership works to create an important foundation for organised activity'.

The notion of sensemaking draws attention to leadership as a process of 'meaning-making' rather than an essential quality of the leader. Emphasis is placed not on 'being' a leader, that is, leader traits or behaviours, but, rather, on the 'doing' of leadership (Pye, 2005; Silvestri, 2006). Leadership is conceived as expressive and performative practice; the role of the leader is to convey meanings and understandings in order to legitimatise activities and priorities (Mastrofski, 2002). From this perspective, social cues inform the interpretation and behaviour of followers. The sensemaking literature therefore considers the power of language, symbols and rituals in defining situations and communicating expectations of behaviours within those situations (Weick, 1995; Pye, 2005). Understandings of leadership are shaped by the processes of 'meaning-making': the management of the meaning of situations so that forms of leadership are considered appropriate and alternatives are restricted.

Critical leadership scholars argue that dominant narratives of leadership, which locate leadership as a property of the individual, draw heavily on notions of heroism. Here, leadership is idealised, and the leader is, as Barnard (1997: 89) explains, 'confused with pre-eminence or extraordinary usefulness'. Critical leadership research is therefore situated within a paradigm of leadership studies known as 'post-heroic'. These perspectives challenge the individualist, heroic and authoritarian assumptions of conventional discourse, and instead emphasise leadership in terms of social networks and dynamic social practices (Fletcher, 2004; Crevani et al, 2010). As Pearce and Manz (2005: 132) explain:

This is the basis for what we call the myth of heroic leadership – that the source of all wisdom is the designated leader. We believe this myth flies in the face of the needs of many modern organisations. In contemporary knowledge-based, dynamic and complex team environments, both the cognitive and the behavioural capabilities of the wider workforce are needed to achieve optimal effectiveness and competitiveness.

Leadership as power-centric

Like critical management studies, a central thread of critical leadership work is the problematisation of traditional notions of power and resistance. Conventional theory has typically assumed that power in leadership is inherent but unproblematic and uncomplicated. Leadership is largely accepted as 'all about' power. As Gardner (1990: 57) concludes:

> To say a leader is preoccupied with power is like saying that a tennis player is preoccupied with making shots an opponent cannot return. Of course leaders are preoccupied with power! The significant questions are: What means do they use to gain it? How do they exercise it? To what ends do they exercise it?

Critical leadership scholars instead emphasise power as central to the nature and practice of leadership. The consideration of power in leadership is not from a dualistic position of powerful–powerless, such as the 'superior' leader compared with the 'inferior' follower of conventional theory. As Collinson (2014: 37) argues, the practices of leadership 'are typically not so asymmetrical and top-down that they are invariably one-way and all-determining'. Instead, critical leadership scholars consider the complexities and tensions, the dilemmas and contradictions, and explore how power in leadership is used, negotiated and resisted. An important contribution from critical theorists for police leadership has therefore been the consideration of the capacity of followers to construct and adapt, oppose and resist leadership.

For critical leadership scholars, the conventional understanding of leadership assumes leadership to be overwhelmingly positive, valuable, necessary and beneficial to individuals and organisations. As Ford and Harding (2011: 465) argue, the leader is assumed to be 'a highly virtuous and self-regulating individual who strives for utmost standards of moral leadership'. Consequently, conventional theory positions conformity and compliance as universally desirable, and resistance is regulated as 'abnormal' and 'problematic' (Alvesson and Spicer, 2012). In contrast, critical leadership scholars explore leadership in its destructive and coercive forms. In *The Dark Side of Transformational Leadership*, Tourish (2013) examines the damaging consequences of conformity as preserving unethical business practices through absolving individuals of moral responsibility. In theorising what he terms 'Prozac Leadership', Collinson (2012) similarly exposes how narratives of 'positive psychological capital', such as descriptions of leaders as 'charismatic', 'visionary' or 'authentic', dissolve the credibility of acts of resistance. Those who challenge in organisations, Collinson (2012) goes on to explain, are labelled as 'whingers' or 'troublemakers' in order to maintain the status quo. From this perspective, assumptions about leadership as inherently positive have silencing effects (Calas and Smircich, 1991). Critical leadership studies therefore build on feminist traditions to examine power relations and the ideological and institutional assumptions inherent in the dominant discourse of leadership (Billing and Alvesson, 2000). Ford and Harding (2007: 476) confirm that critical leadership scholars should 'challenge some of the taken-for-granted, hegemonic concepts of leadership and ... introduce them to other ways of seeing, interpreting and understanding themselves and their work organisations'.

However, the 'problems' of power in police leadership is a neglected area of research (Davis, 2019). Police leaders are in command of large police bureaucracies, with access to considerable resources (Reiner, 1991). Hough et al (2018) provided a rare insight into the negative consequences of power in leadership in their study of the misconduct of chief officers and staff in the UK. The study identified the ethical culture of police organisations as a fundamental determinant of misconduct in police leadership, and the lack of challenge as particularly relevant. Reflective of the work of critical leadership scholars, the study therefore highlights the problematic implications of 'excessive' conformity for improving standards and integrity in police leadership. As Hough et al (2018: 541) concluded:

> Chief officers need to recognise the specific risks of cognitive failure that organisational leaders face, and the temptations of excepting themselves from rules and norms. There also needs to be an organisational ethos in which leaders can be challenged and in which leaders are given the right sort of support when faced with ethical challenges.

The literature on police occupational culture has revealed the power of the police to 'close ranks' to outsiders and conceal malpractice, deviance and corruption, where solidarity and resistance to challenge are recognised as pervasive features (Van Maanen, 1978b; Punch, 1985). Westmarland (2005), for example, captured a 'blue code' of silence to defend against rule breaking in the police. Power therefore appears as an inherent feature of police occupational culture but, importantly, an under-explored area of police leadership. As Van Dijk et al (2015: 134) conclude: 'there is much evidence to warn us that the power that leaders gain at the top of an organisation may have distorting influence on their behaviour and this requires serious attention'.

In problematising the essentialism of conventional theory, critical leadership theorists have also contributed to a more critical understanding of gender and leadership. There is an inherent gender-blindness within conventional theory. Where gender features in mainstream leadership research, it is typically underpinned with essentialist assumptions. Empirical studies, for example, have explored the ways in which men and women 'lead' differently, with mixed results (such as Petty and Lee, 1975; Dobbins and Platz, 1986; Eagly and Johnson, 1990). Critical theorists emphasise that understandings of leadership are intertwined with stereotypical beliefs about gender and management (Billing and Alvesson, 2000; Sinclair, 2005). Leadership is typically defined as an instrumental, autonomous and results-oriented endeavour. Schein (2001: 675) refers to this as the 'think manager–think male' phenomenon: effective leadership is more consistently associated with male characteristics rather than female. Rosener's (1991) study identified descriptors such as 'strong', 'rational', 'independent' and 'linear thinker' associated with the word 'leader', which have strong resonance with the words that women used to describe men: 'strong', 'in control', 'macho' and 'rational'. Rosener (1991: 214) concludes that 'this simple exercise shows why women are not seen in terms of leadership potential; they don't exhibit male attributes'. In police leadership, Silvestri (2003) reveals the highly gendered nature of credibility in leadership through narratives of the 'ideal' police leader as tough, forceful, strong, aggressive, determined and competitive. Critical scholars therefore emphasise the need to uncover and challenge stereotypical assumptions underpinning our belief systems about the nature and practice of leadership (Gemmill and Oakley, 1997; Ford, 2006). As Fletcher (2004: 647) argues, leadership is 'not gender, power, or sex neutral but instead ... rooted in a sect of social interactions in which "doing gender", "doing power" and "doing leadership" are linked'.

Despite the emergence of social–constructionist perspectives in leadership research, the principles are largely absent in leadership development programmes. Rather, leadership programmes are dominated by the typologies, models and principles of conventional theory. While communication is an inherent feature of leadership and the use of language in terms of the 'management of meaning' to frame situations and experiences, this theoretical understanding is not yet embedded in leadership practice. As Fairhurst (2005: 166) confirms: 'framing was foundational to all but missing in action'. However, critical leadership scholars advocate the utility and application of these principles to leadership training. As Fairhurst (2005: 167) goes on to explain: 'If ever there was an academic warrant for a leadership skill quite new to practicing managers, managing meaning or "framing" was it.' The concept of social constructionism is therefore an important component in the development of leadership training in the police.

Followership

In leadership studies, followers are defined as 'subordinates who have less power, authority, and influence than do their superiors and who therefore usually, but not invariably, fall into line' (Kellerman, 2008: xix). This dichotomy between leaders and followers, with followers positioned as subordinate, powerless and deferent, is complicated in the police workplace. The literature on police occupational culture has long recognised the power of junior officers, as followers, to adapt and resist managerial policy (Rowe, 2006; Skogan, 2008). Reuss-Ianni's (1983) work captures the resistance of 'street cops' to managerial reforms through strategies such as foot dragging and sabotage. More recently, a study of New Public Management (NPM) reforms in a Swedish police force illustrated the different forms of resistance across the organisation, where middle managers responded to reforms by distancing themselves from senior ranks and embracing traditional, less managerialist, working practices (Andersson and Tengblad, 2009). The role of the follower in the success of managerial reform is therefore well acknowledged in the police occupational literature; yet, the experience and contribution of the follower is virtually absent in studies of police leadership. Followership challenges the conventional understanding of leadership, which has typically conceived of followers as conformist, submissive or passive recipients, or moderators of leaders' influence and vision (Shamir, 2007; Uhl-Bien et al, 2014). This perspective has an important contribution to make to police leadership studies.

An appreciation of followership equips senior leaders with a greater understanding of the complexity of follower experiences and engagement in leadership, as well as the values and motivations of their staff, thereby enhancing leadership practices. This section describes the key theoretical models in the followership literature and considers their application to leadership in the police.

The notion of followership emerged in the 1920s and 1930s, but studies during this time failed to provoke change in understandings of leadership (Bligh, 2011). It was not until the late 20th century that the notion of followership developed a more significant presence in the study of leadership. In his article 'In Praise of Followers', Kelley (1988: 142) argued that 'organisations stand or fail partly on the basis of how well their leaders lead, but partly on the basis of how well their followers follow'. Rather than focusing on the attributes of the leader, Kelley considered the characteristics of followers that differentiated them from other followers; as such, followers were not conceived of as a single, homogeneous group. In his later work, *The Power of Followership*, Kelley (1992) distinguished followers in terms of the degree of independent critical thinking and their passive or active behaviours, and presented these in a model comprising of quadrants of dependent–independent and passive–active. According to the model, there are five followership styles; alienated followers, exemplary followers, conformist followers, passive followers and pragmatist followers (see Figure 3).

According to Kelley, *passive followers* are the most passive and uncritical type of follower, with limited initiative and sense of responsibility. This group of followers requires close supervision. *Conformists* are more active than passive followers; they have the energy to 'get the job done' but lack initiative and defer to their leaders for inspiration and direction. They often finish a task and then return to the leader for direction. *Alienated followers* are critical and independent thinkers but passive in their role. They are cynical, often seeing themselves as mavericks, but do not participate in the organisation and do not provide solutions or support the organisation to move in a positive direction. *Pragmatists* are at the centre of the model and preserve the status quo, attempting to survive organisational change by 'keeping their head down'. *Exemplary followers* are very active and think independently. These followers consider the validity of a leader's decision before supporting it, offering constructive alternatives. Kelley (2008: 8) later refers to this group of followers as 'leaders in disguise', described by leaders as a 'go-to person'. A leader to exemplary followers is conceived of as an 'overseer' of change rather than 'a hero'.

Figure 3: Kelley's followership styles

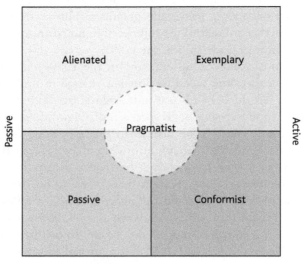

Source: Kelley (1992: 97)

These follower types allow police leaders to understand how best to utilise the skills and experiences of their staff. By presenting the different followership styles in a quadrant, the approaches to followership are not positioned as a hierarchy from the most to the least desirable; rather, value is assigned to all five styles, even the seemingly unfavourable styles, for example, conformists are also described as loyal and dependable. The model captures the interdependence of the leader and follower in 'effective leadership'. At a time when the leader was the primary focus of leadership theorists, Kelley's work was perceived as controversial. Therefore, this work reveals the stereotypical assumptions underpinning the understanding of the different styles and encourages leadership scholars to rethink the role of the follower in the leadership relationship.

In *The Courageous Follower*, Chaleff (2009) depicts the role of the follower as being as equally important as that of the leader for organisational success, where followers do not serve leaders in a traditional top–down process. Instead, he argues that those interested in leadership should 'get comfortable with the idea of powerful followers supporting powerful leaders' (Chaleff, 2009: 3). Chaleff explains that processes of socialisation condition followers to act obediently, which, he argues, is problematic for organisations. From this perspective, leaders rarely use their power wisely and consistently over long periods of time without the support of followers. This is particularly relevant to contemporary police organisations and attempts to develop a culture of questioning and challenge 'upwards' in the police hierarchy (Davis, 2018). Courage is therefore required to challenge dominant assumptions in the leader–follower relationship. In contrast to Kelley, rather than capturing the behaviours that followers exhibit, Chaleff describes ideal follower behaviours. As such, this work can be understood as aspirational – a call for followers to understand their power and accept their mutual responsibility for organisational practices – and describes courage in followership in five dimensions:

- *Courage to assume responsibility:* this includes assuming responsibility for themselves and creating new opportunities to maximise value to the organisation.
- *Courage to serve:* this includes supporting and advocating for leader decisions and assuming additional responsibilities to achieve common purpose.
- *Courage to challenge:* this includes acting with integrity and standing up for what is right.
- *Courage to participate in transformation:* this includes supporting and championing organisational change and the reflexivity of individual change.
- *Courage to take moral action:* this includes commitment to moral and ethical actions, at times, with personal risk.

Chaleff presented a model of followership in terms of the level of support provided by the follower and the extent to which the follower challenges the leader. The model depicts four followership styles: implementer, partner, resource and individualist (see Figure 4).

The partner provides a high level of support and challenge, depicting many of the traits of the 'courageous follower'. *Implementers* are characterised by high support and, as such, leaders depend on them to 'get things done' with minimal supervision. However, these followers are not likely to question problematic decisions; consequently, he recommends development in order to foster the confidence to challenge for this group of followers. *Individualists* are highly challenging, which provides an important balance and 'reality check' to teams and organisations. However, because of their lack of support for leadership initiatives and decisions, this group of followers is often marginalised; their challenge is understood as confrontational and becomes tiresome

Figure 4: Chaleff's model of followership styles

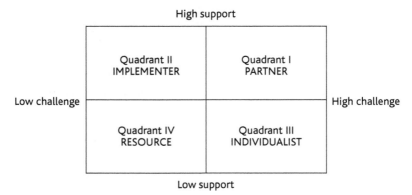

and predictable. Development for individualists should therefore focus on improving their visible support in order to demonstrate their commitment towards a shared organisational purpose. Finally, *the resource* meets the minimum expectations of their role; their priorities lie elsewhere and so they do not go 'above and beyond'. The resource follower, such as volunteers who commit a set number of hours, might be understood as uncommitted, so career progression and making a substantial contribution to an organisation are difficult. For this group, Chaleff recommends focusing first on providing support to the leader in order to earn the credibility to challenge.

Chaleff's model draws attention to the disempowering effects of assuming that followers are passive recipients, which is particularly relevant to traditional conceptualisations of police leadership in command-based terms. However, the model is based on how followers should, rather than do, behave (Crossman and Crossman, 2011). Followers should understand their sense of agency and their role in terms of power, responsibility and influence. However, these aspirations are particularly challenging in the context of police occupational culture, which places emphasis on conformity, solidarity and the 'blue code of silence' rather than questioning or influencing 'upwards' (Westmarland, 2005; Davis, 2018). The followership literature highlights the value of the 'responsibilisation' of the police workforce as an essential precursor to organisational reform in the police. As Chaleff (2009: 78) explains: 'Followers who operate from unexamined and disempowering rule sets toward authority relinquish their natural adult sense of responsibility for productively dealing with situations that arise. They regress to ineffective complaining without acting to remedy the situation.'

Collinson's (2006) post-structural analysis provides a further contribution to the understanding of followership in terms of a typology of 'follower selves': conformist selves, resistant selves or dramaturgical selves:

- *Conformist selves:* this describes the process whereby mechanisms of workplace surveillance and regulation produce 'disciplined selves'. This is particularly relevant to the police organisational workplace. Research on the impact of NPM on the police, for example, draws attention to the 'pedagogic function' of performance management regimes that value and reward conformity over 'difference' and innovation (Butterfield et al, 2004; Cockcroft and Beattie, 2009; Diefenbach, 2009).
- *Resistant selves:* resistance is considered an inevitable and necessary feature of organisational life. Opposition and challenge, Collinson (2006) argues, are important for legitimacy in organisational practices but can be problematic for the individual. This is pertinent to policing as ethics and integrity are increasingly centralised in police leadership practice. Hough et al (2018), in a study of chief officer misconduct, recommended an 'organisational ethos' in which leadership decision-making and practices can be challenged. In other words, resistance and challenge can be valuable organisational products.
- *Dramaturgical selves:* increased workplace surveillance constructs a 'heightened self-consciousness' in which individuals are aware of themselves as 'visible objects'. In this context, Collinson (2006: 186) describes the 'performance' whereby individuals negotiate and manipulate their environment to 'disclose, exaggerate, or deliberately neglect information' in order to present a favourable image of themselves. Dramaturgy is a well-established component of classic ethnographies of police occupational culture (Manning, 1977; Holdaway, 1983). From this perspective, attention is paid to the interactional and performative processes inherent in leadership, as evident in Van Hulst's (2017) study exploring the importance of 'backstage storytelling' in leadership. As Collinson (2006: 186) confirms: 'followers can become skilled choreographers of their own practices, learning over time to be more self-consciously strategic in response to "the gaze"'.

The typologies provided by Kelley, Chaleff and Collinson equip police leaders with mechanisms to consider the experience and motivations of followers in the police workplace. The negotiation between the follower and the demands of the workplace is emphasised and reveals the power of workplace surveillance in producing conformity or, alternatively, resistance and dramaturgical representations. The followership models challenge assumptions of followers as a unified, homogeneous group, and equip police leaders with an understanding of the diversity of follower needs and experiences of leadership. Empirical research in followership is still its infancy, and is virtually absent in police leadership studies. However, the emerging interest in followership has revealed the importance of the perceptions, motivations and experiences of followers in understanding leadership practice.

For police leadership studies, the followership literature problematises conventional power relations in leadership and re-imagines leadership in the police as a dynamic, interdependent process. The concept of followership challenges the dominance of the leader-centrism in police leadership. Rather than conceptualising leadership as a top-down process, with leaders positioned as superior, followership allows for the consideration of the equal and essential contribution of followers to organisational performance. Thus, the stereotypical assumptions of followers as passive and submissive are recognised as a barrier to conceiving of leadership as a participatory activity based on mutual influence and meaningful collaboration (Carsten and Bligh, 2008; Rost, 2008). Followers are understood as essential participants; as Uhl Bien et al (2014: 83) explain, leadership 'can only occur if there is followership – without followers and following behaviours there is no leadership'. Both leaders and followers 'do' leadership; the follower is 'responsibilised' as a powerful collaborator (Rost, 2008). In other words, leadership is considered a partnership 'constituted in combined acts of leading and following' (Uhl-Bien et al, 2014: 90). The research in this area also allows for the consideration of followers' understandings of followership: how followers interpret and define their role in terms of followership concepts, and how followers enact their role (Carsten et al, 2010). Uhl-Bien and Pillai (2007) argue that leadership emerges when followers define themselves and behave as followers; these definitions and behaviours are an important source of study. To effectively respond to the complexity of contemporary demand, senior police leaders would be well placed to understand how followers are engaged in and influence leadership. Set against the professionalisation agenda, and an appreciation among policymakers of the value of an organisational culture of learning and challenge, followership furthers understanding of negotiation and resistance as an essential and valuable feature of leadership. While the policing literature recognises that police constables, as the most junior rank in the police organisation, routinely make management and leadership decisions, their experiences, interpretations and understandings of their role in the leadership process are neglected. Therefore, despite the emergence of followership in leadership research, the role and experiences of the follower in police leadership remains an unexplored, yet vitally important, area of empirical study.

Shared and distributed leadership

The theories of shared and distributed leadership represent a further challenge to the conventional leader-centric understanding of leadership. Interest in this area emerged from the mid-1990s and is particularly associated with the theoretical and empirical works of Craig Pearce and Jay Conger. These theories portray leadership as a function or activity that can be shared or dispersed among organisational members (Pearce and Conger, 2003; Gronn, 2011). As Fletcher and Kaufer (2003: 22) explain: 'Models of shared leadership conceptualise leadership as a set of practices that can and should be enacted by people at all levels rather than a set of personal characteristics and attributes located in people at the top.'

Therefore, contrary to conventional theory, shared and distributed leadership is based on the premise that leadership is not the sole responsibility of individuals in formal leadership roles (Alvesson, 1992). Shared leadership is underpinned by principles of collectivity, support, interdependence, cooperation and participation. It reflects a more lateral process between individuals rather than a vertical, one-way, top-down activity between leaders and follows (Raelin, 2011). Overdependence on single individuals in leadership is understood as an organisational risk, for example, in terms of succession planning or staff retention (Pearce et al, 2009). Power, authority and decision-making are not centralised at particular ranks; rather, responsibility and influence are instead shared. Therefore, rather than relying on formal authority, shared leadership describes the informal processes among individuals, such as the influence of peers and influence 'upwards' in organisational hierarchies (Pearce et al, 2009). Shared leadership approaches facilitate creativity and innovation, and build strong working relationships, organisational commitment and motivation, leadership capacity, and organisational adaptability (Gronn, 2002; Day et al, 2004; Pearce and Ensley, 2004). Individuals are empowered to act as owners or entrepreneurs, taking initiative and accepting accountability (O'Toole et al, 2003). Sharing decision-making and responsibility allows senior leadership to focus more explicitly on defining mission and values, as well as strategic planning (Manz and Sims, 1989). In shared leadership, emphasis is therefore placed on skills, expertise and knowledge, rather than organisational hierarchy (Pearce and Conger, 2003).

In practice, shared leadership is evident in two ways. First, leadership is formally distributed within organisations, allocated to strategists or review teams, or evident in democratic structures and processes (Gronn, 2002; Manz et al, 2009). Leadership responsibilities and authorities, for example, can be devolved to 'self-managed teams', where senior leadership sets the initial mission and scope of the team, who then have decision-making authority and responsibility over a small expenditure budget (Yukl, 2013). Rotating the role of chair is an example of a shared leadership practice, where the responsibility to 'manage' the conduct of a meeting is not located with particular senior individuals, but shared equally across a team. Pearce et al (2009) also describe 'cross-functional teams' that bring together a range of experience and expertise to tackle important organisational issues. These teams do not function through hierarchical top-down authority. There is likely to be a formal leader in the team, perhaps positioned as the chairperson, but this role is typically reliant on the knowledge of the team. Unions were typically founded on the basis of what are considered shared leadership principles, such as democratic decision-making and structures, and understanding of the value of cooperation and working in partnership (O'Malley and Hutchinson, 2007; O'Neill and Holdaway, 2007). In higher education, Whitchurch (2008) discusses the concept of 'third space' as a collaborative team of mixed disciplines and backgrounds where traditional organisational structures are bypassed to facilitate participative decision-making. The priorities of formal shared leadership arrangements are therefore knowledge and expertise, rather than formal authority; consequently, the leader is understood as a facilitator or 'sensemaker' of discussion, knowledge and information (Day et al, 2004). As Pearce et al (2009: 235) explain: 'the leader is therefore highly dependent upon the knowledge of all team members. Leadership in these cross-functional team settings is therefore not determined by positions of authority, but rather by individuals' knowledge sets and consequent abilities to influence peers, in accordance with needs of the team in any given moment'.

Second, shared leadership practices are evident in informal, spontaneous and emergent ways. Gronn (2002) describes 'intuitive working relations', whereby individuals develop interdependent and mutually beneficial working partnerships, their roles being understood as 'co-leaders'. The influence of peer leadership is important here, for example, police officers of the same rank, but perhaps longer service, adopting an informal mentoring role to newer recruits, as observed in Charman's (2018) study. As Gronn (2002: 430) explains:

> Shared roles emerge when set members capitalise on their opportunities for reliance on others (e.g. by balancing each other's skill gaps) or because they are constrained to do so (e.g. due to overlapping role responsibilities). Intuitive working relations are analogous to intimate interpersonal relations (e.g. successful marriages and friendships), and two or more members act as a joint working unit within an implicit framework of understanding.

There is emerging empirical interest internationally in shared and distributed leadership practices in the police as police services move from the traditional artisan role to professional status. A study by Steinheider and Wuestewald (2008) explored a shared leadership team in a US police department, the 'Leadership Team', which consisted of a cross-section of all employees in the police department with the aim to improve processes and communication and build unity across the organisation. The authors describe the Leadership Team as 'high involvement' insofar as the team had capacity to share decision-making and direct activities within the organisation, as well as policymaking authority. The authors confirmed that 'rank and seniority play no part in Leadership Team proceedings and all members maintain equal voting rights' (Steinheider and Wuestewald, 2008: 150). The study found improvements in communication, employee perceptions of workplace conditions and labour relations related to the adoption of shared leadership practices, although, importantly, senior leadership support and commitment to shared leadership were defined as critical. The authors conclude that shared leadership is a valuable way for police organisations to bridge the gap between senior management and junior officers. Craig et al (2010) explored the impact of shared leadership on building relationships between the police and minority ethnic communities in the UK and found considerable support for open and consultative practices between the police and minority community representatives. This involved, for example, sharing decision-making with local communities in relation to police priorities, which is a distinctive feature of community policing. The authors explained that police leaders were 'prepared to engage in a transaction which deploys more resources to reduce local crime on the basis of information provided and the demonstration of cooperation from minority ethnic communities' (Craig et al, 2010: 340). The study found particular support for community involvement in influencing policing priorities and agendas. In Germany, Masal (2015) examined how to facilitate shared leadership in the police, such as lateral information exchange, and found that transformational leadership, as a particular type of top-down leadership, has a positive influence on shared leadership practices through goal clarity and job satisfaction. As Masal (2015: 49) explains:

> Transformational leaders who inspire and intellectually stimulate their followers become role models that followers want to identify with and emulate, resulting in team members who are willing to support other team members (shared leadership's affective-motivational function), to share information with other team members (shared leadership's behavioral function), and to engage in team learning (shared leadership's cognitive function).

Shared leadership principles advocate that no individual leader is likely to be able to meet the significant and complex challenges of contemporary demand. There is increasing need to recognise the value of collaborative and democratic approaches to leadership (Lindsay et al, 2011). Contemporary police organisations are large, highly complex bureaucracies; police officers and staff are working in an increasingly complex environment. Policing involves the 'wicked problem' of crime, and the social problems associated with crime cannot be isolated from their environment (Grint, 2010b). Therefore, command and control 'cannot be the only tool in a leader's repertoire' (Herrington and Colvin, 2016: 7). As Kingshott (2006: 130) explains: 'this means that the effective leader does not surrender his authority to a subordinate but recognises the importance of participation and involvement whereby the organisational standards and objectives are met'.

Empirical research on shared and distributed leadership is in its infancy, and the situations in which this approach to leadership is most effective are unclear (Locke, 2003). That said, the principles of shared leadership have intuitive appeal. The police hierarchy typically relies on senior ranks as decision-makers and problem solvers (Roberts et al, 2016). Mechanisms to bypass the quasi-militaristic hierarchical structure facilitate the empowerment of junior officers to respond effectively to contemporary demands (Andersson and Tengblad, 2009;

Davis, 2018). Senior leadership, overseeing large command areas, is not likely to have comprehensive knowledge of all aspects of their business; there is increasingly a need for police leaders to collaborate with subject experts (Lindsay et al, 2011). Collaborative and participatory forms of leadership are therefore particularly relevant in the police. Pearce and Conger (2003: 2) explain 'the realisation the senior-most leaders may not possess sufficient and relevant information to make highly effective decisions in a fast-changing and complex world. In reality, managers down the line may be more highly informed and in a far better position to provide leadership.'

However, there are distinctive challenges to adopting shared leadership in the police, where ability as a commander is considered crucial (Grint and Thornton, 2015). Shared leadership, based on the principles of power sharing, conflicts with traditional ways of practising leadership in the police, where the hierarchical structure, rank-based protocols and unequal power dynamics reinforce traditional, centralised leader-centric practices (Silvestri, 2003; Herrington and Colvin, 2016; Davis, 2018). In the police, success in shared leadership is likely to require senior leadership endorsement, which complicates attempts at achieving meaningful collaboration based on principles of equality (Steinheider and Wuestwald, 2008; Davis, 2018). Shared and distributed leadership is also challenging in environments that require quick responses and decisive action, which capture core elements of policing business (Manz et al, 2009). For these reasons, senior police leaders may be reluctant to distribute leadership authorities (Steinheider and Wuestwald, 2008). Similarly, junior officers may be wary of taking on additional responsibilities for fear of sanctions (Mastrofski, 2002). In critical incidents, designated individuals as leaders provide a clear and recognised structure of accountability. Shared leadership practices in this context are likely to be perceived as a high-risk practice. Reflecting on shared leadership in the military, Lindsay et al (2011: 540) argue that 'the conundrum is that complex, high-threat, and rapidly evolving unfamiliar situations are precisely the circumstances that can overwhelm the leadership capacity of the single designated leader and heighten the need for shared leadership capacity within the team.'

Shared leadership therefore represents a fundamental shift in traditional working practices in the police. Shared leadership is best developed in an organisational environment where unequal power dynamics are managed, and individuals are equipped as skilled, critical and reflexive thinkers in a learning-centred culture. These factors are not characteristic of the police organisation (Herrington and Colvin,

2016; Davis, 2019). The development of shared leadership in the police places considerable demands on current working practices, training, appraisal and promotion systems, and reforms to existing practices are likely to be needed (Craig et al, 2010). Despite the challenges of adopting shared leadership in a hierarchical environment, this type of leadership practice has been shown to facilitate stronger working relationships and organisational commitment, greater job satisfaction, reductions in staff absenteeism, and organisational resilience and flexibility (Yukl, 2013). Shared leadership therefore represents a credible alternative to traditional forms of leadership in the police. As Herrington and Colvin (2016: 10) conclude: 'as organisations increasingly grapple with the very real complexity of the social problems leading to crime, a better understanding and nurturing of shared leadership is vitally important'.

Conclusion

Critical leadership studies, and the alternative theoretical perspectives of followership and shared leadership, challenge the essentialist and deterministic assumptions of the dominant discourse of police leadership. These alternatives draw attention to leadership not as a product of the individual, but as a relationship between people, characterised by participation and co-production, and the dynamics of authority and influence. Leadership is removed from the traits of individuals and understood a dynamic, contested and negotiated collaboration. In transactional leadership, leadership is understood as a contractual relationship between leaders and followers. The role of the follower, while recognised, is still positioned as inferior to or 'responding to' the leader. In contrast, conceptualising leadership as a social relationship situates both leaders and followers as 'co-producers' of leadership. Understanding leadership as a relationship allows for the consideration of the different experiences and meanings of leadership: how, and in what ways, leadership emerges. Rather than focusing on the attributes of the individual leader, leadership practices, processes and interactions are considered an important source of study. This affords a greater appreciation of the distinctiveness of the police organisational environment.

Policymakers celebrate the relevance of non-traditional approaches to leadership to meet the demands of contemporary policing, for example, the importance of collaborative decision-making has been acknowledged to facilitate creativity and innovation (College of Policing, 2015b). Police leaders themselves are also receptive to moving away from a command-and-control style of leadership (Craig et al, 2010). The principles from critical leadership studies and shared and distributed leadership represent credible alternatives to traditional approaches to police leadership. That said, while official discourse calls for a greater appreciation of alternative practices, police organisations continue to cling to traditional, command-based and transactional styles as the dominant form of leadership (Silvestri, 2003; Grint, 2010b). Shared leadership represents a fundamental challenge to the assumptions of what police leadership is, and how it should be practised. Therefore, there remains a discrepancy between official policy, which celebrates collaborative approaches, and the practices and experiences of police leaders, where police leadership remains heavily influenced by dominant leader-centric discourse (Haake et al, 2017). It appears that leadership in the police continues to be understood in binary superior–subordinate, powerful–powerless terms (Gronn, 2011). Greater appreciation of the complex and dynamic nature of leadership, in particular, the value of follower 'resistance' and 'opposition', is essential to support police organisations across the globe to respond innovatively to contemporary demand.

Further reading

Collinson, D. (2011) 'Critical Leadership Studies', in A. Bryman, D. Collinson, K. Grint, B. Jackson and M. Uhl-Bien (eds) *The Sage Handbook of Leadership*. London: Sage Publications, pp 181–94.

Gordon, R. (2011) 'Leadership and Power', in A. Bryman, D. Collinson, K. Grint, B. Jackson and M. Uhl-Bien (eds) *The Sage Handbook of Leadership*. London: Sage Publications, pp 195–202.

Pearce, C.L. and Conger, J.A. (2003) *Shared Leadership: Reframing the Hows and Whys of Leadership*. California, CA: Sage Publications Ltd.

5

Leadership and police culture(s)

Despite a range of diversity initiatives, police leadership has continued to be perceived as a strongly homogeneous group over the past century (Reiner, 1991; Wall, 1998). With the vast majority of police leadership roles occupied by white men, the lack of embodied diversity among police chiefs is a visible and stark reminder of the ongoing inequalities in policing. This chapter draws upon the concept of police occupational culture to explain contemporary developments in leadership selection and promotion processes in England and Wales. Underpinned by the sociology of policing literature on occupational culture, training and socialisation, it considers the barriers and opportunities faced by police leaders. We explore the meanings of diversity in the context of police leadership, and assess how the diversity agenda is understood and enacted within policing. Through a consideration of the criminological and sociological literature on race, ethnicity, gender and sexuality, we argue that contemporary police leadership emphasises diversity in terms of an embodied identity, that is, 'appearance', rather than diversity in terms of alternative 'thinking' or experience. Moreover, we emphasise that the contemporary police diversity agenda is limited in its capacity to fundamentally transform police leadership and, as such, that diversity in police leadership does not necessarily create diverse leadership practices. Rather, we note the powerful nature of occupational culture in shaping leadership practices in the police and conclude that it is not only the person that shapes the leadership role, but also the conventions, expectations, norms and values of the leadership role that shape the person.

Police culture(s) and socialisation

Police culture is a complex concept. The term describes the accepted principles of conduct or 'craft rules' and occupational values, norms and beliefs that inform and legitimatise police practices (Chan, 1996; Loftus, 2009). Cockcroft (2007: 85) defines police culture as 'specific (and almost prescriptive) modes of behaviour, the values that inform such behaviours and the narrative modes used by the police to describe or accommodate them'. Schein (2010) depicts organisational culture in a well-documented model of three levels of culture: artefacts;

espoused beliefs and values; and basic underlying assumptions. At the surface level, artefacts represent the visible products of an organisation, including clothing, language, symbols, rituals and ceremonies. Espoused beliefs and values represent group learning of ideals, values, ideologies and rationalisations. At the deepest cultural level, basic underlying assumptions are unconscious, taken-for-granted beliefs that determine behaviour. These assumptions operate as unquestionable truths and are consequently incredibly resilient to change.

The explanatory power of police occupational culture to understand police working practices has dominated academic discourse for over 50 years. Much of this work has been prompted by concern and interest in the high levels of discretion and autonomy afforded to front-line police officers. In other words, policing practices are only partially determined by managerial or legalistic policy (Bayley and Bittner, 1984; Chatterton, 1995). A long history of empirical research has captured the importance of occupational culture as a framework that shapes understandings and beliefs about the nature and practice of police work, and accepted principles of conduct in the police workplace (Banton, 1964; Cain, 1973; Manning, 1977; Van Maanen, 1978b). These classic ethnographies highlight the inevitability and necessity of police occupational culture as an inherent feature of police work. Skolnick (1975) illustrates this argument through his well-cited thesis of the police 'working personality'. According to Skolnick, the police working personality is a response to the unique combination of danger and authority as integral features of police work. Danger is understood as the risks in the confrontational nature of the police task and authority as the legal and symbolic position of the police as an institution. The police working personality represents a 'defining identity' and a 'style of life', and constructs distinctive ways of seeing and understanding the police working world (Skolnick, 1975, 2008). The features of danger and authority are well documented in studies of police occupational culture (Van Maanen, 1974; Muir, 1979; Paoline, 2003). These are captured in Reiner's (2010) well-cited core characteristics, which summarise the prevailing features of police occupational culture as the characteristics of a sense of mission, cynicism/pessimism, suspicion, isolation/solidarity, machismo and racial prejudice. More recently, Charman's (2018) longitudinal study of new police recruits identified the emerging cultural characteristics of cynicism, communication, comradeship, a code of self-protection, categorisation and compassion. Therefore, as the police occupational literature reveals, police work is understood through the rhetoric of crime fighting, action and excitement, and risk and dangerousness, which are seen as intrinsic and valued aspects of police work (Bittner, 1967; Punch, 1979). These characteristics have provided a conceptual lens that has dominated much of academic understanding of the police occupational world.

Police officers have socially constructed ways of understanding their work and activities that act as taken-for-granted, unquestionable 'common sense' (Holdaway, 1983; O'Neill and Singh, 2007). As Manning (1977: 142) describes, police culture is 'a set of implicit and unexplicated understandings that might be called a "commonsense theory of policing"': what everyone knows and takes for granted as well as the knowledge of skills a policeman must display in order to be viewed as a competent member of the force'. These understandings are not institutionalised in law, policy or training, and are rarely written down; rather, they are learnt through a process of socialisation into a complex arrangement of rituals, symbols, stories, interactions and experiences (Fielding, 1988; Chatterton, 1995). These processes equip new members with the occupational rules necessary to prescribe practice, for example, the appropriate ways to express opinions and use authority (Skolnick, 2008). The sociology of occupations literature explores the socially constructed nature of occupational identity. This body of work examines the way in which individuals demonstrate identification with and commitment to their occupations, which reflects broader assumptions about the nature of work and societal position of the role. As Becker and Carper (1956: 346) explain: 'occupational identities contain an implicit reference to the person's position in the larger society, tending to specify the positions appropriate for a person doing such work or which have become possible for him by virtue of his work'. Van Maanen (1978b), who provides one of the most influential accounts of occupational socialisation in the police, conceptualises the process of the socialisation of new police recruits as a sequence of four stages:

- pre-entry: choice
- admittance: introduction
- change: encounter
- continuance: metamorphosis

The pre-entry stage captures the assumptions, ideals and values that influence the decision to join the police. Van Maanen identifies assumptions about what constitutes police work, in particular, the appeal of the dangerousness, excitement and action of job, as underpinning the motivation to become a police officer. Studies have also found attachment to the concept of service and 'making a difference' as key motivators (Fielding, 1988; Chan et al, 2003). At this stage, the new recruit identifies with the beliefs and assumptions about the police officer role and the nature of police work (Charman, 2018). In other words, potential police officers have a clear narrative about policing. As Van Maanen (1978b: 296) explains: 'most policemen have not chosen their career casually. They enter the department with a high degree of normative identification with what they perceive to be the goals and values of the organisation.'

The second stage – admittance – describes the introduction to the police organisation through initial police training, where the new police recruit learns the formal rules and expectations. Training school provides formal socialisation, establishing commitment to the 'official line' of formal policy, values and expectations (Fielding, 1988). Brown (2007: 215) concludes that 'training school provides a rehearsal of the way the occupational culture can nurture and protect its members, along with the message that being accepted by the group has primacy over individual needs; the training environment serves to reinforce rather than challenge prevailing received police wisdom'. Importantly, it is during this stage that the new recruit is first exposed to the 'war stories' of occupational culture, where details of past situations, events and individuals reveal the organisation's history, norms and values (Manning, 1977; Chatterton, 1995). This stage is underpinned by assumptions of obedience and submissiveness set against adaption and resistance. As Van Maanen (1978b: 299) explains: 'the initiate learns that the formal rules and regulations are applied inconsistently. What is sanctioned in one case with a gig is ignored in another case. To the recruits, academy rules become behavioural prescriptions which are to be coped with formally, but informally dismissed.'

The third stage describes the first experience of street policing, where the new recruit is exposed to the 'realities' of police work and learns the behaviour that is expected to manage these encounters. During this stage, the new recruits build a strong identification with their new role as a police officer. Scholars have described this as a period of 'de-socialisation' from civilian to 'new police family' (Fielding, 1988; Charman, 2018). With continued exposure to 'tales, myths and legends' throughout this stage, the new recruit is 'most susceptible to attitude change' (Van Maanen, 1978b: 301). The tutor constable is especially influential: the reactions of the probationer are scrutinised, their adaptability to situations is evaluated and their involvement in risk-taking is appraised. This experience constitutes the shared beginnings and common 'test' endured by police officers in which they demonstrate commitment and kinship with colleagues. The influence of the tutor constable ensures the continuity of occupational cultural values, ideals and expectations, overshadowing the experience of formal training in the academy. As Van Maanen (1978b: 300) concludes: 'this traditional feature of police work – patrolmen training patrolmen – ensures continuity from class to class of police officers regardless of the academic instruction. In large measure, the flow of influence from one generation to another accounts for the remarkable stability of the pattern of police behaviour.'

The final stage, which Van Maanen describes as 'metamorphosis', refers to the acceptance of occupational ideologies. This perspective echoes observations made by other policing scholars. Fielding (1988: 16) describes socialisation as a cumulative process of identity transformation, a 'stripping away of the old', whereby police officers are assimilated into the occupational culture, with characteristic ways of seeing and understanding the world. For Van Maanen (1978b), during the metamorphosis stage, the new police officer learns that the reality of police work is far removed from the assumptions underpinning the motivations to join. In contrast to expectations, the job consists of routine, mundane and administrative tasks, as well as highly scrutinised, bureaucratic regulatory procedures, interspersed with the unpredictability of patrol work. The high levels of scrutiny and regulation are particularly important. The policing literature captures the repressive and punitive but unpredictable nature of supervision as a defining feature of the police organisational environment (Paoline, 2003). Consequently, police officers develop coping strategies to successfully negotiate the mundanity and scrutiny through, for example, approaches of 'lay low' and 'don't make waves' to protect oneself from sanction. These coping strategies become inherent features of navigating the police occupational environment, 'doing' police work and 'being' a police officer. As Van Maanen (1978b: 305) confirms:

> Since the vast majority of time is spent on tasks other than real police work, there is little incentive for performance. In other words, the young patrolman discovers the most satisfying solution to the labyrinth of hierarchy, the red tape and the paperwork, the plethora of rules and regulations, and the 'dirty work' which characterise the occupation is to adopt the group norm stressing staying out of trouble.

The experiences at each stage of the socialisation process shape the norms and values about the nature of police work, and ideals about what it means to be a police officer. Van Maanen's work documents the process by which the shared beginnings of police officers construct a sense of 'sameness' in understandings, sentiments and practices, with solidarity and group acceptance as defining features. Police officers learn to adapt to the nature of the police working environment as 'punishment-centred bureaucracy' by demonstrating similarity in attitudes and behaviour with colleagues to 'avoid censure' from the organisation, supervisors and peers (Van Maanen, 1974; Waddington, 1999a). These principles of 'sameness' are a prevailing feature of the police occupational culture. Manning (1977), in a seminal study of police work in London and the US, describes police socialisation as the construction of 'collectively oriented individuals'. Likewise, Fielding's (1988: 16) study of police training documents the elimination of difference inherent in the socialisation process, noting that 'trainers seek to reduce any diversity among recruits'. In addition to the more recent literature therefore, Van Maanen's account of socialisation captures the importance of conformity to shared understandings about the nature of police work, the police workplace and the role and requirements of a police officer (Chan et al, 2003; Charman, 2018).

Informed by Van Maanen's earlier work, the process of socialisation is captured in Charman's (2018) study, where police recruits described six ways of learning: learning from doing, learning from watching, learning from mistakes, learning from common sense, learning from experience and learning from adapting. These concepts are set against a model, the square of police learning (see Figure 5), which combines the style (formal and informal) and the direction (vertical and horizontal) of learning to depict the process of learning as an inherently social process. This reveals the tensions and symmetry between formal and informal learning, and the key influencers of the tutor, the police trainer, the sergeant and colleagues in the socialisation of new police recruits.

Despite the high degree of consensus about police culture within the literature, recent years have witnessed an increasing critique of such accounts. Traditional accounts have typically understood police occupational culture through a 'cultural inheritance model' in which values and beliefs are 'transmitted' from one generation to the next (Charman, 2018). This perspective neglects to consider the variation and diversity of experiences, interpretations and behaviours in the police in favour of focusing on the factors of commonality in the police occupational world (Cockcroft, 2007). While there is an emphasis on solidarity as a prevailing theme, academic writers also understand the police occupational environment in terms of multiple and fluid

Figure 5: The square of police learning

	'FORMAL' LEARNING	'INFORMAL' LEARNING
VERTICAL LEARNING	Classroom-based learning focusing upon the acquisition of skills and knowledge, passed on from 'expert' to 'novice'. This is exemplified by *police trainers* at force training schools and by the new pre-join qualifications, studies either in a classroom setting or online	Non-prescriptive direction and advice during early placements within police stations, most notably from the *sergeant* in charge of the shift.
HORIZONTAL LEARNING	'On-the-job' learning through a process of tutelage or 'shadowing'. The *tutor* period is an aspect of formal learning processes where new recruits spend approximately ten weeks under the supervision of another constable on shift. Part of the process involves completion of the prescribed tasks on the Police Action Checklist.	Non-prescriptive direction and advice during early placements within police stations. This comes from other constables who are *colleagues* of the same rank as the new recruits, although with more experience. There are therefore no line-management responsibilities.

Source: Charman (2018: 320)

cultures, as well as divergent, and at times conflicting, expressions of police culture (Chan, 1997; Paoline, 2003; Loftus, 2009). Police occupational culture does not describe a unified and monolithic entity; rather, there are variations or 'subcultures' depending on factors such as specialism, gender or geography (Westmarland, 2002; Foster, 2003). As Fielding (1988: 185) argues, scholars recognise police culture in terms of 'its internal variations and textures'. The police organisational environment is understood in terms of 'subcultures', for example, related to urban/rural location (Cain, 1973; Young, 1993), role (Hobbs, 1988; Loftus et al, 2016) and rank (Punch, 1983; Reuss-Ianni, 1983; Van Maanen, 1997). Silvestri (2003, 2007, 2017) also emphasises the plurality of police cultures in her work on gender and police leadership, noting that the 'cult of masculinity' and its attendant association with physicality is characteristic of the culture of the lower ranks and not that of those in senior roles. She argues that police leaders are subject to different organisational and cultural expectations that have little to do with physical presence, but are rather best characterised through a 'smart macho' culture. As such, theorists acknowledge the importance of understanding the variation within police occupational culture and consider the police organisation in terms of police *cultures*. Police occupational environment is therefore conceptualised as a complex and fragmented space; a 'multitude of contradictions' exist (Charman, 2018).

Similarly, assumptions of the timeless and unchanging nature of police culture are also challenged. Police occupational culture is not isolated from wider social, political, economic and cultural contexts, yet dominant conceptualisations of police occupational culture do not sufficiently capture the influence of these external forces (Chan, 1997; Charman, 2018). The embedding of community policing, for example, represents a shift away from centralised decision-making and the crime-fighting focus of police work, and challenges dominant characteristics of police occupational culture (Brogden, 1999; Manning, 2002; Paoline et al, 2006). Likewise, contemporary policies, such as the Direct Entry scheme in England and Wales, also have the potential to disrupt dominant norms, values and ideologies in the police workplace (Silvestri, 2018b). That said, theorists also accept that the intrinsic characteristics of police occupational culture are notoriously resistant to change (Skogan, 2008; Skolnick, 2008; Loftus, 2010). While the wider social context undoubtedly has an influence on the police working environment, it is less likely that these influences will provoke a fundamental transformation of the basic underlying assumptions shaping policing practices. As Charman (2018: 339) concludes: 'the new characteristics do not replace the old, but over time, may gradually diminish their prevalence'.

Theorists have also challenged the assumed passivity of traditional depictions of police socialisation. Here, individuals do not passively absorb cultural influences, but have agency to interpret, adapt to and respond to their occupational environment. As Reiner (2010: 116) explains, culture is 'embodied in individuals who enjoy autonomy and creativity'. The sensemaking literature has made an important contribution to understanding organisations and organisational practices. This body of work conceptualises individuals not as fixed or unchangeable entities, but as social actors who 'make sense' of organisational environments and their position within them (Weick, 1995; Pye, 2005). Police occupational culture forms a powerful framework for understanding police practices, but as Fielding (1988: 10) explains, 'the individual officer is the final arbiter or mediator of these influences'. Police officers actively construct and sustain meanings in police work (Holdaway, 1983). Chan (1996: 111) concludes that 'while the culture may be powerful, it is nevertheless up to individuals to accommodate or resist its influence'.

Finally, contemporary theorists are critical of the problematisation of police occupational culture. Unlike other organisational cultures that tend to be framed in a positive light, police occupational culture has largely been conceived in negative terms (Alvesson, 2011; Cockcroft, 2017). Indeed, academic interest in police occupational culture emerged in the 1960s and 1970s through concern over the nature of police discretion and controversies regarding police violence and corruption (Reiner, 2000; Westmarland, 2005). As Van Maanen (1978b: 307) explains: 'most police reformers view the behaviour of individual patrolmen as a problem for the department or society, not vice versa'. Police culture has been used to explain malpractice and deviance, as well as the negative attitudes and values of police officers (Chan, 1997; Westmarland, 2008). The positive aspects of police occupational culture have largely been neglected in dominant discourse. Waddington (1999b) highlights the important function of police occupational culture as a 'repair shop', where storytelling and jokes, both integral features of police culture, are used to release tension. Aspects of police occupational culture are understood to help police officers cope with the emotional realities of police work and the strains of the police working environment (Van Maanen, 1978b; Paoline, 2003). Assumptions of police culture as inherently negative neglect to consider the beneficial and functional aspects that sustain components of occupational culture(s) in the police.

Overall, therefore, contemporary theorists challenge reductionist and deterministic interpretations of police occupational culture. Assumptions of policing practices in terms of a causal relationship between culture and behaviours are critiqued as these approaches fail to capture the complexity of police work and the police organisation (Cockcroft, 2007). Sklansky (2007) critiques the deterministic ideas about police occupational culture as 'cognitive burn in', where conventional understanding of the police as a distinct, unified and isolated occupational group in which police officers' 'minds are dyed blue', has diverted attention from the empirical exploration of the differences between officers. As Sklansky (2007: 41) explains: 'the problem with a burned-in image, even a good one, is what it prevents us from seeing'. Manning (2007: 50) argues that dominant conceptualisations of police culture have therefore 'stripped the organisation of its politics and nuance'. Police occupational culture is not an absolute, fixed determinant of practice; instead, the police organisation is a fragmented, segregated and contested space. Yet, as Fielding (1988: 15) reminds us, members of the police organisation 'are hardly free to fashion their world entirely by their own lights'.

The police occupational environment is therefore understood as a space in which the 'ordering' and 'rule-making' of police occupational culture is actively interpreted and negotiated. The police organisation is a workplace of simultaneous acceptance and rejection, consent and resistance.

Contemporary theorists therefore recognise the importance of local dynamics and the variation of cultural expressions. Despite the debate about the explanatory power of police occupational culture, and the recognition of the complexity and nuance within police culture, the enduring influence on police practices is also well acknowledged (Cockcroft, 2007; Skolnick, 2008). The theoretical concepts in the police occupational culture literature retain important explanatory value. Loftus (2010: 16) observes the 'remarkable continuities and inertia within police values, assumptions and practices'. Over 30 years ago, the working personality thesis revealed police culture as an inherent feature of the fundamentals of the danger and authority of police work (Skolnick, 1975), as well as the world view of police officers as shaped by the position of police in wider social and political structures (Reiner, 2016). Therefore, the prevailing aspects of police culture endure because the fundamental nature of the police role remains the same (Loftus, 2010). Changing police culture therefore requires a redefinition of the police mandate (Chan, 1996). As Van Maanen (1978b: 307) concludes: 'regardless of how well-educated, well-equipped or professional the patrolman may become, his normative position and task within society will remain unchanged'.

Socialisation and police leadership

Police leadership is not independent of police occupational culture, but rather shaped and performed within the distinctive occupational environment. As Adlam (2003: 205) observes: 'police leaders and their styles are constructed within and spring from a distinct cultural milieu. Police culture impresses as unique, multiform and complex. Police leadership reflects this complexity.' In particular, the nature of progression in the police forms part of a powerful process of socialisation into the leadership role, which Wall (1998: 315) describes as 'lengthy and supervised professional socialisation'. As noted in Chapter 2, the police have historically functioned on the basis of internal recruitment; consequently, all chief constables began their careers as front-line police officers. This constructs distinctive experiences through which police leaders establish and demonstrate credibility and legitimacy in leadership. First, the internal process of progression places emphasis on shared beginnings and common experiences. The common occupational history is a powerful occupational narrative to understand career trajectory in the police (Van Maanen, 1977; Bacon, 2014). The importance of 'time served' in street policing is central in the construction of identity as an effective and legitimate police leader (Silvestri, 2003, 2006). The prestige and necessity of the experience of street policing for police leaders is understood as a taken-for-granted 'truth' in the police. As Wall (1998: 307) explains, this ideology 'naturalises the assumption that chief police officers must have previously been police officers' and 'creates a degree of false consciousness by precluding any competing theories from the debate'.

Intense career scrutiny is another integral feature of the process of the socialisation of aspiring leaders. Routinised supervision and monitoring functions to craft the philosophies, perceptions and practices of senior police leaders, and ensures that those in senior ranks acquire a shared world view, a 'collective consciousness', to inform their leadership practice (Van Maanen, 1975; Reiner, 1991). Professional socialisation in police leadership functions as a system of 'checks' to 'filter out' maverick or rogue chief officers (Savage et al, 2000). Emphasis is therefore placed on the demonstration of 'sameness' rather than difference. As Wall (1998: 315) concludes: 'the lengthy and supervised professional socialisation does, however, negate the effect of social origin and ensures that all senior police managers possess a similar *weltanschauung*, speak a common occupational language and share broad assumptions about policing'.

The route to chief officer rank requires a series of systematic and timely promotions, and this can be a long and arduous process (Caless, 2011; Silvestri et al, 2013). Reiner's (1991) study found that the initial promotion to sergeant took the longest amount of time: an average of seven years. Chief constables then have to progress quickly through the middle-management ranks: an average of two to three years at each rank from sergeant to assistant chief constable (Reiner, 1991). The pressure and management of time is a further feature of the socialisation process, which is captured in Silvestri's (2003) study of senior policewomen. Therefore, a sense of speed and urgency underpins the management of a career in policing; the time taken to achieve promotions determines the final rank that an officer is likely to achieve in their career (Bland et al, 1999). Consequently, the strategic use and management of time is a prerequisite to successfully progressing through the police hierarchy. Silvestri (2006: 268; original emphasis) analyses the importance of time as an essential resource for a successful career in police leadership, noting that 'by *doing* and *managing* "time", police officers are able to accomplish organisational commitment and credibility, two fundamental yet essentially informal competencies necessary for police leadership'.

The process of socialisation into leadership in the police is constructed as an 'endurance test'. The prevailing image in the discourse of leadership progression is one of resilience, commitment and competition. Van Maanen (1977) describes the unpredictable and 'capricious character' of a successful career in policing, where candidates successful through the selection processes describe themselves as survivors. Similarly, Manning (2007: 56) describes the negotiation of the police career as 'a series of gambles and bargains'. However, this is framed in terms of strength and resilience, rather than luck. In an empirical study of chief officers in England and Wales, Caless (2011) describes the process of becoming a chief officer as 'arduous and prolonged'. Characterised by emotional and psychological demand, Caless (2011: 12) confirms that 'the overwhelming consistent impression of those who have undergone selection is of pressure'. Chief officers in Caless's study used terms such as 'weary', 'stressful', 'nerve-racking' and 'tough' to describe the process. Likewise, Savage et al (2000) describe the experience of chief officers as 'surviving' various hurdles to achieve their senior position. Consequently, there is a requirement for leadership candidates to demonstrate resilience; as Caless (2011: 40) notes, 'only the most resilient and single-minded' achieve appointment to senior office.

Achieving a senior leadership position in the police also requires the demonstration of a commitment to policing. Historically, chief constables were appointed from outside the police force area, so it was typical that successful candidates relocate in pursuit of desirable opportunities. Reiner (1991) and Caless (2011) emphasise the importance of geographical mobility for prospective chief constables as indicative of commitment to 'the job' and credibility as a senior police leader. Indeed, the majority of chief constables in Reiner's (1991) study were defined as 'cosmopolitans', rather than 'locals', having moved between police forces in their careers. Progression to senior leadership is therefore underpinned with notions of dedication and commitment. As Silvestri (2006: 274; original emphasis) concludes: 'one of the key features in marking the transition to the ACPO [Association of Chief Police Officers] ranks is the demonstration of the ability and commitment to *do* policing "anytime" and "anywhere"'.

The police workplace places considerable emphasis on high levels of commitment, as demonstrated in the normalisation of the long working hours of police leaders. In a two-year study of a UK police constabulary, Davies and Thomas (2003: 696) highlight presenteeism as a pervasive feature of the police working environment, as well as strong attachment to 24-hour availability and 'being seen to be keen'. Enthusiasm for long working hours and the occupational values of the police officer as never 'off duty' and available 'all the time' are integral to establishing credibility as a police leader (Dick and Jankowicz, 2001). In this context, as Silvestri (2006: 274) observes, alternative working practices, such as part-time working, are perceived as 'part able, part-committed and part credible'. Credibility in the police leadership role therefore requires expressions of commitment and dedication.

Progression in police leadership is also constructed in terms of competition. The nature of the police hierarchy dictates that there are increasingly limited opportunities at the more senior levels of the organisation. The reality is that few police officers succeed upwards through the rank-based hierarchy to chief office; therefore, the dominant rhetoric is that senior office is increasingly reserved for the 'select few' (Adlam, 2002). As Smith (2008: 218) observes: 'the system can best be described as being a guarded ladder in that one can see the path to the top but cannot set foot onto the first rung of the ladder unless allowed to do so by the hierarchy'. Internal recruitment processes, and competition for limited opportunities, consequently privilege those with strong connections and networks. Studies have highlighted the importance of the early identification of leadership talent and the necessity of the 'permission giving' of senior recommendation to pursue promotion, revealing the prevalence of patronage and nepotism in leadership selection (Manning, 2007; Caless and Tong, 2015). To successfully negotiate the police hierarchy, the police leader is required to 'pick a sponsor, and mimic their leadership style' (Smith, 2008: 218). Caless's (2011) study identified the importance of 'the golden finger' of a senior ranking officer identifying potential; likewise, Savage et al's (2000) study highlighted the importance of senior officers acting as a mentor to prospective senior leaders. In other words, upwards mobility in the police is strongly regulated. This reveals underlying assumptions of exclusivity, exclusion and competitiveness as inherent features of the leadership selection processes, and, importantly, the influence of social networks in realising leadership ambitions in the police.

The occupational attachment to demonstrations of resilience, commitment and competitiveness reveal basic assumptions and expectations of what police leadership is and what police leaders do. Beliefs about credibility in police leadership are intertwined with the process and characteristics required to successfully achieve senior position. The promotion process therefore acts as preparation for 'being' and 'doing' police leadership. For senior leaders in the police, Silvestri (2006: 276; original emphasis) explains, 'achieving leadership *is* and *should be* characterised by those who demonstrate a "total commitment" to the job, underlined by a sense of "single-mindedness", "ruthlessness", "determination", and "ambition with a hunger and thirst" for the power that high office may bring'.

When taken together, these processes construct a common understanding of credibility in police leadership, and shared experiences and strategies to demonstrate this. Senior police leaders have earned their position, having successfully demonstrated that they meet the expectations of leadership through a series of promotions and careful vetting at each rank to reach senior office. Scholars have argued that these processes of leadership promotion and development typically value commonality and 'sameness'; in this context, non-conformity is understood as a risk (Panzarella, 2003). Police leaders are assessed in relation to their level of conformity to the prevailing system, and the prospective police leader is required to 'blend in with the crowd' (Smith, 2008). The system rewards those who display the cultural ideals of a 'good police leader' and inhibits those leaders who do not 'fit the mould' (Savage et al, 2000; Silvestri et al, 2013). Processes of leadership selection therefore emphasise and reinforce the 'status quo', which creates a sense of continuity and stability in the police organisation (Foster, 2003; Smith, 2008; Cockcroft, 2017). Rowe's (2006) ethnographic study of policing shows that police officers value qualities in leadership that reflect dominant and established perceptions of policing and police work. In a qualitative study of a Canadian police department, Campeau (2019) argues that the police organisation represents a site of 'cultural inertia'. This inertia is maintained through police leaders negotiating old and new 'cultural scripts': the simultaneous display of 'social fitness' with contemporary expectations and demand while also demonstrating commitment to traditional values in policing. Senior police leaders, Campeau continues, are those who most embody these cultural values. The power and prestige of beliefs, values and assumptions associated with police occupational culture is reinforced.

The contemporary trend towards the 'professionalisation' of the police, with its emphasis on the values of ethics, diversity and transparency, sits in direct conflict with traditional cultural values, such as solidarity and machismo. The occupational culture in the police has a powerful influence on the underlying assumptions about the nature and practice of leadership, and notions of the 'ideal police leader' are framed through distinctive occupational narratives (Cockcroft, 2013; Bacon, 2014; Silvestri, 2018b). The value of conformity, reinforced through leadership selection processes, exposes the fundamental challenges of creating difference in leadership in the police.

Creating difference in leadership

The development of different, non-hierarchical approaches in leadership has been identified as an important step in equipping police organisations to respond to the increasing complexity of contemporary policing (Panzarella, 2003; Herrington and Colvin, 2016). Police organisations can no longer depend exclusively on traditional command-based transactional approaches to leadership. The contemporary landscape requires a broader range of leadership skills and capabilities, and 'different people'. Diverse representation is therefore understood as a mechanism to challenge existing ways of working in the police and achieve difference in leadership practices (Silvestri et al, 2013).

As this chapter has explored, social processes and interactions construct, maintain and regulate legitimacy and credibility in police leadership. The ideal police leader identity is based on notions of hegemonic masculinity, which emphasise assumptions of physical strength, heterosexuality, individualism and competitiveness, and marginalise displays of femininity as 'weakness' or 'inferior' (Heidensohn, 1996; Martin, 1980; West and Zimmerman, 1987; Brown, 2007). Commentators have long argued that, as a reproduction of wider societal processes, social differences of gender, race and sexuality form organising mechanisms for the workplace (Kanter, 1977; Connell, 1987; Holdaway and Parker, 1998). Acker (1990) argues that organisations are highly gendered spaces, underpinned by notions of hegemonic masculinity and based on control, segregation and exclusion. As Acker (1990: 146) explains: 'to say that an organization, or any analytic unit, is gendered means that advantage and disadvantage, exploitation and control, action and emotion, meaning and identity are patterned through in terms of a distinction between male and female, masculine and feminine'.

Within this context, various strategies and policies have attempted to challenge conventional working practices in the police. The police strategy *Equality, Diversity and Human Rights Strategy for the Police Service* (ACPO, 2010) maintains that greater diversity in the police workforce leads to improvements in organisational performance, including improved decision-making, greater willingness to challenge and better staff management. The College of Policing (2017b) continues to support initiatives and strategies to improve diversity and inclusion in the police service in England and Wales, and calls for a greater understanding of the representation of the protected characteristics of ethnicity, gender, age, disability, religion and belief, and sexual orientation. In response to a myriad of legislative developments and organisational change initiatives, including the development of police associations for minority groups, the police service in England and Wales has been under increased pressure to demonstrate its representativeness (Rowe, 2002; O'Neill and Holdaway, 2007). Workforce data show marginal improvements. In 2018, 6.6 per cent of all police officers in England and Wales were from a black and minority ethnic (BME) background compared with 4.4 per cent in 2009, and 30 per cent of police officers were women compared with 25 per cent in 2009 (Hargreaves et al, 2018). However, under-representation at senior leadership roles is particularly striking: BME officers account for only 2.6 per cent of chief officers and only 27.1 per cent of chief officers are women (Hargreaves et al, 2018). Therefore, despite considerable focus on diversity in the police, the lack of representation in leadership roles continues to be particularly problematic.

The discrimination and prejudice experienced by female, BME and lesbian, gay, bisexual and trans (LGBT) police officers is well acknowledged in police studies (Holdaway, 1993; Burke, 1994; Heidensohn, 1996; Jones and Williams, 2013). Scholars have examined access to leadership positions in the police and recognise the persistent barriers to the progression of BME, LGBT and female officers (Dick and Cassell, 2002; Van Ewijk, 2011; Haake, 2018). Taken-for-granted, racialised, gendered and heteronormative assumptions underpin the construction of credibility in police leadership. As Miller et al (2003: 357) confirm: 'qualifications for particular jobs are infused with conscious and unconscious images of the appropriate gender, race, ethnicity, class and sexual orientation of the "winning" applicant'.

The dominance of men and masculinity in leadership creates distinctive challenges for women in establishing credibility as 'good' leaders. When women engage in masculine jobs, they experience gender and occupational role conflicts (Brown, 2007). Dick and Jankowicz's (2001) study of a UK police constabulary found that characteristic features of the police leadership role, such as long working hours, militate against the retention and promotion of women. Silvestri's (2003) work provides a unique contribution to the academic evidence on the experience of senior policewomen and documents the challenges for senior policewomen to establish credibility in leadership. As Silvestri (2003: 117) observes: 'One of the most commonly cited barriers experienced by women is that senior management is perceived to be a "club", with its own distinctive set of rituals, symbols and behavioural prescriptions that need to be learnt and enacted for the process of acceptance to take place.'

Studies also show that retention and progression is problematic for BME police officers (Holdaway, 1993; Foster et al, 2005). Bland et al (1999), for example, found that, on average, BME officers took 12 months longer than their white counterparts to reach the rank of sergeant. However, while there is evidence on the barriers to progression for women and BME officers, there is less research on the experience of LGBT officers as police leaders. Assumptions about minority groups conflict with dominant ideologies of police occupational culture. Decades of empirical research has demonstrated the challenges experienced by minority groups in negotiating the police workplace, characterised by a 'cult of masculinity' (Martin, 1980; Heidensohn, 1996; Brown, 2007; Rabe-Hemp, 2009). Fielding (1994: 47) explains the cult of masculinity as having four manifestations:

• aggressive, physical action;
• a strong sense of competitiveness and preoccupation with imagery of conflict;
• exaggerated heterosexual orientations, often articulated in terms of misogynistic and patriarchal attitudes towards women; and
• the operation of rigid in-group/out-group distinctions, whose consequences are strongly exclusionary in the case of out-groups and strongly assertive of loyalty and affinity in the case of in-groups.

Therefore, the pervasiveness of hegemonic masculinity in police occupational culture has important implications for the experiences of minority groups in the police. Holdaway (1997) describes the relationship between racialised stereotypes and 'team membership' as a barrier to the inclusion and acceptance of BME officers. This is a particularly relevant point considering the importance of trust and solidarity as defining features of police occupational culture. As Holdaway (1997: 26) explains: 'membership of the work group implies a significant measure of acceptance of the rank-and-file culture, including its racialised elements, which makes it difficult for a black or Asian officer to find an agreeable reception from colleagues'.

Similarly, Jones' (2014: 153) study of LGB police officers captures their experience of being judged against their ability to 'conform, perform and be accepted within traditionally masculinist police structures'. LGB officers risk being excluded from the police 'team', and their professional integrity and personal safety being threatened. LGBT police officers challenge the stability of hegemonic masculinity in the police, and consequently experience hostility. In Miller et al's (2003: 369) study, the authors concluded that 'there was little room for alternative or oppositional forms of masculinity'. Likewise, Burke (1992, 1994), in one of the few empirical studies of LGB police officers, describes the experience of LGB officers as in direct conflict with the conservatism and hyper-masculinity of police occupational culture. For Burke (1992), in the context of police occupational culture, 'difference' in terms of sexuality is conceptualised as 'deviant'. Therefore, LGB police officers in the study described experiences of the police workplace as tension, segregation, resistance and suspiciousness. As Burke (1992: 38) explains:

> The police and the gay community represent two distinct groups, separated by a chasm through which members of neither group can pass. It suggests that homosexuals and police officers come from, and live in, separate worlds; that their essential selves are fundamentally different, and that there is no overlap of thought or ideology between these two mutually exclusive groups.

It therefore seems that individuals of 'difference' continue to experience challenges in gaining acceptance in the police workplace and demonstrating leadership credibility within an occupational culture premised on powerful assumptions of hegemonic masculinity. Dominant discourse therefore equates leadership with men and masculinity, with notions of 'good' leadership perceived in masculine and patriarchal terms (Rosener, 1991; Billing and Alvesson, 2000; Sinclair, 2005). Leadership is positioned as an exclusively masculine enterprise, and 'non-masculine' leadership is subordinated in organisational practice (Billing and Alvesson, 2000; Eagly and Carli, 2003; Silvestri, 2003).

The diversity agenda is underpinned by assumptions that those from minority backgrounds practise leadership differently and can therefore have a transformative impact on the working environment in the police. Individuals from minority backgrounds are conceptualised as 'change agents' that challenge the dominance of hegemonic masculinised practices (Kingshott, 2009; Haake et al, 2017). Jones (2014), for example, argues that LGB police officers believe that they encourage a greater emphasis on supportive and problem-oriented discourse in the workplace. The assumption of diversity as change is particularly evident in the literature on gender, where in order to challenge the gender-blindness of conventional discourse, leadership scholars have examined the ways in which men and women lead differently. Bartol and Butterfield (1976) found differences between men and women in 'consideration style' and 'initiating structure'; similarly, Petty and Lee (1975) found differences in satisfaction, with rates being higher for followers with female supervisors. In contrast, Dobbins and Platz's (1986) meta-analysis found that the sex of the leader did not affect perceived leadership influence or follower satisfaction; likewise, Eagly and Johnson (1990) also found that male and female leaders did not differ significantly in leadership style. In policing, scholars have explored the role of policewomen in developing more participatory and collaborative practices in the police (Rabe-Hemp, 2008; Kingshott, 2009; Dick et al, 2014). This body of work challenges the masculine assumptions of effective leadership through championing the value of women's contribution in leadership and encouraging a greater appreciation of a 'feminine' approach to leadership (Grant, 1988; Alimo-Metcalfe, 2004).

However, critical leadership scholars critique this position and argue that assumptions of women 'doing' leadership differently perpetuate stereotypical beliefs about gender and management (Powell et al, 2002; Ford, 2006). Gender stereotypes, which communicate expectations about gender roles, typically assume women as communal, emotional and expressive, reflecting an inclusive and sympathetic manner, with men assumed to be instrumental, assertive, authoritative, competitive and task-focused (Heidensohn, 1996; Scott and Brown, 2006). Eagly and Carli (2003: 810) confirm that 'sex-typed leadership styles invite careful scrutiny'. Celebration of 'feminine leadership' does little to elevate the gender stereotypes and conventional assumptions about the nature of leadership. Critical leadership theorists therefore continue to problematise the biological essentialism and determinism of mainstream research on gender and leadership (Ford, 2006; Collinson, 2011). While the examination of 'feminine' leadership is a helpful contrast to the gender-blindness of conventional discourse, Billing and Alvesson (2000: 155) argue that the gender labelling of leadership reproduces gendered stereotypes, and recommend 'a move away from conventional ideas on management, not so much a move to celebrating a feminine model intimately coupled to stereotypical, idealised and essentialist views on talents and orientations contingent upon female sex'.

Prevailing features of police occupational culture are powerful in shaping how 'difference' is experienced and enacted. Holdaway (1997:

31), for example, argues that characteristics of police occupational culture 'construct and sustain racialised relations with the police workforce'. Scholars therefore recognise the complexity in negotiating 'difference' in the police workplace. Martin (1979) captured the role dilemmas experienced by women in the police in the ideal types of *police*women and police*women*. These concepts, situated on a spectrum, describe the strategies of defeminisation or deprofessionalisation enacted by women in order to gain acceptance in the workplace. According to Martin (1979: 316), *police*women 'strongly embrace the prevailing enforcement-oriented view of policing held by the men', while police*women* adopt a more service-oriented and traditionally 'feminine' approach. These approaches, Martin argues, are coping strategies in response to the pressures, expectations and isolation of difference in the police. However, adopting different coping strategies minimises the potentially transformative impact of women as a group on the police working environment. Martin (1979: 323) concludes that 'the contrasting coping strategies adopted by *police*women and police*women* have also resulted in a lack of unity among the female officers which, in turn, limits the ability of women to act as an effective political function or group in departmental politics'.

Martin's discussion of *police*women reveals the extent to which minority groups enact and reinforce, rather than challenge, the dominant ideologies of police occupational culture. Strategies of 'laying low' – minimising the visibility of difference – preserve the prevailing features of police occupational culture. In rejecting the hegemonic masculine leadership practices of competitiveness and individualism, senior policewomen in Silvestri's (2003) study experienced tensions and resistance. Silvestri (2003: 117) describes senior policewomen adopting strategies of 'being a man' and male behaviours to secure 'organisational belongingness', explaining that 'senior policewomen were characterised by a desire to "fit in" within prevailing cultures and power structures of the organisation, to integrate themselves within it and not look for visibility as women'.

Similarly, LGB police officers in Burke's (1994: 199) study constructed 'double-lives' because 'the invisibility of an individual's sexual orientation makes it inevitable that many officers will choose to "pass" as heterosexual rather than display their deviance'. Rather than integrate their LGB status into their working life, LGB police officers in the study maintain the invisibility of their 'difference' and adopt 'role appropriate behaviours' (Burke, 1994; Jones and Williams, 2013). Therefore, through strategies of invisibility, dominant ideologies within police occupational culture are preserved, rather than challenged. This work on gender and sexuality in the police therefore captures how strategies to adapt to the police working environment function to preserve and sustain the prevailing features of police occupational culture.

Negotiating difference in the police is therefore a complex activity involving both resistance and adherence to dominant practices. In leadership, individuals make sense of their working world and negotiate differential power dynamics in multiple ways (Alvesson, 1998; Dick and Jankowicz, 2001). Rabe-Hemp (2009: 114) confirms that women in the police engaged in both challenging and sustaining dominant practices: 'women actively resisted and adopted stereotypical norms of femininity and policing, broadening their opportunities for work in the male dominated occupation while reinforcing their traditional conception of gender difference'. Similarly, senior policewomen in Silvestri's (2003: 136) study performed leadership in masculine and feminine ways, both 'adapting to' the policing working environment and 'adopting new' approaches to leadership.

The complexities of women's identities in the police workplace, Morash and Haarr (2012: 3) conclude, cannot be understood solely in terms of the adherence to and reproduction of gender stereotypes: 'women do not simply reproduce old female–male stereotypes and the hierarchies that devalue female-associated traits. They fashion complex, positive occupational identities that are not necessarily tied to their sex category.' This body of work therefore draws attention to the complexity and fragmentation in managing difference in leadership in the police. However, as Campeau (2019) argues, the balance between the same and different practices in leadership, or old and new cultural scripts, continues to preserve dominant institutional ideologies and maintains the police in a state of 'cultural inertia'. Despite the increasing recognition and enactment of 'difference' in the police organisation, dominant cultural ideologies retain considerable power to shape legitimacy and credibility in leadership (Silvestri, 2003; Loftus, 2009). Rather than focusing on difference as a mechanism of change, critical leadership scholars instead challenge our belief systems about the nature of leadership. As Gemmill and Oakley (1997: 283) argue, the meaningful reform of police leadership requires 'new forms of leadership by redefining the meanings attached to leadership behaviour'.

Conclusion

This chapter has examined the ways in which police socialisation has a powerful influence on the nature and practice of leadership in the police. A long history of policing studies has captured the prevailing features of police occupational culture as a powerful framework for understanding the police working world. Legitimacy and credibility in police leadership is underpinned by normative assumptions about the 'ideal police leader' that draw on hegemonic masculine ideologies about the role of the police and the nature of police work.

There is no doubt that the police service in England and Wales has made considerable progress towards the greater diverse representation of its officers and staff. There has been a plethora of policies and strategies to address the lack of diversity in the police service. However, we argue that such change has been directed at the surface-level 'artefacts' (Schein, 2010) of police occupational culture and, as such, does little to dismantle or transform the basic underlying assumptions, conventions and expectations associated with the nature and practice of leadership. Those basic assumptions continue to be heavily influenced by normative expectations of police culture and the nature of police work. Despite attempts to challenge this, police leadership continues to be understood in hegemonic masculine terms.

Further reading

Charman, S. (2018) *Police Socialisation, Identity and Culture: Becoming Blue*. Basingstoke: Palgrave Macmillan.

Cockcroft, T. (2013) *Police Culture: Themes and Concepts*. Abingdon: Routledge.

Silvestri, M. (2017) 'Police Culture and Gender: Revisiting the "Cult of Masculinity"', *Policing* 11: 289–300.

6

Leadership, well-being and resilience

Well-being and resilience in the police have garnered much attention among academics and policymakers. For police leaders, their personal resilience and the well-being of their staff is increasingly recognised as fundamental to successful organisational performance. In this chapter, we problematise the conventional rhetoric of well-being and resilience in the police through an analysis of the steadfast attachment to 'heroism' in leadership. We argue that the introduction of well-being policy is difficult in a police occupational culture that prioritises romanticised and idealised versions of leadership. The chapter begins with a critical consideration of the stress literature, followed by an overview of the 'romance of leadership' thesis. We emphasise the problematic consequences of the contemporary well-being and resilience rhetoric for both individuals and organisations, and argue that such rhetoric reinforces unhelpful and regressive notions of heroism in police leadership. The final part of this chapter considers the challenges for police leadership in adopting alternative 'post-heroic' forms of leadership, and makes recommendations for future practice.

Stress, well-being and resilience

There is an established interest in the nature of stress in policing. This body of work explores assumptions about police work as inherently stressful, and more stressful than other occupations, and examines the negative effects of stress experienced by the police, as well as the relationship between stress and police occupational culture (Brown and Campbell, 1994; Chan, 2007b). In understanding the nature of stress in policing, Stinchcomb (2004) distinguishes between *episodic stressors* and *chronic organisational stressors*. Episodic stressors refer to the traumatic aspects of policing and the emotional and psychological strains of police work, which are not necessarily regularly encountered by police officers. These episodic stressors relate stress to the distinctive role of the police. Studies have examined the impact on police officers of major disasters (Alexander and Wells, 1991; Carlier et al, 1998), shooting incidents (Gersons, 1989; Strahler and Ziegert, 2015), violent public disorder (Beagley et al, 2018) and assaults (Fielding et al, 2018; West et al, 2017). This body of research, some of which draws on

109

psychology and neuroscience, has captured the relationship between exposure to traumatic events and sleep problems, fatigue, depression, burnout and neurological disorders, and firmly positions the nature of stress in the police as unique (Violanti et al, 2017). With episodic stress well recognised by the police service, most constabularies have policies and procedures in place to provide psychological support in response to traumatic incidents. However, and perhaps contrary to conventional wisdom, episodic stress is not the most prevalent source of stress in the police. Liberman et al (2002) found that continued exposure to routine work stress was a strong predictor of psychological distress, the routinised nature being the distinguishing feature. As Stinchcomb (2004: 264; original emphasis) explains: 'these are the types of stressors that, at least to some degree, are *expected* in policing. What they did not expect was to have to cope with chronic organizational irritants: the demanding supervisor; the difficult co-worker; the micro-managing administrator.'

Chronic organisational stressors are the everyday, routine stressors of the bureaucratic work environment, 'the product of a slow, continual process of erosion that occurs over time', the 'push and pull' of competing demands, and the expectations of organisational management practices (Stinchcomb, 2004: 263). Police, organisational and leadership studies have investigated the impact of the organisational environment on the individual. This work includes an examination of the impact of leadership on the well-being, motivation and satisfaction of individuals. Stinchcomb (2004), for example, identified micromanagement as a source of organisational stress; likewise, studies have explored the relationship between staff empowerment and job satisfaction (Brunetto and Farr-Wharton, 2003; Johnson, 2012). In a study of stress in a UK police constabulary, Brown and Campbell (1990) found that police officers were more likely to identify organisational and management issues as key stressors rather than routine operational duties. Staff shortages, shift work, time pressures, managing people, poor supervision and leadership, and a lack of consultation are among the commonly cited routine organisational stressors in the police (Brown and Campbell, 1994; Abdollahi, 2002). Therefore, for episodic stressors, police leadership is, in part, situated as the 'solution' through, for example, the provision of adequate psychological and supervisory support or 'better' leadership. Leaders in the police are influential in developing a supportive workplace environment where colleagues are able to identify signs of stress in one another (Hesketh et al, 2019). Research evidence suggests that senior leaders are an important source of support in the management of stress and the return to work following stress-related absences (Alexander and Wells, 1991; Paton, 2006). In contrast, chronic organisational stressors, such as managerial styles and systems, reveal police leadership practices and policies as the source of, rather than the solution to, occupational stress.

Set against a climate of unprecedented change to policing in England and Wales, the well-being agenda has emphasised the importance of the mental health of police officers and staff as a priority for policymakers. The National Police Chiefs Council set up the first well-being working group in 2013, and in 2017, the College of Policing developed a policing-specific strategy, the *Blue Light Wellbeing Framework*, which includes requirements for police organisations to have, for example, flexible working and anti-bullying policies in place, as well as effective strategies to identify high-risk areas of work. Well-being in the police has also been highlighted in the National Policing Vision 2025 and forms part of the HMICFRS (Her Majesty's Inspectorate of Constabulary and Fire and Rescue Services) annual inspections. Responding to stress, mental health and well-being is therefore an accepted principle of police organisations and a priority for police leadership, and staff welfare is clearly positioned as a leadership responsibility. As Smith and Charles (2015: 132) explain: 'organisations can embed policies, practices and a culture to enable the organisation as a whole to be more resilient in coping with the various stressors employees encounter'.

Much of the research on stress in policing is focused on the operational ranks; less is known about the impact of stress in leadership roles. Brown and Campbell (1990, 1994) provide a unique contribution to understanding the impact of stress on police leaders. Their work shows that while the levels of operational stressors are lower among the higher ranks compared with junior officers, management-generated stressors increase. The sergeant rank, where the operational and managerial stressors were found to intersect, was identified as an acutely stressful supervisory rank. Brown et al (1994) examined the sources and impacts of work pressures among chief superintendents and superintendents. Here, the most frequent source of stress related to workload, insufficient finances and resources, and a lack of consultation and communication. This reflects Reiner's (1991) study, which identified organisational communication as a key challenge for chief constables. Set against the emphasis on episodic stressors that privileges the stress associated with occupational trauma, the stress experienced in leadership is relatively unacknowledged. Yet, understanding the nature of stress in leadership is an important precursor to designing effective support provision. The distinctive patterns of stress related to leadership roles, and the adverse consequences for police leaders, is therefore an important source of future study.

Resilience is central to the contemporary rhetoric of stress management. Referring to the ability of police leaders to successfully adapt to stressors while maintaining psychological balance, Luthans (2002) defines resilience as 'the positive psychological capacity to rebound, to "bounce back" from adversity, uncertainty, conflict, failure or even positive change, progress and increased responsibility'. Resilience is therefore most typically understood in individualised and psychological, rather than organisational, terms. Burke et al (2006), for example, examined the individual characteristics of resilience in new recruits in Australia and developed a personality profile of 'the resilient officer'. Here, the focus is on the ability of individuals to 'bounce back' from stress and trauma. Part of this 'bouncing back', Conn (2018: 2) explains, is re-establishing psychological balance. Resilience is not about the avoidance of stress and trauma, but, rather, the process of psychological and emotional recovery from these experiences. Consequently, there is a growing interest in personal resilience in the contemporary mainstream literature, particularly from popular management and coaching commentators. Police leaders can access numerous 'self-help' resources that claim to be able to teach the 'tools' of resilience, self-care and mindfulness, such as *Build Your Resilience* (Robertson, 2012), *Developing Resilience* (Neenan, 2017) and *Resilient: 12 Tools for Transforming Everyday Experiences into Lasting Happiness* (Hanson, 2018). Empirical research, most of which is based on studies of policing in the US, has also examined the characteristics of individual resilience and the vulnerability or risk factors among police officers. This research identifies influences such as emotional stability, self-awareness and tolerance of ambiguity as key protective factors in stress management and indicators of personal resilience, all of which are relevant to resilience among police leaders (Flin, 1996; Linley and Joseph, 2004). Paton (2006) provides a stress risk management model for police organisations. This model documents the balance of resilience and vulnerability factors, which are conceptualised in terms of personal, team and environmental issues. These factors are considered in relation to negative outcomes, such as hyper-vigilance, and the more positive outcome referred as 'adaption growth'. According to Paton (2006: 204), the model provides police organisations and police leadership with 'a basis for auditing existing cultures, practices, and competencies'.

Within this context, greater emphasis is placed on understanding and building personal resilience within police organisations. Resilience training programmes are recommended to equip police leaders to effectively support staff through contemporary organisational change (Hesketh et al, 2005; Robertson et al, 2015). Emotional and cognitive training is said to promote resilience in police leadership, so leaders are able to model and support resilient behaviours across the organisation (Conn, 2018). However, research evidence on the effectiveness of resilience training programmes is limited (Robertson et al, 2015). Hesketh et al's (2019: 63) study of personal resilience training in a UK police constabulary found improvements in perceptions of resources and communications, work relationships, workload, and job conditions, concluding that 'resilience training ought to be incorporated into leadership inputs, with the aim of better preparing leaders for the pressures and challenges of the modern working environment'.

The contemporary well-being agenda in the police challenges traditional assumptions about stress as just 'part of the job' and traditional coping strategies in the police. Staff well-being is a leadership and organisational priority and police constabularies across the country are now required to demonstrate understanding of and commitment to workforce well-being. Alongside this, strategies to support personal resilience are increasingly understood as a legitimate response to effectively manage stress in the police. In what follows, we critically consider these policy trends through a discussion of the romanticised and heroic cultural ideologies of 'the police leader'.

Well-being, resilience and the heroic leader

The dominant discourse of leadership is infused with notions of heroism. The 'romance of leadership' thesis exposes the social fascination of leadership and the cultural beliefs about the limitless potential of leadership (Meindl, 1995; Mastrofski, 2002). Meindl and Ehrlich (1987: 93) explain that 'leadership has assumed a special status – not merely a prosaic alternative that people dispassionately consider on an equal footing with other explanations, it has achieved a heroic, larger-than-life value'. Conventional theory, as Chapter 3 explored, conceptualises leadership in heroic terms: leadership is located as a property of the individual leader and observable in their exceptional traits, personality or behaviours. Leadership is assumed as a natural quality of the person. Gardner (1990: xv), for example, defines leaders as those 'who are exemplary, who inspire, who stand for something, who help us set and achieve goals'. Such characterisations also assume the leader as the initiator of change and determinant of individual, team or organisational performance. Leadership is signalled as both the source of and solution to organisational problems (Barker, 1997; Grint, 2010a). As Pfeffer (1977: 110) confirms: 'the leader as a symbol provides a target for action when difficulties occur, serving as a scapegoat when things go wrong'. Assigned with the power to bring about change, leadership is understood as instrumental, affirmative and transformational. Indeed, Bennis (1989: 15) emphasises that a leader is responsible for the effectiveness of organisations, noting that 'The success or failure of all organisations, whether basketball teams, moviemakers, or automobile manufacturers, rests on the perceived quality at the top.'

Notions of heroism also underpin police occupational culture. Research literature has long captured the emphasis on toughness and aggressiveness as characteristic features of police culture, with police work understood in terms of action, danger and risk (Heidensohn, 1996; Brown, 2007). The sharing of 'war stories' that glorify the exceptional experiences of violence and conflict, and the emphasis of the police as 'the thin blue line' between order and chaos, position the police as 'valiant protectors' (Fielding, 1994; Waddington, 1999a). The use of physical force is a valued aspect of police work. The physicality of street police work, with an emphasis on 'strong', 'fit' and 'capable' bodies, further communicates notions of heroism (Morash and Haarr, 2012; Sinclair, 2015; Westmarland, 2017). The police and policing, Heidensohn (2003: 574) confirms, 'remain gendered in the twenty-first century. The macho culture is still alive in some forces even now.' The quasi-militaristic hierarchical structure and the demarcation by rank reinforce notions of leadership in heroic 'commander' terms (Cowper, 2000; Panzarella, 2003). In leadership, conventional understandings, as Collinson (2005b: 245) explains, are 'saturated with the gendered, masculine imagery of the assertive, heroic and individualistic male'. The police leader encapsulates ideals about both the heroism of the police *and* the heroism of leadership. Embodying the imagery of the militaristic 'commander', the police leader is conceived of as a brave, charismatic and visionary individual able to take decisive action in response to crisis (Mastrofski, 2002; Grint, 2010b; Sinclair, 2015). As Silvestri (2018b: 315) explains:

> The presence and pervasiveness of such heroic narratives has much resonance within the police organization where the police leader has been conceived of through romanticized symbols of heroic importance. The heroic aspects of the police leader stem not only from the power inherent

within the role itself but also from the associated masculine attributes of strength, stamina, and endurance required to climb to leadership ranks. The construction of police leaders as a power elite more generally has undeniably done much to cultivate the idea of the 'heroic male.'

The contemporary emphasis on resilience in police leadership is also underpinned by assumptions of heroism. Research has pointed to the extent to which occupational stress and resilience in the police are understood as status symbols (Terry, 1981; Stinchcomb, 2004). Cultural assumptions about the police as the 'thin blue line' situate stress and vulnerability as an inherent yet celebrated and ritualised part of the police role. Although there are characteristic features of stress experienced in the police, some of the routine and organisational stressors, such as shift work or poor communication, are not distinctive to the police (Brown and Campbell, 1994). Indeed, Stinchcomb (2004: 263) argues that the type of occupational stress experienced in the police is 'glamorised and highly publicised as a significant problem', which creates a self-fulfilling prophecy whereby police officers view their work as uniquely stressful. Conn (2018: 4) argues that the contemporary emphasis on well-being and resilience in the police perpetuates the belief that stress in the police is inevitable. According to Conn, this leads to 'pathology-based' messages and 'disorder-focused', 'deficit-based' practices that emphasise difficulties rather than strengths. Ironically, this position preserves masculinised notions of strength as 'overcoming' problems and difficulties, and of resilience as 'bouncing back'. This is particularly noticeable in popular discourse on resilience. In *Resilience: The Science of Mastering Life's Greatest Challenges*, Southwick and Charney (2012) discuss 'brain fitness'; likewise, Conn (2018) writes of personal resilience in the police as building 'mental armour'. These resources speak to the dominant understanding of policing in militaristic 'crime-fighting' terms. Beliefs about the distinctive nature of stress in the police reinforce notions of the 'special social status' of the police, underpinned by idealised and romanticised assumptions. Since leadership is positioned both as the source of and the solution to organisational stress in the police, organisational resilience is similarly understood as a leadership responsibility, with leaders perceived as role models for resilient behaviour. Leadership is conceived of as creating 'order' and 'calm' in uncertainty, ambiguity and complexity (Tourish, 2013). This personification of leadership as the cause or solution to complex processes, like organisational and individual resilience, further perpetuates the 'social myth' of leadership as heroic (Pfeffer, 1977). As Gemmill and Oakley (1997: 276) confirm:

> This attributional social bias creates the illusion that 'leaders' are in control of events. The use of leadership as a cause or social myth seems to stem, in part, from the natural uncertainty and ambiguity embedded in reality which most persons experience as terrifying, overwhelming, complex and chaotic.... The attribution of omnipotence and omniscience allows the terror to be focused in one place instead of it being experienced as diffused in a seemingly random universe.

A critical perspective challenges the romanticised assumptions of the excessive influence and limitless capabilities of police leadership. Rather than focusing on the exclusive power of the leader, this perspective re-imagines leadership as the management of meanings and appearances, and as the framing of situations, experiences and activities (Grint, 2005a; Manning, 2012). Leadership is understood as symbolic and expressive rather than instrumental. As Mastrofski (2002: 154) explains, the role of leaders is 'to convey meaning for the organisation, its activities, and their consequences – to construct a way for others to identify what is significant and to understand it'. The power of leadership, critical scholars argue, lies not in heroic notions of excessive leadership capacity, but, rather, in the ability of leadership to frame realities and, by doing so, to regulate alternative perspectives and critical voices. As Grint (2010a: 101; original emphasis) explains:

> There is more to sense-making than its literal interpretation because the act of leadership is as much to do with sense-*breaking* as sense-making. In other words, it is not simply that leaders make sense of the world but that they make particular sense of the world by silencing alternative versions.

The thesis of the romance of leadership provides a useful theoretical framework to problematise the contemporary discourse of well-being in the police. It exposes the power of the dominant discourse in constructing, as Grint (2010a: 101) argues, a 'particular sense of the world'. Alternatives are marginalised, regulated and silenced, and understood as 'ineffective' or 'undesirable' leadership.

The problem with heroism and leadership

The notion of heroism in leadership positions leaders at a distance; here, leadership is understood as a senior position within a hierarchy, superior and beyond reach. This perspective equates effective leadership with 'professional distance' between leaders and their staff (Alimo-Metcalfe and Alban-Metcalfe, 2005; Collinson, 2005b). Leadership is also considered 'distant' through assumptions of the elevated power and social status of leaders, whereby leadership is understood as the domain of the 'elite few' (Antonakis and Atwater, 2002). The distance between senior and junior levels of the police organisation is also well acknowledged within the policing literature, with accounts of senior leadership working in the 'ivory tower', being out of touch and removed from the realities of street police work (Holdaway, 1977; Punch, 1983).

Romanticised notions of leadership, which position leaders at a distance, assume that 'closeness' in leadership is ineffective and undesirable. As Shamir (1995: 22) confirms: 'close leaders and supervisors cannot hide their weaknesses from followers and, therefore, they are perceived to be very human and very fallible'. Collinson (2005b) problematises assumptions of distance in leadership as exaggerating and reproducing social divisions between leaders and followers. Relationships and interactions between leaders and followers are a fundamental and valuable part of leadership, yet professional distance in leadership undermines this. This positioning of leaders 'at a distance' conflicts with alternative approaches to leadership that emphasise accessibility, inclusivity and 'closeness' in leadership. Assumptions of 'distance as desirable' in leadership also act as a barrier to meaningful understanding and engagement with staff well-being, which requires a prioritisation of relationships and an element of 'closeness'. The thesis of the romance of leadership contributes to challenging dominant leader–centric assumptions about the superiority of the leader and the necessity of physical, psychological and emotional distance in leadership practice.

The emphasis on heroism within leadership creates three fundamental problems for the acceptance of well-being policies in police organisations: first, the fact of vulnerability as an inherent and valued part of leadership is not fully appreciated; second, the implications for police leadership in accessing support for stress is neglected; and, third, the problematic consequences of the unequal power dynamics for organisations are unacknowledged. The vision of leadership in heroic terms overshadows the appreciation of fallibility, vulnerability or ambiguity as an inherent, even desirable, part of leadership. Leaders are assumed to be strong, resilient and decisive. Anything less than that, such as indecisiveness or making mistakes, is interpreted as a sign of fragility, weakness and poor leadership. Critical leadership scholars challenge assumptions of the unconstrained capacity of leaders to manage workplace stress and bring about organisational change (Gronn, 2002; Collinson, 2011). Beyer (1999: 311) argues that 'it makes no sense to assume that all or even most of people's behaviors are caused by something some kind of leader does'. The contemporary rhetoric of resilience perpetuates assumptions of the causal influence of leadership; leaders are thought of as responsible for workplace stress, rather than the wider social, economic or organisational context. Yet, as Tourish (2013: 23) recognises, 'most of us stumble and fall on a regular basis. Leaders are no different.' As Grint (2010b: 313) explains:

> Leaders are not heroic knights on horseback rescuing damsels in distress, they are instead more likely to be Stockmannesque figures, fighting both their own demons and the small-minded nature of their neighbours. This is necessary work, but it is not heroic because, as the title reminds us, often leadership is not perceived by the people for the people but against the people.

The romanticisation of leaders results in the construction of leadership as either strong or weak, seen as binary opposites. The reliance on such dichotomies is a central critique of conventional leadership studies. Similarities in behaviours or characteristics are manufactured under the label 'strong' or 'weak', and differences between them are emphasised. This process oversimplifies the nature of leadership and neglects to consider the complexity of leadership as an interconnected and dynamic process (Bolden and Gosling, 2006; Collinson, 2014). It privileges certain characteristics, such as strength, as 'the best way' of being a leader, which fails to take into account the situated nature of understanding 'what works' (Grint, 2005b). In other words, the analysis of alternative perspectives beyond the dominant dichotomy is marginalised and excluded. Understanding leadership in heroic terms therefore excludes consideration of emotion, fallibility, doubt and 'weakness' as an indication of 'good' leadership.

Collinson (2012) uses the term 'Prozac Leadership' to describe the contemporary emphasis on 'positive psychological capital', such as resilience, in leadership. Prozac, referring to the medication used to manage depression, is used as a metaphor to challenge the social attachment to the pursuit of excessive happiness and positivity in leadership. The power of positive thinking, like personal resilience, is a recurring theme in popular leadership and management books. There is a collective, taken-for-granted acceptance of the value of positivity for organisations. This, scholars argue, can encourage leaders to engage in risk-taking behaviours (Collinson, 2012; Tourish, 2013). This perspective also excludes critical consideration of the impact of the pervasiveness of heroism on individual leaders. The responsibility and pressures on leadership, assumed as the source of reassurance in situations of uncertainty, are ignored and experiences of pressures, loneliness and vulnerability among leaders are silenced (Gemmill and Oakley, 1997; Grint, 2010a).

Understanding leadership in heroic and idealised terms also militates against the critical self-reflection of leaders. As Collinson (2012: 87) argues, leaders foster a belief in their own narratives and 'that everything is going well'. Critical reflection is an important part of contemporary leadership practice (Kilgallon et al, 2015; Wood and Bryant, 2016). Goleman (1995) popularised the term 'emotional intelligence', which further situates self-reflection as indicative of effective leadership. From this perspective, effective leaders should exert high levels of self-awareness and empathy. Reflexivity, it appears, is an important strategy to achieve this. As Goleman (1995: 84) explains: 'self-awareness means having a deep understanding of one's emotions, strengths, weaknesses, needs, and drives. People with strong self-awareness are neither overly critical nor unrealistically hopeful. Rather, they are honest – with themselves and with others.' The concept of the 'reflective practitioner' is increasingly present in leadership development programmes (Schon, 1983; Beckley, 2004). However, set against the rise of evidence-based policing and the privileging of positivistic methodologies, reflexivity in the police appears to have developed as a somewhat sanitised and managerialist, rather than critical, process. Meaningful reflexivity is 'messy'; it requires criticality, vulnerability and an appreciation of positionality (Letherby, 2002; Harding, 2018; Souhami, 2019). As Schon (1983: 61) explains: 'through reflection, he [the reflective practitioner] can surface and criticise the tacit understandings that have grown up around the repetitive experiences of a specialised practice, and can make new sense of the situations of uncertainty or uniqueness which he may allow himself to experience.' This is difficult to achieve in an occupational environment characterised by 'heroic' practices of resilience and strength. Understanding leadership in heroic or 'smart macho' terms is therefore a barrier to the adoption of alternative, more reflective, forms of leadership practice (Silvestri, 2007).

The second fundamental problem with the romanticised version of leadership is the extent to which the emphasis on heroism discourages police leaders from disclosing their experience of stress. Values, beliefs and assumptions about being 'a police officer' stigmatise mental health issues as weakness and act as a disincentive to seeking support. There is a tendency in the police to display what has been described as a 'John Wayne Syndrome': maintaining a macho image by denying or avoiding the emotional and psychological impact of stress and trauma (Gresty and McLelland, 1989; Brown and Campbell, 1994; Stinchcomb, 2004). Police officers are socialised to avoid displays of overt emotion, with humour, for example, considered a more socially acceptable form of tension release (Holdaway, 1988; Waddington, 1999b; Souhami, 2019). Neutrality, rationality and objectivity are understood as valued characteristics in the professional police officer, and emotion is interpreted as unprofessional, unreliable, weak and 'losing control' (Silvestri, 2003). As Drodge and Murphy (2002: 425) confirm: 'the emotional prescription of police work is tacitly understood: calm disengagement, affectless order, an unquestioning obeisance'. Police leaders learn the value of emotional regulation, detachment and distance as a signifier of strength and capability (Silvestri, 2003). Chan's (2007b) study of stress in policing found that assumptions of 'toughness' in policing meant that police officers choose to hide their feelings of stress. A study of UK police personnel found that mental ill-health was stigmatised in the police workplace; those who had been diagnosed with mental health issues experienced feelings of 'status loss', with mental ill-health in the police assumed to be a sign of 'poor character', leading to concerns about their performance in their work and ability to do their job (Bullock and Garland, 2018). As Bullock and Garland (2018: 177) conclude:

> The organizational environment comes to shape how mental illness is understood and interpreted by officers and helps to explain how a diagnosis can come to spoil the identity of a police officer. The primary theme in the accounts of participants was that a diagnosis of mental ill-health stood in contrast to what was perceived to be culturally expected of a police officer.

However, occupational stress is higher in working environments in which emotional and psychological reactions to stressors are problematised and regulated. Therefore, there may be additional stress in keeping mental ill-health secret. Paton (2006: 203) explains that 'vulnerability increases if experience is interpreted in an organizational culture that discourages emotional disclosure, focuses on attributing blame to staff, or minimizes the significance of peoples' [sic] reactions or feelings'. Notions of heroism perpetuate beliefs about stress as a sign of individual weakness. Organisational responses to stress and the rhetoric of resilience function to 'reify the ideal of the officer as a stalwart figure who is able to cope in the face of adversity' (Bullock and Garland, 2018: 186). These beliefs regulate against expressions of overt emotions in the police; stress reactions are therefore kept hidden. Emotional detachment and distance are understood as strength and capability in leadership (Silvestri, 2003). These perceptions therefore challenge the openness of police officers to access support.

The third and final problem with the heroism inherent in leadership is the lack of consideration of the implications of the unequal power dynamics between leaders and followers for embedding learning in organisations. Conventional theory, based on romanticised notions of leadership, emphasises coherence and consensus between the needs of leaders and followers, and leadership as an inherently positive process. The problematic consequences of these assumptions, and the repressive nature of power in organisations, are unexplored. As Silvestri (2018b) argues, alternative realities are masked. Idealised notions of heroism in leadership, particularly in hierarchical organisations, stifle learning and challenge, and silence dissent, resistance and opposition (Calas and Smircich, 1991; Grint, 2010a). Contemporary police leaders are being encouraged to learn from 'failures'. Matthew Syed's (2015) *Black Box Thinking* is a popular example of a resource to 'create a climate where it's safe to fail'. In England and Wales, the College of Policing (2015b) calls for police organisations to develop a culture of learning and challenge as a mechanism to alleviate organisational stress and improve morale. In this context, police leaders are encouraged to value 'canaries in the mine' and those in their organisation who 'challenge the system, ask the questions, spot the faults' (Tuffin, 2016). At the 2016 Police Federation Conference, Alex Marshall (2016), the then Chief Executive Officer of the College of Policing, confirmed that 'at the heart of it is the ability to challenge, to ask why, to have a culture in policing where the hierarchy doesn't mean you're not allowed to ask a difficult question, where we listen'. The assumption is that the credibility to challenge and influence is not equally distributed across the police hierarchy, and is interrupted by the unequal power dynamics in police organisations (Davis, 2019).

However, within the police, research has consistently demonstrated that value is placed on conformity and compliance, rather than criticality and challenge (Panzarella, 2003; Herrington and Colvin, 2016). Leadership practices in the police are heavily informed by assumptions about the necessity of command and control, and beliefs about the power and authority of senior rank (Silvestri, 2003; Davis, 2018). These assumptions place value on the deference and respect of junior officers who know and respect 'their place' in the rank hierarchy and regulate against challenge and questioning 'upwards' (Adlam, 2002; Silvestri, 2018b). Communication 'upwards' in police organisations is heavily shaped by 'rank etiquette'; who is afforded legitimacy to challenge and influence is laden with the authority of rank (Dick and Jankowicz, 2001; Davis, 2018). Junior officers may be given permission to challenge but within the context of 'constructive challenge' or 'respectful challenge', and, as such, this does little to fundamentally transform organisational practices. Challenge and criticality in hierarchical organisations are not risk-free, or indeed stress-free, endeavours. On the contrary, adopting such an approach is laden with personal risk, especially for those officers seeking promotion to leadership ranks. Studies have documented the career-damaging consequences of challenging poor leadership, such as studies of whistle-blowing that reveal the detrimental consequences on individuals (Alford, 2001). How power is enacted and experienced is therefore fundamental to understanding the nature of challenge and criticality in police organisations. Where 'heroic leaders' are assumed to be beyond criticism, questioning or resistance is interpreted as 'a problem' and those who challenge are labelled 'troublemakers' or 'whingers' (Grint, 2010b; Collinson, 2012; Tourish, 2013). As Collinson (2012: 95) explains: 'courage can be redefined as betrayal, and explicit dissent may have damaging effects on an individual's reputation and career'.

Tourish (2013), in *The Dark Side of Transformational Leadership*, describes the negative consequences of excessive compliance and conformity for organisations. Over time, the idealisation of leadership creates an organisational culture where upward communication is flattering rather than critical, constructive or meaningful. Decision-making, innovation and creativity are stifled. As Tourish (2013: 77) concludes:

> When sufficient and timely critical feedback is curtailed or eliminated, such leaders deprive themselves of a crucial means of ascertaining how viable their strategies are. Flattery constitutes a perfumed trap for decision makers. It improves the odds of organisational failure, separates leaders even further from non-leaders, institutionalises dysfunctional

power differences and ensures that leaders develop ever more elaborate plans and strategies with which their followers profoundly but silently disagree.

Likewise, Collinson's (2012: 93) analysis of 'Prozac Leadership' reveals how an organisational emphasis on 'excessive positivity' acts as a form of social control that regulates against criticism, and notes that 'by insisting that subordinates' upward communication is exclusively positive, Prozac leaders and the uncritical cultures they encourage can silence committed and concerned followers'. Therefore, romanticised notions of leadership have censuring and regulatory effects on organisational members. By conceptualising challenge from junior officers in negative terms, different and critical perspectives are therefore problematised and controlled, and the 'status quo' in leadership is maintained.

We have argued that romanticised beliefs about police leadership are therefore powerful in shaping understandings and practices in stress management. The individual police leader is expected to manage organisational well-being and act as a role model for stress management while being regulated from the disclosure of personal stress. As a mechanism to empower the workforce and improve morale, learning and challenge in police organisations are silenced in favour of compliance.

Leadership and relationships: a post-heroic alternative?

Critical leadership scholars call for 'no more heroes' in response to romanticised understandings of leadership (Collinson et al, 2018). These 'post-heroic' interpretations of leadership conceptualise leadership as a shared or distributed practice and a social process, which draws on notions of leadership as a collective, interdependent and power-neutral activity (see Chapter 4). Post-heroic perspectives consider alternative forms of leadership, such as servant leadership, and recognise the value of humility, emotion, relationships and community in leadership (Greenleaf, 1970; Murphy, 2008; Martin et al, 2017). However, despite this, the way in which leadership is constructed continues to draw heavily on notions of heroism, with leaders assigned an almost omnipotent status, and afforded authority as persons of exceptional qualities, attributes and influence.

The importance of relationships in leadership, in particular, within the context of stress management, is now well recognised. Leadership is relational insofar as it is conceived as an interdependent relationship between social actors, which is a process requiring participation and contribution (Collinson, 2006; Raelin, 2011). Shamir (2007) argues for the mutual influence of leaders and followers in leadership: the behaviours of followers are influenced by the leader and, likewise, the leader's behaviours are influenced by followers. Relationships form the basic premise of authentic leadership; this type of leadership is understood in terms of the acceptance of personal responsibility, motivations and actions, and the 'non-manipulation' of followers (Avolio and Gardner, 2005; Gardner et al, 2011). In contrast to conventional discourse, the followership literature elevates the role of the follower as an equal contributor in leadership and leadership is conceived as a joint production between the leader and the follower (Kelley, 1988; Shamir, 2007; Rost, 2008). The theories of shared and distributed leadership are based on assumptions of equality, collectivism and collaboration (Conger and Pearce, 2003; Gronn, 2011). These theories therefore prioritise the relational aspects of leadership.

However, studies of policing have captured how hegemonic masculine beliefs and values intrinsic to police occupational culture disrupt leadership relationships (Reuss-Ianni, 1983; Adlam, 2002; Silvestri, 2003). Relationships in the police workplace have historically been constituted in hierarchical terms to respect the demarcation of rank. These relationships, as Gordon (2010: 265) states, are 'unproblematically accepted as the way things are'. Developing an organisational culture of learning and challenge, which prioritises the relational aspects of leadership, depends on creating conditions where knowledge can be co-constructed. This requires a shift from hierarchical power relations in leadership, or 'power over' approaches, towards practices that emphasise collaboration and participation, or 'power with' (Gordon, 2002). The disruptive influence of rank as an authority in leadership cannot be transformed solely through policies aimed at flattening the hierarchical rank structure. Rather, critical consideration of how rank, as an authority, is enacted and experienced is essential, as well as, importantly, the implications of this for the development of collaborative relationships in leadership.

Police occupational culture is therefore a fundamental barrier to the prioritisation of well-being. It appears that the legitimacy of well-being initiatives in the police requires challenging the conventional assumptions underpinning the 'heroic police leader' and the negotiation of rank-centric beliefs and practices. As a study by Dick and Jankowicz (2001) found, rank has a significant influence over perceptions of job-related performance. Leaders, at all levels of the police organisation, experience considerable pressures, scrutiny and vulnerabilities (Brown et al, 1994; Haake et al, 2017). Therefore, a 'safe space' is required in which police officers and leaders can meaningfully engage with issues related to stress and well-being. Davis (2018) developed the Situated Authority Model of Leadership to depict the relationship between rank as an authority, context and leadership (see Figure 6). The model captures how the authority of rank is heightened and emphasised using the concept of the 'doing' of rank in leadership, as compared with the 'undoing' of rank to describe strategies to minimise the influence of rank in leadership. The doing and undoing of rank are situated in the context of audience and risk; situations are defined in terms of high or low audience and high or low risk. Low audience situations, such as informal interactions between senior and junior officers, are considered protected spaces free of independent or powerful 'outsiders', as compared with the highly visible, public encounters of high audience situations. Risk is conceptualised using time; high risk situations are emergency and critical situations, such as firearms or public order incidents, where there is a high risk to officer or public safety.

The hierarchical rank structure in the police can inhibit innovation and criticality (Silvestri, 2003; Gundhus, 2013; Hallenberg and Cockcroft, 2017). The Situated Authority Model of Leadership describes the construction of 'rank-neutral spaces' as mechanisms of 'undoing' rank. These spaces act as safe and protected environments

Figure 6: The Situated Authority Model of Leadership

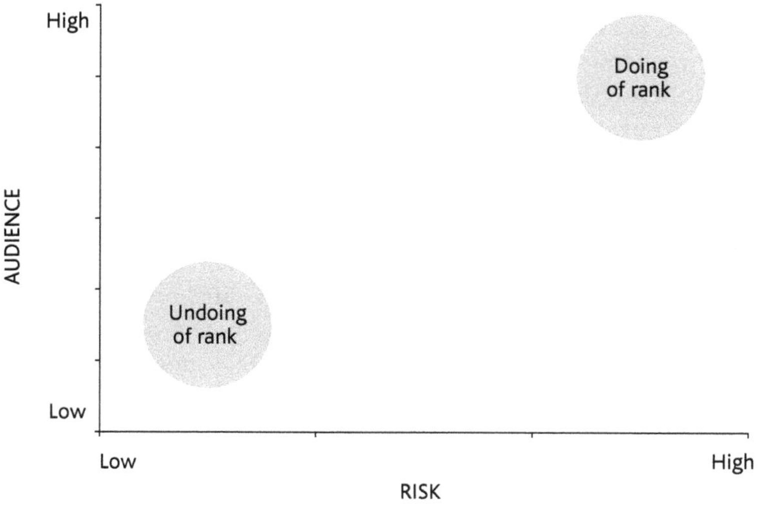

Source: Davis (2018: 5)

where permission is afforded to challenge conventional rank-centric practices in leadership and alternative approaches can 'safely' emerge. In other words, the 'etiquette' of rank is situationally suspended. Herrington and Colvin (2016) similarly describe the use of 'innovation laboratories' in an Australian police department to develop collaboration and participation in leadership. Learning and challenge – the co-construction of knowledge – can occur in these environments where the barrier of rank is minimised. Free of the expectations associated with senior rank, these rank-neutral spaces may also represent sites where leaders feel safe to critically reflect on their leadership practice, exhibit 'weakness' and seek support. As the leadership literature demonstrates, this self-awareness is an important precursor to the development of alternative 'authentic' leadership practices (Avolio and Gardner, 2005; Gardner et al, 2011). These 'safe spaces' therefore represent environments where 'post-heroic' leadership practices are privileged and the unequal power dynamics in the police workplace are navigated. Relationships and authenticity can be prioritised. As Davis (2018: 11) explains: 'in a hierarchical organisation, these low-risk and low-audience situations allow for leaders to suspend traditional top-down leadership in favour of a more collaborative approach'.

For police constabularies to develop as learning organisations, practices of critical self-reflection need to be embedded in organisational practices as 'business as usual'. This is problematic in disciplined, hierarchical organisations. Meaningful reflexivity requires vulnerability (Ellis and Bochner, 2000; Letherby, 2002), utilising a 'pervasive nervousness' (Geertz, 1977) or 'systematic doubt' (Agar, 2008) to encourage looking at situations in different and alternative ways. In leadership, this demands critical reflection on the impact of a leader's power and privileged position on their leadership practices and relationships; central to this is greater recognition of the influence of the unequal dynamics of rank. This version of reflexivity is an uncomfortable fit with conventional romanticised notions of leadership and assumptions of 'the leader knows best'. An important part of this reflective process is a genuine openness and responsiveness to critical voices and feedback 'upwards' in the police organisation. In leadership development, 360-degree feedback is not uncommon in organisations outside policing and is considered an essential feature of professional development. However, this practice is virtually absent in police constabularies. Embedding processes of critical reflective practices, such as 360-degree feedback, conflicts with the rank-based occupational culture and traditional approaches to leadership. Silvestri's

(2003: 177) study challenges the rank-oriented nature of leadership in the police and concludes that 'rank mentality does little to foster openness and honesty, nor does it allow a team-based approach to problem solving'. Likewise, Davis (2018) calls for greater awareness of the problematic influence of rank in leadership. To manage the complexity of contemporary demand, police leaders would be well placed to critically consider the implications of 'rank consciousness' for the police workplace and their leadership practice. Rather than continue to resort to structural solutions in response to the 'problem' of rank in leadership, policing policymakers and senior practitioners would be better placed to begin to have critical and meaningful discussions about how to make best use of rank in police leadership (Davis and Bailey, 2018). Rank-neutral spaces, as 'safe spaces', represent an opportunity to navigate the disruptive influence of rank and construct an environment that facilitates critical reflection and learning, and a protected site to understand and engage meaningfully with the management of stress.

Conclusion

The recognition of stress and trauma in policing, together with a focus on the well-being of staff, represent a welcome shift in resisting dominant assumptions of the 'ideal' police officer. If accepted uncritically, at first glance, such recognition represents a significant challenge to conventional ideologies that conceptualise police leadership in heroic terms. However, closer inspection reveals that notions of heroism underpin much of the contemporary discussion of well-being and resilience in the police. Understanding resilience in person-centred terms, in which the individual is positioned as both 'the problem' and 'the solution', is reminiscent of the criticism levied at conventional leadership theory. In policing, demonstrations of emotion and 'closeness' in relationships by leaders are understood as weakness, so these practices are marginalised. Rather, the credibility of leadership is performed in relation to strength, distance and the ability to 'bounce back'. In emphasising the individualised qualities and characteristics of 'bouncing back' and 'coping', resilience draws on idealised notions exposed by the thesis of the romance of leadership. The emphasis on personal resilience may therefore function to preserve, rather than transform, assumptions of hegemonic masculinity in leadership. As Collinson et al (2018: 1638) conclude: 'oppositional practices may unintentionally reinforce the very conditions of power and control that stimulated resistance in the first place'.

As this chapter has argued, romanticised notions of the ideal, heroic police leader act as an inhibitor to the prioritisation of well-being in the police workplace and the legitimacy of well-being policies. Meaningful acceptance of well-being initiatives in the police requires a challenge to the dominant underlying assumptions of what it means to be a police leader, and how police leaders think about themselves. This requires a fundamental shift from conventional assumptions of leadership towards a re-imagining of police leadership from a post-heroic perspective. To achieve this, police leaders are required to navigate rank-centric understandings and practices in their leadership. The construction of rank-neutral spaces affords an opportunity to create protected environments to challenge heroic practices in police leadership, to re-imagine the conventions and expectations of police leadership, and to 'do' leadership differently.

Further reading

Brown, J.M. and Campbell, E.A. (1994) *Stress and Policing: Sources and Strategies*. West Sussex: John Wiley & Sons Ltd.

Bullock, K. and J. Garland (2018) 'Police Officers, Mental (Ill-)Health and Spoiled Identity', *Criminology & Criminal Justice* 18(2): 173–89.

Collinson, D. (2012) 'Prozac Leadership and the Limits of Positive Thinking', *Leadership* 8(2): 87–107.

7

Conclusion and future directions

Understandings and practices of police leadership are informed by powerful, taken-for-granted ideologies. This book has problematised the fundamental assumptions underpinning conventional leadership discourse and theorised police leadership as a socially constructed activity. This concluding chapter provides a summary of the key arguments and debates presented in the book. Future challenges facing police leaders are examined to illustrate that conventional practices in police leadership are no longer appropriate. We conclude by making a case for alternative approaches to police leadership based on the shared leadership principles of collectivism and interdependence.

Contemporary constructions of police leadership are heavily influenced by the beliefs and assumptions inherent in conventional leadership theory. Transformational leadership, for example, is a popular endorsement for police leaders, and transformational qualities, such as innovation, inspiration and charisma, form part of the dominant contemporary leadership narrative (Dobby et al, 2004; Neyroud, 2011b; Swid, 2014). Police leadership is typically conceptualised in leader-centric terms, as person-centred and positional, and as firmly situated as a product of the traits and behaviours of individual leaders in formal positions of authority. Conventional theory also perpetuates assumptions of causality in leadership, with leadership understood as outcome-oriented, which places primacy on the capacity of leaders to inspire change, improve team performance and 'get the job done'. In other words, leadership is about 'getting results', the assumption being that leadership *can* get results. Dominant discourses of police leadership therefore assume leadership as residing in 'the person' and 'the position', and evident in the production of 'results'.

In such conventional discourse, leadership is typically conceptualised as a one-way process. This position neglects to consider junior officers and staff as co-producers of leadership and their agency to adapt, negotiate and resist leadership influence. Likewise, conventional theory assumes leadership to be a power-neutral activity, and where power in leadership is considered, it is typically done so uncritically; power in leadership is conceived as unproblematic (Gordon, 2011). In contrast, critical leadership scholars problematise the power dynamics inherent in leadership and highlight the destructive consequences of emphasising conformity and obedience. Challenge and resistance, as acts of follower power, are understood as necessary and important, rather than dysfunctional, in the police workplace. Greater understanding of the nuances of power in leadership, and the ways in which power is negotiated in the police workplace, is therefore needed.

Conventional theory also presumes police leadership to be a generic and universal quality, where leadership principles and practices from outside industry are transferred into the police organisation. Yet, resistance to such external initiatives, such as the Direct Entry scheme and New Public Management (NPM), demonstrates the normative 'special status' of police leadership. The criminalisation of leadership decisions in the police, as a legacy of the Hillsborough Inquiry, places a unique and unprecedented pressure on the activities of contemporary police leaders. While there are many comparable elements to the leadership role in the police within other public and private sector organisations, we argue that policing represents a distinctive occupational and political field, given its use of legitimate state-sanctioned force and unique political scrutiny. The activity of the police, and consequently of police leaders, distinctively 'matters' in the public consciousness.

Conventional theory, as the thesis of the romance of leadership demonstrates, also perpetuates notions of heroism in leadership (Mastrofski, 2002). Traditionally, leadership has been conceived in exclusively masculine terms: the 'think manager–think male' phenomenon (Schein, 2001). As Meindl and Ehrlich (1987: 92) noted, leadership 'has assumed a special status – not merely a prosaic alternative that people dispassionately consider on an equal footing with other explanations, it has achieved a heroic, larger-than-life value'. Police leadership in particular, drawing on hegemonic masculinity, is understood in terms of strength, resilience and 'grip', where leaders are expected to act decisively as 'all-knowing' problem solvers (Grint, 2010b; Silvestri, 2018b). The list of desirable leadership qualities appears endless; whether it is charisma or being visionary or inspirational, Grint (2005b: 34) explains, the expectations of leader capabilities mean that 'by the time the list is complete the only plausible description of the owner of such a skill base is "god"'. Overall, therefore, the police leader is positioned as 'the answer' to the problem (Panzarella, 2003; Grint and Thornton, 2015).

Within this context, emotion, humility, indecisiveness, criticality and uncertainty are not qualities understood in leadership terms, and demonstrating them in leadership is positioned as a 'weakness'. However, a continued attachment to 'heroism' has important implications for police leadership. These expectations legitimatise command-based approaches to police leadership and reduce the capacity of junior officers and staff to meaningfully engage in and contribute to leadership. Similarly, notions of heroism reinforce pressures on leaders to act in accordance with dominant hegemonic practices, which, in turn, limits the ability of the police workplace to respond effectively to stress in policing. Stress and vulnerability in leadership is problematised as an indicator of poor leadership performance and poor character, rather than as symptomatic of broader structural or ideological processes. Likewise, in privileging certain expressions of leadership over others, ideologies of heroism undermine policies aimed at improving diversity in leadership and leadership practices. Uniformity, conformity and leaders who 'fit the mould' are valued, rather than those demonstrating difference (Wall, 1998; Savage et al, 2000). Therefore, the dominant discourse of heroism reinforces assumptions that legitimacy in police leadership is gained through the expression and demonstration of practices that most closely relate to traditional masculinity. Difference, in other words, is marginalised. An alternative conceptualisation of police leadership is therefore needed. As Crevani et al (2010: 78) conclude: 'we must challenge our deeply rooted tendency to make the abstract notion of "leadership" concrete in the guise of individual managers ... [and] instead try to redefine leadership in terms of processes and practices organised by people in interaction.'

Adopting a more critical lens provides a valuable contribution to the understanding of contemporary police leadership. In contrast to traditional leadership theorists, critical perspectives characterise leadership in terms of participation and co-production, as well as the dynamics of authority and influence. A considerable body of work has drawn attention to the influence of rank as an authority on the practices within the police workplace (Adlam, 2002; Silvestri, 2003). From this perspective, the legitimacy to challenge and question is not equally distributed across the police organisation but heavily influenced by the seniority of rank (Davis, 2018). That said, the police occupational culture literature reminds us of the power of junior officers and staff to resist and negotiate organisational reform (Chan, 2007a; Skogan, 2008). Power, it appears, is a central and yet relatively unexplored feature of police leadership practices.

Police leadership can therefore usefully be theorised as socially constructed, and a contested and negotiated activity, whereby the meanings of leadership are informed by historical, cultural, political and institutional processes. A critical examination of the history of police leadership reveals that contemporary or 'new' problems have historical legacies. As Fairhurst and Grant (2010: 172) explain, leadership 'is co-constructed, a product of sociohistorical and collective meaning making, and negotiated on an ongoing basis through a complex interplay among leadership actors, be they designated or emergent leaders, managers, and/or followers'. Understanding leadership as a socially constructed, power-centric process challenges the essentialist and deterministic assumptions of conventional theory and the uncritical acceptance of the mutuality and compliance between the needs of leaders and followers. This perspective makes three important contributions to the understanding of police leadership. First, a socially constructed perspective challenges leader-centric assumptions and shifts the focus away from 'being' a leader towards the performance and expressions of leadership, or the 'doing' of leadership (Silvestri, 2003; Pye, 2005). Leadership is not understood exclusively in terms of the traits or behaviours of the individual leader; rather, broader social and cultural processes define the meaning of leadership – leadership is 'in the eyes of the beholder' (Meindl, 1995: 331). A socially constructed approach draws attention to leadership as a process of sensemaking and the management of meanings. Therefore, from this perspective, police leadership is best understood as a relationship, a practice or a presentation rather than 'a person' or 'a position'. As Smircich and Morgan (1982: 259) explain: 'authority relationships institutionalise a hierarchical pattern of interaction in which certain individuals are expected to define the experience of others – to lead, and others to have their experience defined – to follow'.

A socially constructed perspective also places primacy on the situated nature of leadership as the context or 'surrounds' of leadership function to legitimatise particular leadership practices while marginalising and excluding others. Davis (2018), for example, reveals that understandings of context in terms of risk and audience inform how rank as an authority is used in leadership. Grint (2005a: 1470) concludes that 'leadership involves the social construction of the context that both legitimates a particular form of action and constitutes the world in the process'. Finally, conceptualising police leadership as socially constructed reveals the fluidity and multiplicity of understandings and experiences. Leadership is positioned as a dynamic process that emerges and unfolds within everyday experience of the police workplace (Wood and Ladkin, 2008; Crevani et al, 2010). Junior officers and staff are understood as active participants in leadership, with leadership understood as a process of acceptance, adaption and resistance.

The future of policing demands different approaches to leadership. As the role and activities of contemporary policing expand, police organisations in England and Wales are having to adapt to economic austerity and drives for efficiency, respond effectively to global crime within a regional police force structure with diminishing resources, and embed technology, higher education and research evidence into policing practices (Neyroud, 2015). Contemporary police leadership is performed in an increasingly networked and inter-organisational public service environment in which police leaders are required to respond, as part of a collective, to complex social problems. Police leadership also needs to demonstrate commitment to 'public-oriented' leadership with a clear responsiveness and accessibility to citizens (Brookes and Grint, 2010). This requires understanding problems as dynamic, interdependent and multi-causal, and a 'systems thinking' approach rather than practices or responding to problems in organisational silos (Senge, 1999; Marion and Uhl-Bien, 2001). A systems-thinking approach is a fundamentally different way of 'doing' leadership in the police. As Bennington and Hartley (2010: 190) explain, this involves 'the capacity to analyse and understand the inter-connections, inter-dependencies and interactions between complex issues, across multiple boundaries'. Therefore, to work effectively within the complexity of the changing policing landscape, the police service would be better placed to consider leadership as 'asking the right questions' within a network of subject experts rather than the traditional leader-centric practice of 'knowing the answers' (Grint and Thornton, 2015).

We have also yet to see the full impact of the politicised context in policing sparked by the introduction of Police and Crime Commissioners (PCCs). Police leaders are increasingly confronted with senior politicians and civilians with enhanced control over police organisations and decision-making (Van Dijk et al, 2015). The relationship between politics and policing continues to challenge the 'sacred status' of British policing as apolitical; the implications of this for police legitimacy, police leadership and police–community relations are not yet known. The future of policing in a post-Brexit era, the implications for the policing of borders and immigration, policing and globalisation, and what this means for the expectations of police leaders across regional, national and international boundaries are also unknown. However, what is known is that policing is in a state of perpetual turbulence and that traditional approaches to leadership are not fit for purpose. Command-based approaches, which rely on the hierarchical rank structure, can no longer be the privileged and exclusive leadership practice in the police. Therefore, in this complex contemporary context, leadership across all public services requires stronger collective and participatory practices.

Shared or distributed leadership practices, as Chapter 4 examined, have been demonstrated to facilitate creativity and innovation, and support improved working relationships and organisational commitment, in industry and other public service organisations (Gronn, 2002; Pearce and Ensley, 2004). There is emerging recognition of the value of shared leadership practices in the police. The College of Policing's (2016: 18) *Competency and Values Framework*, for example, identified collaboration as a key competency within 'inclusive, enabling and visionary leadership'. According to these competencies, police leadership should 'provide space and encouragement to help others stand back from day-to-day activities, in order to review their direction, approach and how they fundamentally see their role in policing. This helps them to adopt fresh perspectives and identify improvements' (College of Policing, 2016: 18). Shared leadership shifts the focus from a 'power over' model of leadership towards a 'power with' approach (Salovaara and Bathurst, 2018). The principles of shared leadership can support police organisations to respond flexibly, reflectively and innovatively to the demands of the contemporary policing context.

In the Situated Authority Model of Leadership (see Figure 6 on p 125), Davis (2018) describes the concept of 'rank-neutral spaces' as a precursor to the development of alternative practices in police leadership. These rank-neutral spaces act as protective and safe environments in which cultural and ideological barriers related to rank and police leadership are removed and alternative practices, based on shared leadership principles, can emerge. The concept of 'safe spaces' is evident in leadership in other organisational spheres. In higher education, for example, Whitchurch (2008: 379) discusses the concept of 'third space' as a space of mixed teams where organisational structures and conventions are bypassed and negotiated, and collaborative working relationships are encouraged. The protected nature of these spaces affords permission to challenge conventional leadership processes and practices, encouraging collaborative working and building communicative and participatory networks. Emphasis is placed on lateral influence and working practices, rather than traditional hierarchical processes. According to Whitchurch, these spaces develop in spite of, rather than as a result of, the formal leadership and organisational structures, which alludes to the agency of junior officers in the 'co-production' of leadership. These 'safe spaces' reveal the extent to which environments can be constructed within the police hierarchy that foster innovation, creativity and credible alternative professional knowledge and practices.

Much of the consideration of rank and police leadership has concerned the structural solution of reform to the police hierarchy. The rank structure is accepted as a barrier to participatory, collaborative and innovative approaches to leadership (Herrington and Colvin, 2016). The College of Policing (2015b), for example, recognises that the rigid structure in the police can 'clog up' decision-making and communication, and calls for a 'flattening' of the hierarchy in line with outside industry. As the College of Policing (2015b: 22) confirms: 'there is evidence from the commercial sector to suggest that flatter structures may allow organisations to be more responsive to social shifts and agile in meeting market demands, because they have fewer levels of decision making and therefore fewer communication barriers.' However, reforms to the rank structure in isolation will not fundamentally transform the basic underlying assumptions about rank and leadership. Structural reform neglects to consider the socially constructed nature of police leadership and, importantly, the navigation, negotiation and politics of rank. The Situated Authority Model of Leadership provides an analytical framework to theorise police leadership as a rank-centric activity, placing emphasis on rank as an authority rather than a structure, where rank is conceptualised as an 'organising device' or 'meaning-making' that informs the assumptions, interactions and experiences in leadership in the police (Davis, 2018). The model also provides a structure to support police leaders to critically reflect on their approach to leadership. Embedding critical self-reflection is an essential precursor for meaningful and sustainable change in police leadership.

In emphasising the principles of collaboration and participation, shared leadership represents a fundamental challenge to assumptions of the nature of police leadership and the way it should be practised. Dominant understandings of police leadership act as a barrier to developing leadership as a shared process, as well as the acceptance and success of collaborative and participatory leadership practices in the police. Despite the call from policymakers for a greater appreciation of alternative practices in leadership in the police, the police organisations continue to consider leadership through the dominant leader-centric discourse that legitimises traditional and command-based approaches (Silvestri, 2003). A history of police research has demonstrated that without the meaningful engagement and understanding of front-line policing experiences, top-down, external reform imposed onto the police organisation will not fundamentally transform leadership practices. For shared leadership practices to be accepted as a legitimate approach to police leadership, the practice needs to 'make sense' in the context of the lived experiences and occupational realities of police officers. Imposing shared leadership 'onto' the police not only contradicts the basic principles of shared leadership, but is also likely only to meet resistance, as decades of police research has documented.

However, the contemporary context represents distinctive challenges in developing shared leadership in the police. The decisions and activities of police leaders are highly scrutinised on a global platform, and information is readily available through which citizens can experience the impact of police leadership without ever personally encountering a police officer (Mawby, 2002; Bullock, 2018). The high level of discretion afforded to front-line police officers, and the power of junior officers to 'close ranks', places police leaders in the difficult position of being responsible and accountable for a resource with considerable discretionary power but with limited information and influence. Police leaders are not only responsible for present-day practice; a series of high-profile police failings in England and Wales has demonstrated that senior police leaders are also held accountable for historical decision-making and policing practices (Hough et al, 2018). The introduction of PCCs has situated a powerful political actor as a central component in police governance to an unprecedented degree. This is set against the accountability pressures from 'within' the organisation, where senior police leaders are increasingly called to 'speak out' and represent their workforce, particularly in response to occupational stress (Blader and Tyler, 2003; Bradford and Quinton, 2014). Therefore, the contemporary policing landscape exposes police leaders to powerful competing and contradictory pressures. Moreover, in the current political and economic climate, competition for limited opportunities to reach senior ranks is characteristic of the contemporary police service; senior rank is increasingly reserved for the 'select few'. In this context, it is difficult to foresee a widespread acceptance of 'difference' in leadership practice. Alternative expressions and demonstrations of leadership continue to be an uncomfortable challenge to the 'status quo' of how leadership authority is enacted in the police; participative or collaborative practices are perceived as 'out of the norm' in leadership practice. The development of alternative leadership practices based on collaboration and the sharing of decision-making is likely to be understood as a risk, and, consequently, may strengthen the risk-averse leadership culture in the police. There is 'protection' and 'safety' afforded to the traditional command structures and rank-based approaches in police leadership. Therefore, we may observe a greater emphasis on, and reward for, dominant expressions of police leadership and a continued 'reverting back' towards conventional, command-based approaches to leadership.

Contemporary understanding of police leadership is incomplete, and we therefore call for a greater appreciation of the socially constructed nature of leadership in the police. The discussions in this book have highlighted that legitimacy in police leadership is underpinned by values and beliefs about the 'ideal police leader' that draw heavily on hegemonic masculinity. A socially constructed perspective, as we have demonstrated, challenges conventional understanding of police leadership in leader-centric terms and shifts the focus away from conceiving leadership in abstract, context-free lists of desirable leadership behaviours and capabilities. We have instead re-imagined police leadership as a co-produced relationship. Central to this, we have argued, is a critical understanding of the dynamics of power. Police leadership is a product of historical, social and institutional influences, as well as the agency of individuals to negotiate and resist authority in the police workplace. Police leadership is reformed not solely through a focus on structural solution, but, rather, through meaningful and critical debate about the experience of power and authority in leadership in the police. To develop leadership practice in the police, greater attention should therefore be paid to transforming the beliefs and assumptions underpinning the 'ideal' police leader.

However, conventional understandings of police leadership inhibit the acceptance of collaborative, participatory or transformational leadership. The endorsement of such approaches from policymakers has, to date, been removed from the realities of understanding leadership in the context of police occupational culture and police work. Here, it is important to consider police officers and staff as 'co-producers' and 'knowledge holders' whose contribution to leadership reform is valued. The contemporary context, while presenting distinctive challenges for the police, also creates an opportunity for police organisations to facilitate and value leadership in relational and collective terms. Leadership recruitment, training and development would be well placed to incorporate the principles of social constructionism in order to facilitate understanding of leadership as a process. It is hoped that leadership selection, recruitment and development will reflect the socially constructed nature of police leadership and challenge the idealised and romanticised notions of leadership. As such, recommendations for reform will be grounded in the realities of police officers' experiences and understandings of leadership.

Further reading

Brown, J.M. (2014) *The Future of Policing*. London: Routledge.
Davis, C. (2018) 'Rank Matters: Police Leadership and the Authority of Rank', *Policing and Society* (advanced access).

References

Abdollahi, M.K. (2002) 'Understanding Police Stress Research', *Journal of Forensic Psychology Practice* 2(2): 1–24.

Acker, J. (1990) 'Hierarchies, Jobs and Bodies: A Theory of Gendered Organizations', *Gender & Society* 4(2): 139–58.

ACPO (Association of Chief Police Officers) (2010) *Equality, Diversity and Human Rights Strategy for the Police Service.* London: Home Office.

Adlam, R. (2002) 'Governmental Rationalities in Police Leadership: An Essay Exploring some of the "Deep Structure" in Police Leadership Praxis', *Policing and Society* 12(1): 15–36.

Adlam, R. (2003) 'This Complex Thing, Leadership', in R. Adlam and P. Villiers (eds) *Police Leadership in the Twenty-First Century: Philosophy, Doctrine and Developments.* Hampshire: Waterside Press, pp 204–22.

Adlam, R. and Villiers, P. (eds) (2003) *Police Leadership in the Twenty-First Century: Philosophy, Doctrine and Developments.* Hampshire: Waterside Press.

Agar, M.H. (2008) *The Professional Stranger* (2nd edn). Bingley: Emerald Publishing.

Alexander, D.A. and Wells, A. (1991) 'Reactions of Police Officers to Body Handling after a Major Disaster: A Before and after Comparison', *British Journal of Psychiatry* 159: 517–55.

Alford, C. (2001) *Whistleblowers: Broken Lives and Organizational Power.* Ithaca, NY: Cornell University Press.

Alimo-Metcalfe, B. (2004) *'Leadership: A Masculine Past, but a Feminine Future?' Gender and Excellence in the Making.* Luxembourg: Office for Official Publications of European Communities.

Alimo-Metcalfe, B. and Alban-Metcalfe, J. (2005) 'Leadership: Time for a New Direction?', *Leadership* 1(1): 51–71.

Allen, G. and Zayed, Y. (2019) 'Police Service Strength', House of Commons Research Briefing Paper, 31 July.

Alvesson, M. (1992) 'Leadership as Social Integrative Action: A Study of a Computer Consultancy Company', *Organization Studies* 13(2): 185–209.

Alvesson, M. (1998) 'Gender Relations and Identity at Work: A Case Study of Masculinities and Femininities in an Advertising Agency', *Human Relations* 51(8): 969–1005.

Alvesson, M. (2011) 'Leadership and Organizational Culture', in A. Bryman, D. Collinson, K. Grint, B. Jackson and M. Uhl-Bien (eds) *The Sage Handbook of Leadership.* London: Sage Publications, pp 151–64.

Alvesson, M. and Spicer, A. (2012) 'Critical Leadership Studies: The Case for Critical Performativity', *Human Relations* 65(3): 367–90.

Alvesson, M. and Sveningsson, S. (2003) 'The Great Disappearing Act: Difficulties in Doing "Leadership"', *The Leadership Quarterly* 14(3): 359–81.

Andersson, T. and Tengblad, S. (2009) 'When Complexity Meets Culture: New Public Management and the Swedish Police', *Qualitative Research in Accounting & Management* 6(1/2): 41–56.

Andreescu, V. and Vito, G.F. (2010) 'An Exploratory Study on Ideal Leadership Behaviour: The Opinions of American Police Managers', *International Journal of Police Science & Management* 12(4): 567–83.

Antonakis, J. (2011) 'Predictors of Leadership: The Usual Suspects and the Suspect Trait', in A. Bryman, D. Collinson, K. Grint, B. Jackson and M. Uhl-Bien (eds) *The Sage Handbook of Leadership*. London: Sage, pp 269–85.

Antonakis, J. and Atwater, L.E. (2002) 'Leader Distance: A Review and a Proposed Theory', *Leadership Quarterly* 13(6): 673–704.

Antonakis, J., Cianciolo, A.T. and Sternberg, R.J. (2004) 'Leadership: Past, Present and Future', in J. Antonakis, A.T. Cianciolo and R.J. Sternberg (eds) *The Nature of Leadership*. Thousand Oaks, CA: Sage, pp 3–16.

Antonakis, J., Ashkanasy, N.M. and Dasborough, M.T. (2009) 'Does Leadership Need Emotional Intelligence?', *The Leadership Quarterly* 20(2): 247–61.

Audit Commission (1990) *Effective Policing: Performance Review in Police Forces*. London: Audit Commission.

Avolio, B.J. and Gardner, W.L. (2005) 'Authentic Leadership Development: Getting to the Root of Positive Forms of Leadership', *The Leadership Quarterly* 16(3): 315–38.

Avolio, B.J., Waldman, D.A. and Yammarino, F.J. (1991) 'Leading in the 1990s: The Four I's of Transformational Leadership', *Journal of European Industrial Training* 15(4): 9–16.

Ayman, R. (2004) 'Situational and Contingency Approaches to Leadership', in J. Antonakis, A.T. Cianciolo and R.J. Sternberg (eds) *The Nature of Leadership*. Thousand Oaks, CA: Sage, pp 148–70.

Bacon, M. (2014) 'Police Culture and the New Policing Context', in J.M. Brown (ed) *The Future of Policing*. London: Routledge, pp 103–19.

Banton, M. (1964) *The Policeman in the Community*. London: Tavistock.

Barker, R.A. (1997) 'How Can We Train Leaders if We Do Not Know What Leadership Is?', *Human Relations* 50(4): 343–62.

Barker, R.A. (2001) 'The Nature of Leadership', *Human Relations* 54(4): 469–94.

Barlow, C. and Walklate, S. (2018) 'Policing Intimate Partner Violence: The "Golden Thread" of Discretion', *Policing: A Journal of Policy and Practice* (advanced access).

Barnard, C. (1997) 'The Nature of Leadership', in K. Grint (ed) *Leadership: Classical, Contemporary and Critical Approaches.* Oxford: Oxford University Press, pp 89–111.

Bartol, K.M. and Butterfield, D.A. (1976) 'Sex Effects in Evaluating Leaders', *Journal of Applied Psychology* 61(4): 446–54.

Bass, B.M. (1985) *Leadership and Performance beyond Expectations.* New York, NY: The Free Press.

Bass, B.M. (1990) 'From Transactional to Transformational Leadership: Learning to Share the Vision', *Organizational Dynamics* 18(3): 19–31.

Bass, B.M. (2008) *The Bass Handbook of Leadership: Theory, Research and Managerial Applications* (4th edn). New York, NY: Free Press.

Bayley, D.H. (2016) 'The Complexities of 21st Century Policing', *Policing* 10(3): 163–70.

Bayley, D.H. and Bittner, E. (1984) 'Learning the Skills of Policing', *Law and Contemporary Problems* 47(4): 35–59.

Beagley, M.C., Peterson, Z.D., Strasshofer, D.R. and Galovski, T.E. (2018) 'Sex Differences in Posttraumatic Stress and Depressive Symptoms in Police Officers Following Exposure to Violence in Ferguson: The Moderating Effect of Empathy', *Policing: An International Journal* 41(5): 623–35.

Becker, H.S. and Carper, J.W. (1956) 'The Elements of Identification with an Occupation', *American Sociological Review* 21(3): 341–8.

Beckley, A. (2004) 'Police Training – Can it Cope?', *Police Research & Management* 6(2): 1–17.

Behague, D., Tawiah, C., Rosato, M., Some, T. and Morrison, J. (2009) 'Evidence-Based Policy Making: The Implications of Globally-Applicable Research for Context-Specific Problem-Solving in Developing Countries', *Social Science & Medicine* 69(10): 1539–46.

Bennington, J. and Hartley, J. (2010) 'Knowledge and Capabilities for Leadership across the Whole Public Service System', in S. Brookes and K. Grint (eds) *The New Public Leadership Challenge.* London: Palgrave Macmillan, pp 187–98.

Bennis, W. (1989) *On Becoming a Leader.* Massachusetts, MA: Addison-Wesley Publishing.

Bennis, W. (1999) 'The End of Leadership: Exemplary Leadership Is Impossible without Full Inclusion, Initiatives, and Cooperation of Followers', *Organizational Dynamics* 28(1): 71–9.

Berger, P. and Luckmann, T. (1967) *The Social Construction of Reality*. Middlesex: Penguin Books.

Beyer, J.M. (1999) 'Taming and Promoting Charisma to Change Organizations', *The Leadership Quarterly* 10(2): 307–30.

Biggart, N.W. and Hamilton, G.G. (1987) 'An Institutional Theory of Leadership', *The Journal of Applied Behavioral Science* 23(4): 429–41.

Billing, Y.D. and Alvesson, M. (2000) 'Questioning the Notion of Feminine Leadership: A Critical Perspective on the Gender Labelling of Leadership', *Gender, Work and Organization* 7(3): 144–57.

Bittner, E. (1967) 'The Police on Skid-Row: A Study of Peace Keeping', *American Sociological Review* 32(5): 699–715.

Blader, S. and Tyler, T.R. (2003) 'What Constitutes Fairness in Work Settings? A Four Component Model of Procedural Justice', *Human Resource Management Review* 13(1): 107–26.

Blake, R.R. and Mouton, J.S. (1978) *The New Managerial Grid*. Houston, TX: Golf Publishing Company.

Bland, N., Mundy, G., Russell, J. and Tuffin, R. (1999) *Career Progression of Ethnic Minority Police Officers*, Police Research Series Paper 107. London: Home Office.

Bligh, M.C. (2011) 'Followership and Follower-Centred Approaches', in A. Bryman, D. Collinson, K. Grint, B. Jackson and M. Uhl-Bien (eds) *The Sage Handbook of Leadership*. London: Sage Publications, pp 425–54.

Blumer, H. (1969) *Symbolic Interactionism: Perspective and Method* (2nd edn). Berkeley, CA: University of California Press.

Bolden, R. and Gosling, J. (2006) 'Leadership Competencies: Time to Change the Tune?', *Leadership* 2(2): 147–63.

Bowling, B. and Weber, L. (2011) 'Stop and Search in Global Context: An Overview', *Policing and Society* 21(4): 480–8.

Boyatzis, R.E., Passarelli, A.M., Koenig, K., Lowe, M., Mathew, B., Stoller, J.K. and Phillips, M. (2012) 'Examination of the Neural Substrates Activated in Memories of Experiences with Resonant and Dissonant Leaders', *The Leadership Quarterly* 23(2): 259–72.

Boyne, G.A. (2002) 'Public and Private Management: What's the Difference?', *Journal of Management Studies* 39(1): 97–122.

Bradford, B. and Quinton, P. (2014) 'Self Legitimacy, Police Culture and Support for Democratic Policing in an English Constabulary', *British Journal of Criminology* 54(6):1023–46.

Bradley, D. and Nixon, C. (2009) 'Ending the "Dialogue of the Deaf": Evidence and Policing Policies and Practices. An Australian Case Study', *Police Practice and Research* 10(5/6): 423–35.

Bradley, D., Walker, N. and Wilkie, R. (1986) *Managing the Police: Law, Organisation and Democracy*. Sussex: Wheatsheaf Books.

Brain, T. (2013) *A Future for Policing in England and Wales*. Oxford: Oxford University Press.

Brogden, M. (1999) 'Community Policing as Cherry Pie', in R.I. Mawby (ed) *Policing Across the World: Issues for the Twenty-First Century*. London: UCL Press, pp 167–86.

Brogden, M. and Ellison, G. (2013) *Policing in an Age of Austerity: A Postcolonial Perspective*. London: Routledge.

Brookes, S. and Grint, K. (2010) 'A New Public Leadership Challenge?', in S. Brookes and K. Grint (eds) *The New Public Leadership Challenge*. London: Palgrave Macmillan, pp 1–16.

Brown, J.M. (2007) 'From Cult of Masculinity to Smart Macho: Gender Perspectives on Police Occupational Culture', in M. O'Neil, M. Marks and A.M. Singh (eds) *Police Occupational Culture: New Debates and Directions*. Oxford: Elsevier JAI, pp 205–28.

Brown, J.M. and Campbell, E.A. (1990) 'Sources of Occupational Stress in the Police', *Work & Stress* 4(4): 305–18.

Brown, J.M. and Campbell, E.A. (1994) *Stress and Policing: Sources and Strategies*. Chichester: John Wiley & Sons.

Brown, J.M., Cooper, C. and Kirkcaldy, B. (1994) 'Impact of Work Pressures on Senior Police Managers in the United Kingdom', *Policing and Society* 4(4): 341–52.

Brown, J.M., Belur, J., Tompson, L., McDowall, A., Hunter, G. and May, T. (2018) 'Extending the Remit of Evidence-Based Policing', *International Journal of Police Science & Management* 20(1): 38–51.

Brunetto, Y. and Farr-Wharton, R. (2003) 'Commitment and Satisfaction of Lower-Ranked Officers: Lessons for Management', *Policing: An International Journal of Police Strategies & Management* 26(1): 43–63.

Bryant, R., Cockcroft, T., Tong, S. and Wood, D. (2014) 'Police Training and Education: Past, Present and Future', in J.M. Brown (ed) *The Future of Policing*. Routledge: London, pp 383–97.

Bryman, A. (2011) 'Research Methods in the Study of Leadership', in A. Bryman, D. Collinson, K. Grint, B. Jackson and M. Uhl-Bien (eds) *The Sage Handbook of Leadership*. London: Sage, pp 15–28.

Bullock, K. (2018) '(Re)Presenting "Order" Online: The Construction of Police Presentational Strategies on Social Media', *Policing and Society* 28(3): 345–59.

Bullock, K. and Garland, J. (2018) 'Police Officers, Mental (Ill-)Health and Spoiled Identity', *Criminology & Criminal Justice* 18(2): 173–89.

Bullock, K. and Tilley, N. (2009) 'Evidence-Based Policing and Crime Reduction', *Policing* 3(4): 381–7.

Burke, K.J., Shakespearce-Fierce, J., Paton, D. and Ryan, M. (2006) 'Characterizing the Resilient Officer: Individual Attributes at Point of Entry to Policing', *Traumatology* 12(3): 178–88.

Burke, M. (1992) 'Cop Culture and Homosexuality', *Police Journal* 65(1): 30–40.

Burke, M. (1994) 'Homosexuality as Deviance: The Case of the Gay Police Officer', *British Journal of Criminology* 34(2): 192–203.

Burns, J.M. (1978) *Leadership*. New York, NY: Harper Perennial Political Classics.

Butterfield, R., Edwards, C. and Woodall, J. (2004) 'The New Public Management and the UK Police Service', *Public Management Review* 6(3): 395–415.

Butterfield, R., Edwards, C. and Woodall, J. (2005) 'The New Public Management and Managerial Roles: The Case of the Police Sergeant', *British Journal of Management* 16(4): 329–41.

Cain, M. (1973) *Society and the Policeman's Role*. London: Routledge & Kegan Paul.

Calas, M.B. and Smircich, L. (1991) 'Voicing Seduction to Silence Leadership', *Organization Studies* 12(4): 567–602.

Caless, B. (2011) *Policing at the Top: The Roles, Values and Attitudes of Chief Police Officers*. Bristol: Policy Press.

Caless, B. and Owens, J. (2016) *Police and Crime Commissioners: The Transformation of Police Accountability*. Bristol: Policy Press.

Caless, B. and Tong, S. (2015) *Leading Policing in Europe*. Bristol: Policy Press.

Campeau, H. (2019) 'Institutional Myths and Generational Boundaries: Cultural Inertia in the Police Organisation', *Policing and Society* 29(1): 69–84.

Carlier, I.V.E., Lamberts, R.D., Van Uchelen, A.J. and Gersons, B.P.R. (1998) 'Disaster-Related Post-Traumatic Stress in Police Officers: A Field Study of the Impact of Debriefing', *Stress & Health* 14(3): 143–8.

Carsten, M.K. and Bligh, M.C. (2007) 'Here Today, Gone Tomorrow: Follower Perceptions of a Departing Leader and a Lingering Vision', in B. Shamir, R. Pillai, M.C. Bligh and M. Uhl-Bien (eds) *Follower-Centered Perspectives on Leadership: A Tribute to the Memory of James R. Meindl*. Connecticut, CT: Information Age Publishing, pp 211–42.

Carsten, M.K. and Bligh, M.C. (2008) 'Lead, Follow and Get out of the Way: Involving Employees in the Visioning Process', in R.E. Riggio, I. Chaleff and J. Lipman-Blumen (eds) *The Art of Followership: How Great Followers Create Great Leaders and Organizations*. New Jersey: John Wiley & Sons.

Carsten, M.K., Uhl-Bien, M., West, B.J., Patera, J.L. and McGregor, R. (2010) 'Exploring Social Constructions of Followership: A Qualitative Study', *The Leadership Quarterly* 21(3): 543–62.

Casey, J. and Mitchell, M. (2007) 'Requirements of Police Managers and Leaders from Sergeant to Commissioner', in M. Mitchell and J. Casey (eds) *Police Leadership and Management*. Sydney: Federation Press, pp 4–20.

Chaleff, I. (2009) *The Courageous Follower* (3rd edn). Oakland, CA: Berrett-Koehler Publishers.

Chan, J. (1996) 'Changing Police Culture', *British Journal of Criminology* 36(1): 109–34.

Chan, J. (1997) *Changing Police Culture: Policing in a Multicultural Society*. Cambridge: Cambridge University Press.

Chan, J. (2007a) 'Making Sense of Police Reforms', *Theoretical Criminology* 11(3): 323–45.

Chan, J. (2007b) 'Police Stress and Occupational Culture', in M. O'Neil, M. Marks and A.M. Singh (eds) *Police Occupational Culture: New Debates and Directions*. Oxford: JAI Press, pp 129–52.

Chan, J., Devery, C. and Doran, S. (2003) *Fair Cop: Learning the Art of Policing*. Toronto: University of Toronto Press.

Chapman, C. (2012) 'Use of Force in Minority Communities Is Related to Police Education, Age, Experience, and Ethnicity', *Police Practice and Research* 13(5): 421–36.

Charman, S. (2018) *Police Socialisation, Identity and Culture: Becoming Blue*. London: Palgrave Macmillan.

Charman, S., Savage, S.P. and Cope, S. (1999) 'Getting to the Top: Selection and Training for Senior Managers in the Police Service', *Social Policy & Administration* 33(3): 281–301.

Chatterton, M. (1995) 'The Cultural Craft of Policing: Its Past and Future Relevance', *Policing and Society* 5(2): 97–107.

Chaturvedi, S., Zyphur, M.J., Arvey, R.D., Avolio, B.J. and Larsson, G. (2012) 'The Heritability of Emergent Leadership: Age and Gender as Moderating Factors', *The Leadership Quarterly* 23(2): 219–32.

Christie, G., Petrie, S. and Timmins, P. (1996) 'the Effect of Police Education, Training and Socialization on Conservative Attitudes', *Australian and New Zealand Journal of Criminology* 29(3): 299–314.

Cockcroft, T. (2007) 'Police Culture(s): Some Definitional, Methodological and Analytical Considerations', in M. O'Neill, M. Marks and A.M. Singh (eds) *Police Occupational Culture: New Debates and Directions*. Oxford: Elsevier JAI, pp 85–104.

Cockcroft, T. (2013) *Police Culture: Themes and Concepts*. Abingdon: Routledge.

Cockcroft, T. (2014) 'Police Culture and Transformational Leadership: Outlining the Contours of a Troubled Relationship', *Policing: A Journal of Policy and Practice* 8(1): 5–13.

Cockcroft, T. (2017) 'Police Culture: Histories, Orthodoxies, and New Horizons', *Policing: A Journal of Policy and Practice* 11(3): 229–35.

Cockcroft, T. and Beattie, I, (2009) 'Shifting Cultures: Managerialism and the Rise of "Performance"', *Policing: An International Journal of Police Strategies & Management* 32(3): 526–40.

College of Policing (2014a) *Five-Year Strategy*. Ryton: College of Policing.

College of Policing (2014b) *Code of Ethics*. Ryton: College of Policing.

College of Policing (2015a) *College of Policing Analysis: Estimating Demand on the Police Service*. Ryton: College of Policing.

College of Policing (2015b) *Leadership Review*. Ryton: College of Policing.

College of Policing (2016) *Competency and Values Framework*. Ryton: College of Policing.

College of Policing (2017a) *Guiding Principles for Organisational Leadership*. Ryton: College of Policing.

College of Policing (2017b) *Valuing Difference*. Ryton: College of Policing.

Collinson, D. (2005a) 'Dialectics of Leadership', *Human Relations* 58(11): 1419–42.

Collinson, D. (2005b) 'Questions of Distance', *Leadership* 1(2): 235–50.

Collinson, D. (2006) 'Rethinking Followership: A Post-Structuralist Analysis of Follower Identities', *The Leadership Quarterly* 17(2): 179–89.

Collinson, D. (2011) 'Critical Leadership Studies', in A. Bryman, D. Collinson, K. Grint, B. Jackson and M. Uhl-Bien (eds) *The Sage Handbook of Leadership*. London: Sage Publications, pp 181–94.

Collinson, D. (2012) 'Prozac Leadership and the Limits of Positive Thinking', *Leadership* 8(2): 87–107.

Collinson, D. (2014) 'Dichotomies, Dialectics and Dilemmas: New Directions for Critical Leadership Studies?', *Leadership* 10(1): 36–55.

Collinson, D., Smolović Jones, O. and Grint, K. (2018) '"No More Heroes": Critical Perspectives on Leadership Romanticism', *Organization Studies* 39(11): 1625–47.

Conger, J.A. and Pearce, C.L. (2003) 'A Landscape of Opportunities: Future Research on Shared Leadership', in C.L. Pearce and J.A. Conger (eds) *Shared Leadership: Reframing the Hows and Whys of Leadership*. California, CA: Sage, pp 285–304.

Conn, S.M. (2018) *Increasing Resilience in Police and Emergency Personnel.* New York, NY: Routledge.

Connell, R.W. (1987) *Gender and Power: Society, the Person and Sexual Politics.* Cambridge: Polity Press.

Cope, S., Leishman, F. and Starie, P. (1997) 'Globalization, New Public Management and the Enabling State: Futures of Police Management', *International Journal of Public Sector Management* 10(6): 444–60.

Cowper, T.J. (2000) 'The Myth of the "Military Model" of Leadership in Law Enforcement', *Police Quarterly* 3(3): 228–46.

Cox, C. and Kirby, S. (2018) 'Can Higher Education Reduce the Negative Consequences of Police Occupational Culture amongst New Recruits?', *Policing: An International Journal* 41(5): 550–62.

Cox, D.J. (2018) '"The Best Chief Constable in the Kingdom?": Recruitment and Retention Problems in an Early English County Constabulary', in K. Stevenson, D.J. Cox and I. Channing (eds) *Leading the Police: A History of Chief Constables 1835–2017.* London: Routledge, pp 33–52.

Craig, C., Marnoch, G. and Topping, I. (2010) 'Shared Leadership with Minority Ethnic Communities: Views from the Police and the Public in the UK', *Policing and Society* 20(3): 336–57.

Crevani, L., Lindgren, M. and Packendorff, J. (2010) 'Leadership, Not Leaders: On the Study of Leadership as Practices and Interactions', *Scandinavian Journal of Management* 26(1): 77–86.

Critchley, T.A. (1978) *A History of Police in England and Wales.* London: Constable.

Crossman, B. and Crossman, J. (2011) 'Conceptualising Followership – A Review of the Literature', *Leadership* 7(4): 481–97.

Currie, G. and Lockett, A. (2007) 'A Critique of Transformational Leadership: Moral, Professional and Contingent Dimensions of Leadership within Public Services Organizations', *Human Relations* 60(2): 341–70.

Davies, A. and Thomas, R. (2003) 'Talking Cop: Discourses of Change and Policing Identities', *Public Administration* 81(4): 681–99.

Davies, C. (1983) 'Professionals in Bureaucracies: The Conflict Thesis Revisited', in R. Dingwall and P. Lewis (eds) *The Sociology of the Professions*. London: Macmillan Press, pp 177–95.

Davis, C. (2018) 'Rank Matters: Police Leadership and the Authority of Rank', *Policing and Society* (advance access).

Davis, C. (2019) 'Police Leadership and the Authority of Rank: A Call for a Critical Perspective', in P. Ramshaw, M. Simpson and M. Silvestri (eds) *Police Leadership: Changing Landscapes*. Basingstoke: Palgrave Macmillan.

Davis, C. and Bailey, D. (2018) 'Police Leadership: The Challenges for Developing Contemporary Practice', *International Journal of Emergency Services* 7(1): 13–23.

Day, D.V., Gronn, P. and Salas, E. (2004) 'Leadership Capacity in Teams', *The Leadership Quarterly* 15(6): 857–80.

Decker, L.K. and Huckabee, R.G. (2002) 'Raising the Age and Education Requirements for Police Officers: Will Too Many Women and Minority Candidates Be Excluded?', *Policing: An International Journal of Police Strategies & Management* 25(4): 789–802.

De Maillard, J. (2015) 'International Perspectives in Policing: Challenges for 2020', in P. Wankhade and D. Weir (eds) *Police Services: Leadership and Management Perspectives*. London: Springer, pp 173–7.

Densten, I. (2003) 'Senior Police Leadership: Does Rank Matter?', *Policing: An International Journal of Police Strategies & Management* 26(3): 400–18.

DeRue, D.S., Nahrgang, J.D., Wellman, N. and Humprey, S.E. (2011) 'Trait and Behavioral Theories of Leadership: An Integration and Meta-Analytic Test of Their Relative Validity', *Personnel Psychology* 64: 7–52.

Diaz-Saenz, H.R. (2011) 'Transformational Leadership', in A. Bryman, D. Collinson, K. Grint, B. Jackson and M. Uhl-Bien (eds) *The Sage Handbook of Leadership*. London: Sage Publications, pp 299–310.

Dick, P. and Cassell, C. (2002) 'Barriers to Managing Diversity in a UK Constabulary', *Journal of Management Studies* 39(7): 953–76.

Dick, P. and Jankowicz, D. (2001) 'A Social Constructionist Account of Police Culture and Its Influence on Representation and Progression of Female Officers: A Repertory Grid Analysis in a UK Police Force', *Policing: An International Journal of Police Strategies & Management* 24(2): 181–99.

Dick, P., Silvestri, M. and Westmarland, L. (2014) 'Women Police: Potential and Possibilities for Police Reform', in J.M. Brown (ed) *The Future of Policing*. London: Routledge, pp 134–48.

Diefenbach, T. (2009) 'New Public Management in Public Sector Organizations: The Dark Sides of Managerialistic "'Enlightenment'"', *Public Administration* 87(4): 892–909.

Digman, J.M. (1990) 'Personality Structure: Emergence of the Five-Factor Model', *Annual Review of Psychology* 87: 417–40.

Dingwall, R. (1976) 'Accomplishing Profession', *The Sociological Review* 24(2): 331–50.

Dingwall, R. (1983) 'Introduction', in R. Dingwall and P. Lewis (eds) *The Sociology of the Professions*. London: Macmillan Press, pp 1–18.

Dinh, J.E., Lord, R.G., Gardner, W.L., Meuser, J.D., Liden, R.C. and Hu, J. (2014) 'Leadership Theory and Research in the New Millennium: Current Theoretical Trends and Changing Perspectives', *The Leadership Quarterly* 25(1): 36–62.

Dobbins, G.H. and Platz, S.J. (1986) 'Sex Differences in Leadership: How Real Are They?', *Academy of Management Review* 11(1): 118–27.

Dobby, J., Anscombe, J. and Tuffin, R. (2004) *Police Leadership: Expectations and Impact*, Home Office Online Report 20/04. London: Home Office.

Dobrow, M.J. Goel, V. and Upshur, R.E.G. (2004) 'Evidence-Based Health Policy: Context and Utilisation', *Social Science & Medicine* 58(1): 207–17.

Drodge, E.N. and Murphy, S.A. (2002) 'Interrogating Emotions in Police Leadership', *Human Resource Development Review* 1(4): 420–38.

Eagly, A.H. and Carli, L.L. (2003) 'The Female Leadership Advantage: An Evaluation of the Evidence', *The Leadership Quarterly* 14(6): 807–34.

Eagly, A.H. and Johnson, B.T. (1990) 'Gender and Leadership Style: A Meta-Analysis', *Psychological Bulletin* 108(2): 233–56.

Electoral Commission (2013) *Police and Crime Commissioner Elections in England and Wales: Report on the Administration of the Elections Held on 15 November 2012*. London: Electoral Commission.

Ellis, C. and Bochner, A.P. (2000) 'Autoethnography, Personal Narrative, Reflexivity: Researcher as Subject', in N.K. Denzin and Y.S. Lincoln (eds) *Handbook of Qualitative Research* (2nd edn). California, CA: Sage, pp 733–68.

Emsley, C. (1996) *The English Police: A Political and Social History*. London: Longman.

Engel, R.S. (2001) 'Supervisory Styles of Patrol Sergeants and Lieutenants', *Journal of Criminal Justice* 29(4): 341–55.

Fairhurst, G.T. (2005) 'Reframing the Art of Framing: Problems and Prospects for Leadership', *Leadership* 1(2): 165–85.

Fairhurst, G.T. and Grant, D. (2010) 'The Social Construction of Leadership: A Sailing Guide', *Management Communication Quarterly* 24(2): 171–210.

Fiedler, F.E. (1997) 'Situational Control and a Dynamic Theory of Leadership', in K. Grint (ed) *Leadership: Classical, Contemporary and Critical Approaches*. Oxford: Oxford University Press, pp 126–54.

Fielding, N. (1988) *Joining Forces: Police Training, Socialization, and Occupational Competence*. London: Routledge.

Fielding, N. (1994) 'Cop Canteen Culture', in T. Newburn and E.A. Stanko (eds) *Just Boys Doing Business? Men, Masculinities and Crime*. London: Routledge, pp 45–63.

Fielding, N., Bullock, K., Fielding, J.L. and Hieke, G. (2018) 'Patterns of Injury on Duty and Perceptions of Support Amongst Serving Police Personnel in England and Wales', *Policing and Society* 28(9): 1005–24.

Fleishman, E.A., Mumford, M.D., Zaccaro, S.J., Levin, K.Y., Korotkin, A.L. and Hein, M. (1991) 'Taxonomic Effects in the Description of Leader Behaviour: A Synthesis and Functional Interpretation', *The Leadership Quarterly* 2(4): 245–87.

Fleming, J. (2014) 'The Pursuit of Professionalism: Lessons from Australasia', in J. Brown (ed) *The Future of Policing*. London: Routledge, pp 355–68.

Fleming, J. (ed) (2015) *Police Leadership: Rising to the Top*. Oxford: Oxford University Press.

Fleming, J. and Lafferty, G. (2000) 'New Management and Techniques and Restructuring for Accountability in Australian Police Organisation', *Policing: An International Journal of Police Strategies & Management* 23(2): 154–68.

Fleming, J., Fyfe, N. and Marshall, A. (2015) 'Making Connections between Research and Practice: Tackling the Paradox of Policing Research', in J. Fleming (ed) *Police Leadership: Rising to the Top*. Oxford: Oxford University Press, pp 237–56.

Fletcher, J.K. (2004) 'The Paradox of Postheroic Leadership: An Essay on Gender, Power, and Transformational Change', *The Leadership Quarterly* 15(5): 647–61.

Fletcher, J.K. and Kaufer, K. (2003) 'Shared Leadership: Paradox and Possibility', in C.L. Pearce and J.A. Conger (eds) *Shared Leadership: Reframing the Hows and Whys of Leadership*. California, CA: Sage Publications, pp 21–47.

Flin, R. (1996) *Sitting in the Hot Seat: Leaders and Teams for Critical Incident Management*. Chichester: Wiley.

Ford, J. (2006) 'Discourses of Leadership: Gender, Identity and Contradiction in a UK Public Sector Organisation', *Leadership* 2(1): 77–99.

Ford, J. (2010) 'Studying Leadership Critically: A Psychosocial Lens on Leadership Identities', *Leadership* 6(1): 47–65.

Ford, J. and Harding, N. (2007) 'Move Over Management: We Are All Leaders Now', *Management Learning* 38(5): 475–93.

Ford, J. and Harding, N. (2011) 'The Impossibility of the "True Self" of Authentic Leadership', *Leadership* 7(4): 463–79.

Foster, J. (1989) 'Two Stations: An Ethnographic Study of Policing in the Inner City', in D. Downes (ed) *Crime and the City*. London: Palgrave Macmillan, pp 128–53.

Foster, J. (2003) 'Police Cultures', in T. Newburn (ed) *Handbook of Policing*. Devon: Willan Publishing.

Foster, J., Newburn, T. and Souhami, A. (2005) *Assessing the Impact of the Stephen Lawrence Inquiry*, Home Office Research Study 294. London: Home Office.

Friedson, E. (1983) 'The Theory of Professions: State of the Art', in R. Dingwall and P. Lewis (eds) *The Sociology of the Professions*. London: Macmillan Press, pp 19–37.

Fyfe, N.R. and Wilson, P. (2012) 'Knowledge Exchange and Police Practice: Broadening and Deepening the Debate Around Researcher–Practitioner Collaborations', *Police Practice and Research* 13(4): 306–14.

Gagnon, S. and Collinson, D. (2014) 'Rethinking Global Leadership Development Programmes: The Interrelated Significance of Power, Context and Identity', *Organization Studies* 35(5): 645–70.

Gambrill, E. (1999) 'Evidence-Based Practice: An Alternative to Authority-Based Practice', *Families in Society* 80(4): 341–50.

Gardner, J.W. (1990) *On Leadership*. New York, NY: The Free Press.

Gardner, W.L., Cogliser, C.C., Davis, K.M. and Dickens, M.P. (2011) 'Authentic Leadership: A Review of the Literature and Research Agenda', *The Leadership Quarterly* 22(6):1120–45.

Geertz, C. (1977) *The Interpretation of Cultures*. New York, NY: Basic Books.

Gemmill, G. and Oakley, J. (1997) 'Leadership: An Alienating Social Myth?', in K. Grint (ed) *Leadership: Classical, Contemporary and Critical Approaches*. Oxford: Oxford University Press, pp 272–92.

Gersons, B.P.R. (1989) 'Patterns of PTSD Among Police Officers Following Shooting Incidents: A Two-Dimensional Model and Treatment Implications', *Journal of Traumatic Stress* 2(3): 247–57.

Gibb, C.A. (1949) 'Some Tentative Comments Concerning Group Rorschach Pointers to the Personality Traits of Leaders', *The Journal of Social Psychology* 30(2): 251–63.

Goldberg, L.R. (1990) 'An Alternative "Description of Personality": The Big-Five Factor Structure', *Journal of Personality and Social Psychology* 59(6): 1216–29.

Golding, B. and Savage, S.P. (2011) 'Leadership and Performance Management', in T. Newburn (ed) *Handbook of Policing* (2nd edn). Abingdon: Taylor & Francis, pp 725–59.

Goldstein, H. (1990) *Problem-Oriented Policing*. New York, NY: McGraw-Hill.

Goleman, D. (1995) *Emotional Intelligence*. New York, NY: Bantam Books.

Gordon, R. (2002) 'Conceptualizing Leadership with Respect to its Historical–Contextual Antecedents to Power', *The Leadership Quarterly* 13(2): 151–67.

Gordon, R. (2010) 'Dispersed Leadership: Exploring the Impact of Antecedent Forms of Power Using a Communicative Framework', *Management Communication Quarterly* 24(2): 260–87.

Gordon, R. (2011) 'Leadership and Power', in A. Bryman, D. Collinson, K. Grint, B. Jackson and M. Uhl-Bien (eds) *The Sage Handbook of Leadership*. London: Sage Publications, pp 195–202.

Gottfredson, L.S. (2002) 'Where and Why g Matters: Not a Mystery', *Human Performance* 15(1/2): 25–46.

Graeff, C.L. (1997) 'Evolution of Situational Leadership Theory: A Critical Review', *The Leadership Quarterly* 8(2): 153–70.

Grant, J. (1988) 'Women as Managers: What They Can Offer Organizations', *Organizational Dynamics* 16(3): 56–63.

Greenleaf, R.K. (1970) *The Servant as Leader*. San Francisco, CA: Jossey-Bass.

Gresty, B. and McLelland, T. (1989) 'Beating the John Wayne Syndrome', *Police Review* 13 January: 72–3.

Grint, K. (2005a) 'Problems, Problems, Problems: The Social Construction of Leadership', *Human Relations* 58(11): 1457–94.

Grint, K. (2005b) *Leadership: Limits and Possibilities*. Hampshire: Palgrave Macmillan.

Grint, K. (2010a) 'The Sacred in Leadership: Separation, Sacrifice and Silence', *Organization Studies* 31(1): 89–107.

Grint, K. (2010b) 'The Cuckoo Clock Syndrome: Addicted to Command, Allergic to Leadership', *European Management Journal* 28(4): 306–13.

Grint, K. (2011) 'A History of Leadership', in A. Bryman, D. Collinson, K. Grint, B. Jackson and M. Uhl-Bien (eds) *The Sage Handbook of Leadership*. London: Sage Publications, pp 3–14.

Grint, K. and Thornton, S. (2015) 'Leadership, Management, and Command in the Police', in J. Fleming (ed) *Police Leadership: Rising to the Top*. Oxford: Oxford University Press, pp 95–109.

Gronn, P. (2002) 'Distributed Leadership as a Unit of Analysis', *The Leadership Quarterly* 13(4): 423–51.

Gronn, P. (2011) 'Hybrid Configurations of Leadership', in A. Bryman, D. Collinson, K. Grint, B. Jackson and M. Uhl-Bien (eds) *The Sage Handbook of Leadership*. London: Sage Publications, pp 437–54.

Gundhus, H.I. (2013) 'Experience or Knowledge? Perspectives on New Knowledge Regimes and Control of Police Professionalism', *Policing* 7(2): 176–92.

Haake, U. (2018) 'Conditions for Gender Equality in Police Leadership – Making Way for Senior Police Women', *Police Practice and Research* 19(3): 241–52.

Haake, U., Rantatalo, O. and Lindberg, O. (2017) 'Police Leaders Make Poor Change Agents: Leadership Practice in the Face of a Major Organisational Reform', *Policing and Society* 27(2): 764–78.

Hallenberg, K.M. and Cockcroft, T. (2017) 'From Indifference to Hostility: Police Officers, Organizational Responses and the Symbolic Value of "in-Service" Higher Education in Policing', *Policing* 11(3): 273–88.

Hanson, R. (2018) *Resilient: 12 Tools for Transforming Everyday Experiences into Lasting Happiness*. London: Ebury Publishing.

Harding, N. (2018) 'Places on Probation: An Auto-Ethnographic Account of Co-Produced Research with Women with Criminal Biographies', in A. Plows (ed) *Messy Ethnographies in Action*. Malaga: Vernon Press, pp 91–100.

Hargreaves, J., Husband, R. and Lineham, C. (2018) *Police Workforce, England and Wales: 31 March 2018*. London: Home Office.

Hawkins, J. and Dulewicz, V. (2007) 'The Relationship between Performance as a Leader and Emotional Intelligence, Intellectual and Managerial Competences', *Journal of General Management* 33(2): 57–78.

Hawkins, J. and Dulewicz, V. (2009) 'Relationships between Leadership Style, the Degree of Change Experienced, Performance and Follower Commitment in Policing', *Journal of Change Management* 9(3): 251–70.

Heidensohn, F. (1996) *Women in Control? The Role of Women in Law Enforcement*. New York, NY: Oxford University Press.

Heidensohn, F. (2003) 'Gender and Policing', in T. Newburn (ed) *Handbook of Policing*. Cullompton: Willan.

Herrington, V. and Colvin, A. (2016) 'Police Leadership for Complex Times', *Policing* 10(1): 7–16.

Hersey, P. (1997) *The Situational Leader*. California, CA: Center for Leadership Studies.

Hersey, P., Blanchard, K.H. and Johnson, D.E. (2008) *Management of Organizational Behavior* (9th edn). New Jersey, NJ: Prentice Hall.

Hesketh, I., Cooper, C.L. and Ivy, J. (2005) 'Well-Being, Austerity and Policing: Is It Worth Investing in Resilience Training?', *The Police Journal* 88(3): 220–30.

Hesketh, I., Cooper, C.L. and Ivy, J. (2019) 'Leading the Asset', *The Police Journal* 92(1): 56–71.

Heslop, R. (2011) 'Reproducing Police Culture in a British University: Findings from an Exploratory Case Study of Police Foundation Degrees', *Police Practice and Research* 12(4): 298–312.

HMIC (Her Majesty's Inspectorate of Constabulary) (2013) *Policing in Austerity: Rising to the Challenge*. London: HMIC.

HMIC (2014) *Policing in Austerity: Meeting the Challenge*. London: HMIC.

Hobbs, D. (1988) *Doing the Business: Entrepreneurship, the Working Class and Detectives in the East End of London*. Oxford: Oxford University Press.

Hoggett, J., Redford, P., Toher, D. and White, P. (2019) 'Challenges for Police Leadership: Identity, Experience, Legitimacy and Direct Entry', *Journal of Police and Criminal Psychology* 34(2): 145–55.

Holdaway, S. (1977) 'Changes in Urban Policing', *British Journal of Sociology* 28(2): 119–37.

Holdaway, S. (1983) *Inside the British Police: A Force at Work*. Oxford: Basil Blackwell.

Holdaway, S. (1988) 'Blue Jokes: Humour in Police Work', in C. Powell and G.E.C. Paton (eds) *Humour in Society: Resistance and Control*. Hampshire: Macmillan Press, pp 106–22.

Holdaway, S. (1993) *The Resignation of Black and Asian Officers from the Police Service*. London: Home Office.

Holdaway, S. (1997) 'Constructing and Sustaining "Race" within the Police Workforce', *British Journal of Sociology* 48(1): 19–34.

Holdaway, S. (2017) 'The Re-Professionalization of the Police in England and Wales', *Criminology & Criminal Justice* 17(5): 588–604.

Holdaway, S. and Parker, S.K. (1998) 'Policing Women Police: Uniform Patrol, Promotion and Representation in the CID', *British Journal of Criminology* 38(1): 40–60.

Home Affairs Select Committee (2013) *Leadership and Standards in the Police*, London: The Stationery Office.

Home Office (2013) *Consultation on the Implementation of Direct Entry in the Police*. London: Home Office.

Home Office (2018) *Crime Recording General Rules*. London: Home Office.

Hood, C. (1991) 'A Public Management for All Seasons?', *Public Administration* 69(1): 3–19.

Hosking, D.M. (1997) 'Organizing, Leadership, and Skilful Process', in K. Grint (ed) *Leadership: Classical, Contemporary and Critical Approaches*. Oxford: Oxford University Press, pp 293–318.

Hough, M. and Stanko, E.A. (2019) 'Designing Degree-Level Courses for Police Recruits in England and Wales: Some Issues and Challenges', *Policing: A Journal of Policy and Practice* (advanced access).

Hough, M., May, T., Hales, G. and Belur, J. (2018) 'Misconduct by Police Leaders in England and Wales: An Exploratory Study', *Policing and Society* 28(5): 541–52.

House, R.J. and Aditya, R.N. (1997) 'The Social Scientific Study of Leadership: Quo Vadis?', *Journal of Management* 23(3): 409–73.

Hudzik, J.K. (1978) 'College Education for Police: Problems in Measuring Component and Extraneous Variables', *Journal of Criminal Justice* 6(1): 69–81.

Huey, L., Kalyal, H., Peladeau, H. and Lindsay, F. (2018) '"If You're Gonna Make a Decision, You Should Understand the Rationale"' Are Police Leadership Programs Preparing Canadian Police Leaders for Evidence-Based Policing?', *Policing: A Journal of Policy and Practice* (advance access): 1–11.

Hunt, J.G. (2004) 'What Is Leadership?', in J. Antonakis, A.T. Cianciolo and R.J. Sternberg (eds) *The Nature of Leadership*. Thousand Oaks, CA: Sage, pp 19–47.

Independent Police Commission (2013) *Policing for a Better Britain: Report of the Independent Police Commission*. London: HMSO.

Innes, M. (2014) 'Reinventing the Office of Constable: Progressive Policing in the Age of Austerity', in J. Brown (ed) *The Future of Policing*, Abingdon, Oxon: Routledge, pp 64–78.

Ireland, R.W. (2018) '"A Nonconformist Must Be Chief Constable": The Historical Challenges of Policing in Rural Wales', in K. Stevenson, D.J. Cox and I. Channing (eds) *Leading the Police: A History of Chief Constables 1835–2017*. London: Routledge, pp 109–24.

Jackson, W. (2019) 'Researching the Policed: Critical Ethnography and the Study of Protest Policing', *Policing and Society* (advance access): 1–17.

Jenkins, W.O. (1947) 'A Review of Leadership Studies with Particular Reference to Military Problems', *Psychological Bulletin* 44(1): 54–79.

Johnson, R.R. (2012) 'Police Officer Job Satisfaction: A Multidimensional Analysis', *Police Quarterly* 15(2): 157–76.

Jones, M. (2014) 'A Diversity Stone Left Unturned? Exploring the Occupational Complexities Surrounding Lesbian, Gay and Bisexual Police Officers', in J.M. Brown (ed) *The Future of Policing*. London: Routledge, pp 149–70.

Jones, M. and Williams, M.L. (2013) 'Twenty Years on: Lesbian, Gay and Bisexual Police Officers' Experiences of Workplace Discrimination in England and Wales', *Policing and Society* 25(2): 188–211.

Jones, T., Newburn, T. and Smith, D.J. (2012) 'Democracy and Police and Crime Commissioners', in T. Newburn and J. Peay (eds) *Policing: Politics, Culture and Control*. Oxford: Hart Publishing Ltd, pp 219–44.

Judge, T.A., Bono, J.E., Ilies, R. and Gerhardt, M.W. (2002) 'Personality and Leadership: A Qualitative and Quantitative Review', *Journal of Applied Psychology* 87(4): 765–80.

Kalyal, H. (2019) 'One Person's Evidence Is Another Person's Nonsense: Why Police Organizations Resist Evidence-Based Practices', *Policing* (advance access): 1–15.

Kanter, R.M. (1977) *Men and Women of the Corporation*. New York, NY: Basic Books.

Kellerman, B. (2008) *Followership*. Boston, MA: Harvard Business Press.

Kelley, R.E. (1988) 'In Praise of Followers', *Harvard Business Review* 66(6): 142–8.

Kelley, R.E. (1992) *The Power of Followership*, New York: Doubleday.

Kelley, R.E. (2008) 'Rethinking Followership', in R.E. Riggio, I. Chaleff and J. Lipman-Blumen (eds) *The Art of Followership: How Great Followers Create Great Leaders and Organizations*. New Jersey, NJ: John Wiley & Sons, pp 5–16.

Kenny, D.A. and Zaccaro, S.J. (1983) 'An Estimate of Variance Due to Traits in Leadership', *Journal of Applied Psychology* 68(4): 678–85.

Kent, T.W. (2005) 'Leading and Managing: It Takes Two to Tango', *Management Decision* 43(7/8): 1010–17.

Kernaghan, P. (2013) 'Police Direct Entry and the Search for Talent – A Historical Perspective', *The Police Journal* 86(1): 7–14.

Kilgallon, M., Wright, M. and Lee, A. (2015) 'Contested Knowledge: Learning to Lead in a Policing Context', in J. Fleming (ed) *Police Leadership: Rising to the Top*. Oxford: Oxford University Press, pp 211–36.

Kingshott, B.F. (2006) 'The Role of Management and Leadership within the Context of Police Service Delivery', *Criminal Justice Studies* 19(2): 121–37.

Kingshott, B.F. (2009) 'Women in Policing: Changing the Organizational Culture by Adopting a Feminist Perspective on Leadership', *Criminal Justice Studies* 22(1): 49–72.

Klein, J. (2012) 'Quiet and Determined Servants and Guardians: Creating Ideal English Police Officers, 1900–1945', in D.G. Barrie and S. Broomhill (eds) *A History of Police and Masculinities: 1700–2010*. London: Routledge, pp 201–34.

Kort, E.D. (2008) 'What, after all, is Leadership? "Leadership" and Plural Action', *The Leadership Quarterly* 19(4): 409–25.

Kuykendall, J. (1985) 'Police Managerial Styles: A Grid Analysis', *American Journal of Police* 4(2): 38–70.

Kuykendall, J. and Roberg, R. (1988) 'Police Managers' Perceptions of Employee Types: A Conceptual Model', *Journal of Criminal Justice* 16(2): 131–7.

Kuykendall, J. and Unsinger, P.C. (1982) 'The Leadership Styles of Police Managers', *Journal of Criminal Justice* 10(4): 311–21.

Larson, M.S. (1977) *The Rise of Professionalism: A Sociological Analysis*. Berkeley, CA: University of California Press.

Lee, M. and Punch, M. (2004) 'Policing by Degrees: Police Officers' Experience of University Education', *Policing and Society* 14(3): 233–49.

Leishman, F. and Savage, S.P. (1993) 'Officers or Managers? Direct Entry into British Police Management', *International Journal of Public Sector Management* 6(5): 4–11.

Leishman, F., Cope, S. and Starie, P. (1995) 'Reforming the Police in Britain: New Public Management, Policy Networks and a Tough "Old Bill"', *International Journal of Public Sector Management* 8(4): 26–37.

Lennon, G. and Murray, K. (2018) 'Under-Regulated and Unaccountable? Explaining Variation in Stop and Search Rates in Scotland, England and Wales', *Policing and Society* 28(2): 157–74.

Letherby, G. (2002) 'Claims and Disclaimers: Knowledge, Reflexivity and Representation in Feminist Research', *Sociological Research Online* 6(4): 81–93.

Lewin, K., Lippitt, R. and White, R.K. (1939) 'Patterns of Aggressive Behavior in Experimentally Created "Social Climates"', *Journal of Social Psychology* 10(2): 271–99.

Liberman, A.M., Best, S.R., Metzler, T.J., Fagan, J.A., Weiss, D.S. and Marmar, C.R. (2002) 'Routine Occupational Stress as and Psychological Distress in Police', *Policing: An International Journal of Police Strategies & Management* 25(2): 421–39.

Lieberson, S. and O'Connor, J.F. (1972) 'Leadership and Organizational Performance: A Study of Large Corporations', *American Sociological Review* 37(2): 117–30.

Likert, R. (1961) *New Patterns of Management.* New York, NY: McGraw-Hill.

Lim, H. and Lee, H. (2015) 'The Effects of Supervisor Education and Training on Police Use of Force', *Criminal Justice Studies* 28(4): 444–63.

Lindebaum, D. (2012) 'Pathologizing the Healthy but Ineffective', *Journal of Management Inquiry* 22(3): 295–305.

Lindsay, D.R., Day, D.V. and Halpin, S.M. (2011) 'Shared Leadership in the Military: Reality, Possibility, or Pipedream?', *Military Psychology* 23(5): 528–49.

Linley, P.A. and Joseph, S. (2004) 'Positive Change Following Trauma and Adversity: A Review', *Journal of Traumatic Stress* 17: 11–21.

Lister, S. (2013) 'The New Politics of the Police: Police and Crime Commissioners and the "Operational Independence" of the Police', *Policing* 7(3): 239–47.

Lister, S. and Rowe, M. (2015) 'Electing Police and Crime Commissioners in England and Wales: Prospecting for the Democratisation of Policing', *Policing and Society* 25(4): 358–77.

Loader, I. (2000) 'Plural Policing and Democratic Governance', *Social & Legal Studies* 9(3): 323–45.

Loader, I. (2014) 'Why Do the Police Matter? Beyond the Myth of Crime-Fighting', in J.M. Brown (ed) *The Future of Policing.* London: Routledge, pp 40–51.

Locke, E.A. (2003) 'Leadership: Starting at the Top', in C.L. Pearce and J.A. Conger (eds) *Shared Leadership: Reframing the Hows and Whys of Leadership.* California, CA: Sage.

Loftus, B. (2009) *Police Culture in a Changing World.* Oxford: Oxford University Press.

Loftus, B. (2010) 'Police Occupational Culture: Classic Themes, Altered Times', *Policing and Society* 20(1): 1–20.

Loftus, B., Goold, B. and Mac Giollabhui, S. (2016) 'From a Visible Spectacle to an Invisible Presence: The Working Culture of Covert Policing', *The British Journal of Criminology* 56(4): 629–45.

Long, M. (2003) 'Leadership and Performance Management', in T. Newburn (ed) *Handbook of Policing.* Devon: Willan Publishing.

Lord, R.G., Foti, R.J. and De Vader, C.L. (1984) 'A Test of Leadership Categorization Theory: Internal Structure, Information Processing and Leadership Perceptions', *Organizational Behavior and Human Performance* 34(3): 343–78.

Lord, R.G., Foti, R.J. and De Vader, C.L. (1986) 'A Meta-Analysis of the Relation between Personality Traits and Leadership Perceptions: An Application of Validity Generalization Procedures', *Journal of Applied Psychology* 73(3): 402–10.

Lotz, R. and Regoli, L.M. (1977) 'Police Cynicism and Professionalism', *Human Relations* 30(2): 175–86.

Loveday, B. (2008) 'Performance Management and the Decline of Leadership within Public Services in the United Kingdom', *Policing* 2(1): 120–30.

Loveday, B. (2013) 'Police and Crime Commissioners: The Changing Landscape of Police Governance in England and Wales: Their Potential Impact on Local Accountability, Police Service Delivery and Community Safety', *International Journal of Police Science & Management* 15(1): 22–9.

Loveday, B. (2017) 'Still Plodding Along? The Police Response to the Changing Profile of Crime in England and Wales', *International Journal of Police Science & Management* 19(2): 101–9.

Lowe, K.B. and Gardner, W.L. (2001) 'Ten Years of *The Leadership Quarterly*: Contributions and Challenges for the Future', *The Leadership Quarterly* 11(4): 459–514.

Lum, C. (2009) *'Translating Police Research into Practice'. Ideas in American Policing*. Washington, DC: The Police Foundation.

Lum, C., Koper, C.S. and Telep, C.W. (2010) 'The Evidence-Based Policing Matrix', *Journal of Experimental Criminology* 7(1): 3–26.

Luthans, F. (2002) 'The Need for and Meaning of Positive Organizational Behavior', *Journal of Organizational Behavior* 23(6): 695–706.

MacVean, A. and Spindler, P. (2015) 'Principled and Ethical Policing: Some Considerations for Police Leaders', in J. Fleming (ed) *Police Leadership: Rising to the Top*. Oxford: Oxford University Press, pp 110–28.

Manis, J., Archbold, C.A. and Hassell, K.D. (2008) 'Exploring the Impact of Police Officer Education Level on Allegations of Police Misconduct', *International Journal of Police Science & Management* 10(4): 509–23.

Mann, R.D. (1959) 'A Review of the Relationship between Personality and Performance in Small Groups', *Psychological Bulletin* 56(4): 241–70.

Manning, P.K. (1977) *Police Work: The Social Organization of Policing*. Massachusetts, MA: The MIT Press.

Manning, P.K. (2002) 'Authority, Loyalty, and Community Policing', in E. Waring and D. Weisburd (eds) *Advances in Criminological Theory Volume 10: Crime and Social Organization*. New Brunswick, NJ: Transaction Publishers.

Manning, P.K. (2005) 'The Study of Policing', *Police Quarterly* 8(1): 23–43.

Manning, P.K. (2007) 'A Dialectic of Organisational and Occupational Culture', in M. O'Neill, M. Marks and A.M. Singh (eds) *Police Occupational Culture: New Debates and Directions*. Oxford: Elsevier JAI, pp 47–84.

Manning, P.K. (2012) 'Drama, the Police and the Sacred', in T. Newburn and J. Peay (eds) *Policing: Politics, Culture and Control*. Oxford: Hart Publishing, pp 173–94.

Manning, P.K. (2014) 'Policing: Privatising and Changes in the Policing Web', in J. Brown (ed) *The Future of Policing*. Abingdon, Oxon: Routledge, pp 23–39.

Manz, C.C. and Sims, H.P. (1989) *Superleadership: Leading Others to Lead Themselves*. San Francisco, CA: Berrett-Koehler.

Manz, C.C., Shipper, F. and Stewart, G.L. (2009) 'Everyone a Team Leader', *Organizational Dynamics* 38(3): 239–44.

Marion, R. and Uhl-Bien, M. (2001) 'Leadership in Complex Organisations', *The Leadership Quarterly* 12(4): 389–418.

Marshall, A. (2016) 'College of Policing', Police Federation Conference 'Believe in Blue', 17–19 May, Bournemouth: Bournemouth International Centre.

Martin, H.C., Rogers, C., Samuel, A.J. and Rowling, M. (2017) 'Serving from the Top: Police Leadership for the Twenty-First Century', *International Journal of Emergency Services* 6(3): 209–19.

Martin, S.E. (1979) 'POLICEwomen and PoliceWOMEN: Occupational Role Dilemmas and Choices of Female Officers', *Journal of Police Science and Administration* 7(3): 314–23.

Martin, S.E. (1980) *Breaking and Entering: Policewomen on Patrol*. Berkley, CA: University of California Press.

Masal, D. (2015) 'Shared and Transformational Leadership in the Police', *Policing: An International Journal of Police Strategies & Management* 38(1): 40–55.

Mastrofski, S.D. (2002) 'The Romance of Police Leadership', in E. Waring and D. Weisburd (eds) *Advances in Criminological Theory Volume 10: Crime and Social Organization*. New Brunswick, NJ: Transaction Publishers, pp 153–96.

Mawby, R.C. (2002) *Policing Images: Policing, Communication and Legitimacy*. Devon: Willan Publishing.

Mawby, R.I. and Smith, K. (2017) 'Civilian Oversight of the Police in England and Wales', *International Journal of Police Science & Management* 19(1): 23–30.

McCauley, M.H. (1990) 'The Myers-Briggs Type Indicator and Leadership', in K.E. Clark and M.B. Clark (eds) *Measures of Leadership*. West Orange, NJ: Leadership Library of America, pp 381–418.

McGregor, D.M. (1989) 'The Human Side of Enterprise', in H.J. Leavitt, L.R. Pondy and D.M. Boje (eds) *Readings in Managerial Psychology*. Chicago, IL: University of Chicago Press.

McLaughlin, E. and Murji, K. (1995) 'The End of Public Policing? Police Reform and "the New Managerialism"', in L. Noaks, M. Levi and M. Maguire (eds) *Contemporary Issues in Criminology*. Cardiff: University of Wales Press.

Mead, G.H. (1934) *Mind, Self and Society*. Chicago, IL: University of Chicago Press.

Meindl, J.R. (1995) 'The Romance of Leadership as a Follower-Centric Theory: A Social Constructionist Approach', *Leadership Quarterly* 6(3): 329–41.

Meindl, J.R. and Ehrlich, S.B. (1987) 'The Romance of Leadership and the Evaluation of Organizational Performance', *Academy of Management Journal* 30(1): 91–109.

Meindl, J.R., Ehrlich, S.B. and Dukerich, J.M. (1985) 'The Romance of Leadership', *Administrative Science Quarterly* 30(1): 78–102.

Miller, S.L., Forest, K.B. and Jurik, N.C. (2003) 'Diversity in Blue: Lesbian and Gay Police Officers in a Masculine Occupation', *Men and Masculinities* 5(4): 355–85.

Millie, A. (2013) 'The policing task and the expansion (and contraction) of British policing', *Criminology and Criminal Justice* 13(2): 143–60.

Ministry of Justice (2015) *Criminal Justice Statistics Quarterly Update to June 2015: England and Wales*. London: Ministry of Justice.

Mintzberg, H. (1998) 'Covert Leadership: Notes on Managing Professionals', *Harvard Business Review* 76(6): 140–7.

Morash, M. and Haarr, R.N. (2012) 'Doing, Redoing, and Undoing Gender: Variation in Gender Identities of Women Working as Police Officers', *Feminist Criminology* 7(1): 3–23.

Muir, W.K. (1979) *Police: Streetcorner Politicians*. Chicago, IL: University of Chicago Press.

Murphy, S.A. (2008) 'The Role of Emotions and Transformational Leadership on Police Culture: An Autoethnographic Account', *International Journal of Police Science & Management* 10(2): 165–78.

Murphy, S.A. and Drodge, E.N. (2004) 'The Four I's of Police Leadership: A Case Study Heuristic', *International Journal of Police Science & Management* 6(1): 1–15.

Myhill, A., Yarrow, S., Dalgleish, D. and Docking, M. (2003) *The Role of Police Authorities in Public Engagement*, Home Office Online Report 37/03. London: Home Office.

Neenan, M. (2017) *Developing Resilience: A Cognitive-Behavioural Approach*. London: Taylor & Francis.

Newburn, T. (2012) 'Police and Crime Commissioners: The Americanization of Policing or a Very British Reform?', *International Journal of Law, Crime and Justice* 40(1): 31–46.

Neyroud, P. (2011a) 'Leading Policing in the 21st Century: Leadership, Democracy, Deficits and the New Professionalism', *Public Money & Management* 31(5): 347–54.

Neyroud, P. (2011b) *Review of Police Leadership and Training*. London: Home Office.

Neyroud, P. (2015) 'Future Perspectives in Policing: A Crisis or a Perfect Storm: The Trouble with Public Policing?' in P. Wankhade and D. Weir (eds) *Police Services: Leadership and Management Perspectives*. London, Springer, pp 161–6.

Neyroud, P. and Beckley, A. (2001) *Policing, Ethics and Human Rights*. Collumpton: Willan.

Office for National Statistics (2015) *Statistical Bulletin: Crime in England and Wales, Year Ending March 2015*. London: Office for National Statistics.

Office for National Statistics (2018) *User Guide to Crime Statistics for England and Wales*. London: Office for National Statistics.

Office for National Statistics (2019) *Crime in England and Wales: Year Ending September 2018*. London: Office for National Statistics.

O'Malley, P. and Hutchinson, S. (2007) 'Converging Corporatization? Police Management, Police Unionism, and the Transfer of Business Principles', *Police Practice and Research* 8(2): 159–74.

O'Neill, M. (2014) 'Playing Nicely with Others: Lessons from Successes in Partnership Working', in J. Brown (ed) *The Future of Policing*. Abingdon, Oxon: Routledge, pp 203–16.

O'Neill, M. and Holdaway, S. (2007) 'Black Police Associations and the Police Occupational Culture', in M. O'Neill, M. Marks and A.M. Singh (eds) *Police Occupational Culture: New Debates and Directions*. Oxford: Elsevier JAI, pp 253–74.

O'Neill, M. and Singh, A.M. (2007) 'Conclusion: Taking Stock and Looking Ahead in Police Culture Studies', in M. O'Neill, M. Marks and A.M. Singh (eds) *Police Occupational Culture: New Debates and Directions*. Oxford: Elsevier JAI, pp 349–68.

Osterlind, M. and Haake, U. (2010) 'The Leadership Discourse amongst Female Police Leaders in Sweden', *Advancing Women in Leadership Journal* 30(16): 1–24.

O'Toole, J., Galbraith, J. and Lawler, E.E. (2003) 'The Promise and Pitfalls of Shared Leadership: When Two (or More) Heads are Better than One', in C.L. Pearce and J.A. Conger (eds) *Shared Leadership: Reframing the Hows and Whys of Leadership*. California, CA: Sage, pp 250–68.

Panzarella, R. (2003) 'Leadership Myths and Realities', in R. Adlam and P. Villiers (eds) *Police Leadership in the Twenty-First Century: Philosophy, Doctrine and Developments*. Hampshire: Waterside Press, pp 119–33.

Paoline, E.A. (2003) 'Taking Stock: Toward a Richer Understanding of Police Culture', *Journal of Criminal Justice* 31(3): 199–214.

Paoline, E.A. and Terrill, W. (2007) 'Police Education, Experience and the Use of Force', *Criminal Justice and Behavior* 34: 179–96.

Paoline, E.A., Myers, S.M. and Worden, R.E. (2006) 'Police Culture, Individualism, and Community Policing: Evidence from Two Police Departments', *Justice Quarterly* 17(3): 575–605.

Paoline, E.A., Terrill, W. and Rossler, M.T. (2015) 'Higher Education, College Degree Major, and Police Occupational Attitudes', *Journal of Criminal Justice Education* 26(1): 49–73.

Paterson, C. (2011) 'Adding Value? A Review of the International Literature on the Role of Higher Education in Police Training and Education', *Police Practice and Research* 12(4): 286–97.

Paton, D. (2006) 'Critical Incident Stress Risk in Police Officers: Managing Resilience and Vulnerability', *Traumatology* 12(3): 198–206.

Pearce, C.L. and Conger, J.A. (2003) 'All Those Years Ago: The Historical Underpinnings of Shared Leadership', in C.L. Pearce and J.A. Conger (eds) *Shared Leadership: Reframing the Hows and Whys of Leadership*. California, CA: Sage Publications, pp 1–18.

Pearce, C.L. and Ensley, M.D. (2004) 'A Reciprocal and Longitudinal Investigation of the Innovation Process: The Central Role of Shared Vision in Product and Process Innovation Teams (PPITs)', *Journal of Organizational Behavior* 25(2): 259–78.

Pearce, C.L. and Manz, C.C. (2005) 'The New Silver Bullets of Leadership: The Importance of Self and Shared Leadership in Knowledge Work', *Organizational Dynamics* 34(2): 130–40.

Pearce, C.L., Manz, C.C. and Sims, H.P. (2009) 'Where Do We Go From Here? Is Shared Leadership the Key to Team Success?', *Organizational Dynamics* 38(3): 234–8.

Petty, M.M. and Lee, G.K. (1975) 'Moderating Effects of Sex of Supervisor and Subordinate on Relationships between Supervisory Behaviour and Subordinate Satisfaction', *Journal of Applied Psychology* 60(5): 624–8.

Pfeffer, J. (1977) 'The Ambiguity of Leadership', *Academy of Management Review* 2(1): 104–12.

Podsakoff, P.M., MacKenzie, S.B., Lee, J.Y. and Podsakoff, N.P. (2003) 'Common Method Biases in Behavioral Research: A Critical Review of the Literature and Recommended Remedies', *Journal of Applied Psychology* 88(5): 879–903.

Podsakoff, P.M., Mackenzie, S.B., Moorman, R.H. and Fetter, R. (1990) 'Transformational Leader Behaviours and Their Effects on Followers' Trust in Leader, Satisfaction, and Organisational Citizenship Behaviours', *The Leadership Quarterly* 1(2): 107–42.

Powell, G.N., Butterfield, D.A. and Parent, J.D. (2002) 'Gender and Managerial Stereotypes: Have the Times Changed?', *Journal of Management* 28(2): 177–93.

Punch, M. (1979) *Policing the Inner City: A Study of Amsterdam's Warmoesstraat*. London: Macmillan Press Ltd.

Punch, M. (1983) 'Officers and Men: Occupational Culture, Inter-Rank Antagonism and the Investigation of Corruption', M. Punch (ed) *Control in the Police Organization*. Cambridge, MA: MIT Press, pp 227–50.

Punch, M. (1985) *Conduct Unbecoming: The Social Construction of Police Deviance and Control*. London: Tavistock Publications.

Punch, M. (2007) 'Cops with Honours: University Education and Police Culture', in M. O'Neill, M. Marks and A.M. Singh (eds) *Police Occupational Culture: New Debates and Directions*. Oxford: Elsevier JAI, pp 105–28.

Punch, M. (2010) 'Policing and Police Research in the Age of the Smart Cop', *Police Practice and Research* 11(2): 155–9.

Pye, A. (2005) 'Leadership and Organizing: Sensemaking in Action', *Leadership* 1(1): 31–49.

Rabe-Hemp, C.E. (2008) 'Survival in an "All Boys Club": Policewomen and their Fight for Acceptance', *Policing: An International Journal of Police Strategies & Management* 31(2): 251–70.

Rabe-Hemp, C.E. (2009) 'POLICEwomen or PoliceWOMEN? Doing Gender and Police Work', *Feminist Criminology* 4(2): 114–29.

Raelin, J. (2011) 'From Leadership-As-Practice to Leaderful Practice', *Leadership* 7(2): 195–211.

Ramshaw, P., Silvestri, M. and Simpson, M. (2019) *Police Leadership: Changing Landscapes*. Basingstoke: Palgrave Macmillan.

Ratcliffe, J.H. (2016) *Intelligence-Led Policing*. London: Routledge.

Rawlings, P. (2002) *Policing: A Short History*. Devon: Willan.

Reiner, R. (1978) *The Blue Coated Worker*. Cambridge: Cambridge University Press.

Reiner, R. (1991) *Chief Constables: Bobbies, Bosses, or Bureaucrats?* Oxford: Oxford University Press.

Reiner, R. (1998) 'Process or Product? Problems of Assessing Individual Police Performance', in J.P. Brodeur (ed) *How to Recognise Good Policing: Problems and Issues*. California, CA: Sage Publications, pp 55–72.

Reiner, R. (2000) 'Police Research', in R.D. King and E. Wincup (eds) *Doing Research on Crime and Justice*. Oxford: Oxford University Press.

Reiner, R. (2010) *The Politics of the Police* (4th edn). Oxford: Oxford University Press.

Reiner, R. (2016) 'Is Police Culture Cultural?', *Policing* 11(3): 236–41.

Reiner, R. and O'Connor, D. (2015) 'Politics and Policing: The Terrible Twins', in J. Fleming (ed) *Police Leadership: Rising to the Top*. Oxford: Oxford University Press, pp 42–70.

Reuss-Ianni, E. (1983) *Two Cultures of Policing: Street Cops and Management Cops*. New Jersey, NJ: Transaction Publishers.

Roberts, K., Herrington, V., Jones, W., White, J. and Day, D. (2016) 'Police Leadership in 2045: The Value of Education in Developing Leadership', *Policing* 10(1): 26–33.

Robertson, D. (2012) *Build Your Resilience*. London: Hodder & Stoughton.

Robertson, I., Cooper, C., Sarkar, M. and Curran, T. (2015) 'Resilience Training in the Workplace from 2003 to 2014: A Systematic Review' *Journal of Occupational Psychology* 88(3): 533–62.

Rojek, J., Alpert, G. and Smith, H. (2012) 'The Utilization of Research by the Police', *Police Practice and Research* 34(4): 328–41.

Rosener, J.B. (1991) *Workforce America: Managing Employee Diversity as Vital Resource*, London: McGraw-Hill.

Rost, J.C. (1993) 'Leadership Development in the New Millennium', *Journal of Leadership & Organizational Studies* 1(1): 91–110.

Rost, J.C. (2008) 'Followership: An Outmoded Concept', in R.E. Riggio, I. Chaleff and J. Lipman-Blumen (eds) *The Art of Followership*. San Francisco, CA: Jossey-Bass, pp 53–66.

Rowe, M. (2002) 'Policing Diversity: Themes and Concerns from the Recent British Experience', *Police Quarterly* 5(4): 424–46.

Rowe, M. (2006) 'Following the Leader: Front-Line Narratives on Police Leadership', *Policing: An International Journal of Police Strategies & Management* 29(4): 757–67.

Salovaara, P. and Bathurst, R. (2018) 'Power-with Leadership Practices: An Unfinished Business', *Leadership* 14(2): 179–202.

Sampson, F. (2012) 'Hail to the Chief? How Far Does the Introduction of Elected Police Commissioners Herald a US-Style Politicization of Policing for the UK?', *Policing: A Journal of Policy and Practice* 6(1): 4–15.

Sarver, M.B. and Miller, H. (2014) 'Police chief leadership: styles and effectiveness', *Policing: An International Journal of Police Strategies & Management* 37(1): 126–43.

Sashkin, M. (2004) 'Transformational Leadership Approaches: A Review and Synthesis', in J. Antonakis, A.T. Cianciolo and R.J. Sternberg (eds) *The Nature of Leadership*. Thousand Oaks, CA: Sage, pp 171–96.

Savage, S.P. (2003) 'Tackling Tradition: Reform and Modernization of the British Police', *Contemporary Politics* 9(2): 171–84.

Savage, S.P. and Charman, S. (1996) 'Managing Change', in F. Leishman, B. Loveday and S.P. Savage (eds) *Core Issues in Policing*. London: Longman, pp 39–53.

Savage, S.P., Charman, S. and Cope, S. (2000) *Policing and the Power of Persuasion: The Changing Role of the Association of Chief Police Officers*. London: Blackstone.

Schafer, J.A. (2010) 'Effective Leaders and Leadership in Policing: Traits, Assessment, Development and Expansion', *Policing: An International Journal of Police Strategies & Management* 33(4): 644–63.

Schein, E.H. (2010) *Organizational Culture and Leadership* (4th edn). San Francisco, CA: Jossey-Bass.

Schein, V.E. (2001) 'A Global Look at Psychological Barriers to Women's Progress in Management', *Journal of Social Issues* 57(4): 675–88.

Schmidt, F.L. and Hunter, J. (2004) 'General Mental Ability in the World of Work: Occupational Attainment and Job Performance', *Journal of Personality and Social Psychology* 86(1): 162–73.

Schon, D.A. (1983) *The Reflective Practitioner: How Professionals Think in Action*. New York: Basic Books.

Schriesheim, C.A. and Bird, B.J. (1979) 'Contributions of the Ohio State Studies to the Field of Leadership', *Journal of Management* 5(2): 135–45.

Scott, J., Evans, D. and Verma, A. (2009) 'Does Higher Education Affect Perceptions Among Police Personnel? A Response from India', *Journal of Contemporary Criminal Justice* 25(2): 214–36.

Scott, K.A. and Brown, D.J. (2006) 'Female First, Leader Second? Gender Bias in the Encoding of Leadership Behavior', *Organizational Behavior and Human Decision Processes* 101(2): 230–42.

Senge, P.M. (1999) *The Fifth Discipline*. New Mexico: Doubleday.

Shamir, B. (1995) 'Social Distance and Charisma: Theoretical Notes and an Exploratory Study', *Leadership Quarterly* 6(1): 19–47.

Shamir, B. (2007) 'From Passive Recipients to Active Co-producers: Followers' Roles in the Leadership Process', in B. Shamir, R. Pillai, M.C. Bligh and M. Uhl-Bien (eds) *Follower-Centered Perspectives on Leadership: A Tribute to the Memory of James R. Meindl*. Connecticut, CT: Information Age Publishing, pp xi–xxxix.

Shamir, B., Dayan-Horesh, H. and Adler, D. (2016) 'Leading by Biography: Towards a Life-Story Approach to the Study of Leadership', *Leadership* 1(1): 13–29.

Shartle, C.L. (1979) 'Early Years of the Ohio State University Leadership Studies', *Journal of Management* 5(2): 127–34.

Sherman, L.W. (1998) *'Evidence-Based Policing': Ideas in American Policing*. Washington, DC: The Police Foundation.

Sherman, L.W. (2013) 'The Rise of Evidence-Based Policing: Targeting, Testing, and Tracking', *Crime and Justice* 42(1): 377–451.

Silvestri, M. (2003) *Women in Charge: Policing, Gender and Leadership*. London: Routledge.

Silvestri, M. (2006) 'Doing Time: Becoming a Police Leader', *International Journal of Police Science & Management* 8(4): 266–81.

Silvestri, M. (2007) '"Doing" Police Leadership: Enter the "New Smart Macho"', *Policing and Society* 17(1): 38–58.

Silvestri, M. (2017) 'Police Culture and Gender: Revisiting the "Cult of Masculinity"', *Policing: A Journal of Policy and Practice* 11(3): 289–300.

Silvestri, M. (2018a) 'Pioneering Women Police Chiefs: A Tale of Conflict and Cooperation', in K. Stevenson, D.J. Cox and I. Channing (eds) *Leading the Police: A History of Chief Constables 1835–2017*. London: Routledge, pp 193–210.

Silvestri, M. (2018b) 'Disrupting the "Heroic" Male within Policing: A Case of Direct Entry', *Feminist Criminology* 13(3): 309–28.

Silvestri, M., Tong, S. and Brown, J. (2013) 'Gender and Police Leadership: Time for a Paradigm Shift?', *International Journal of Police Science & Management* 15(1): 61–73.

Sinclair, A. (2005) *Doing Leadership Differently: Gender, Power and Sexuality in a Changing Business Culture*. Melbourne: Melbourne University Publishing.

Sinclair, A. (2015) 'Possibilities, Purpose and Pitfalls: Insights from Introducing Mindfulness to Leaders', *Journal of Spirituality, Leadership and Management* 8(1): 3–11.

Singer, M.S. and Jonas, A. (1987) 'Perceived Leadership Style in the New Zealand Police', *Police Studies: The International Review of Police Development* 10(3): 118–21.

Sklansky, D.A. (2007) 'Seeing Blue: Police Reform, Occupational Culture and Cognitive Burn-In', in M. O'Neil, M. Marks and A.M. Singh (eds) *Police Occupational Culture: New Debates and Directions*. Oxford: JAI Press, pp 19–46.

Sklansky, D.A. (2014) 'The Promise and the Perils of Police Professionalism', in J.M. Brown (ed) *The Future of Policing*. London: Routledge, pp 343–55.

Sklansky, D.A. and Marks, M. (2008) 'The Role of the Rank and File in Police Reform', *Policing and Society* 18(1): 1–6.

Skogan, W.G. (2008) 'Why Reforms Fail', *Policing and Society* 18(1): 23–34.

Skolnick, J.H. (1975) *Justice without Trial: Law Enforcement in Democratic Society*. New York, NY: John Wiley & Sons Inc.

Skolnick, J.H. (2008) 'Enduring Issues of Police Culture and Demographics', *Policing and Society* 18(1): 35–45.

Smircich, L. and Morgan, G. (1982) 'Leadership: The Management of Meaning', *The Journal of Applied Behavioral Science* 18(3): 257–73.

Smith, J. and Charles, G. (2015) 'Personal Resilience and Policing', in P. Wankhade and D. Weir (eds) *Police Services: Leadership and Management Perspectives*. London: Springer, pp 129–44.

Smith, R. (2008) 'Entrepreneurship, Police Leadership, and the Investigation of Crime in Changing Times', *Journal of Investigative Psychology and Offender Profiling* 5(3): 209–25.

Smith, R. (2015) 'Talent Management: Building the Case for Direct Entry into Leadership Roles in British Policing', *Police Journal* 88(2): 160–73.

Smith, R. (2016) 'Don't Call Me Ma'am: Direct Entry into Leadership Roles in British Policing', *The Police Journal* 89(4): 311–26.

Souhami, A. (2019) 'Constructing Tales of the Field: Uncovering the Culture of Fieldwork in Police Ethnography', *Policing and Society* (advance access): 1–18.

Southwick, S.M. and Charney, D.S. (2012) *Resilience: The Science of Mastering Life's Greatest Challenges*. Cambridge: Cambridge University Press.

Steedman, C. (1984) *Policing the Victorian Community*. London: Routledge & Kegan Paul.

Steinheider, B. and Wuestewald, T. (2008) 'From the Bottom-Up: Sharing Leadership in a Police Agency', *Police Practice and Research* 9(2): 145–63.

Stevenson, K. (2018) 'Chief Constables as "Moral Heroes" and Guardians of Public Morality', in K. Stevenson, D.J. Cox and I. Channing (eds) *Leading the Police: A History of Chief Constables 1835–2017*. London: Routledge, pp 91–108.

Stinchcomb, J.B. (2004) 'Searching for Stress in All the Wrong Places: Combating Chronic Organizational Stressors in Policing', *Police Practice and Research* 5(3): 259–77.

Stogdill, R.M. (1948) 'Personal Factors Associated with Leadership: A Survey of the Literature', *Journal of Psychology* 26: 35–71.

Stogdill, R.M. (1997) 'Leadership, Membership, Organization', in K. Grint (ed) *Leadership: Classical, Contemporary, and Critical Approaches*. Oxford: Oxford University Press, pp 112–25.

Strahler, J. and Ziegert, T. (2015) 'Psychobiological Stress Response to a Simulated School Shooting in Police Officers', *Psychoneuroendocrinology* 51: 80–91.

Swid, A. (2014) 'Police Members' Perception of their Leaders' Leadership Style and its Implications', *Policing: An International Journal of Police Strategies & Management* 37(3): 579–95.

Syed, M. (2015) *Black Box Thinking*. New York, NY: Penguin Random House.

Tannenbaum, R. and Schmidt, W.H. (1958) 'How to Choose a Leadership Pattern', *Harvard Business Review* 36(2): 95–101.

Telep, C.W. (2011) 'The Impact of Higher Education on Police Officer Attitudes toward Abuse of Authority', *Journal of Criminal Justice Education* 22(3): 392–419.

Telep, C.W. (2017) 'Police Officer Receptivity to Research and Evidence-Based Policing: Examining Variability within and across Agencies', *Crime & Delinquency* 63(8): 976–99.

Telep, C.W. and Winegar, S. (2016) 'Police Executive Receptivity to Research: A Survey of Chiefs and Sheriffs in Oregan', *Policing* 10(3): 241–9.

Terry, W.C. (1981) 'Police Stress: The Empirical Evidence', *Journal of Police Science and Administration* 9(1): 61–5.

Tilley, N. (2008) 'Modern Approaches to Policing: Community, Problem-Oriented and Intelligence-Led', in T. Newburn (ed) *Handbook of Policing* (2nd edn). Abingdon: Taylor & Francis, pp 373–404.

Tilley, N. (2009) 'Sherman vs Sherman', *Criminology & Criminal Justice* 9(2): 135–44.

TNS BMRB (2016) *Reporting Victimisation in the Crime Survey for England and Wales*. London: TNS BMRB.

Tourish, D. (2013) *The Dark Side of Transformational Leadership: A Critical Perspective*. London: Routledge.

Tuffin, R. (2016) 'College of Policing', presentation at the Police Federation Conference 'Believe in Blue', 17–19 May, Bournemouth International Centre, Bournemouth.

Uhl-Bien, M. and Pillai, R. (2007) 'The Romance of Leadership and the Social Construction of Followership', in B. Shamir, R. Pillai, M.C. Bligh and M. Uhl-Bien (eds) *Follower-Centred Perspectives on Leadership: A Tribute to the Memory of James R. Meindl*. Connecticut, CT: Information Age Publishing, pp 187–210.

Uhl-Bien, M., Riggio, R.E., Lowe, K.B. and Carsten, M.K. (2014) 'Followership Theory: A Review and Research Agenda', *The Leadership Quarterly* 25(1): 83–104.

Van der Lippe, T., Graumans, A. and Sevenhuijsen, S. (2004) 'Gender Policies: The Position of Women in the Police Force in European Countries', *Journal of European Social Policy* 14(4): 391–405.

Van Dijk, A. and Crofts, N. (2017) 'Law Enforcement and Public Health as an Emerging Field', *Policing and Society* 27(3): 261–75.

Van Dijk, A., Hoogewoning, F. and Punch, M. (2015) *What Matters in Policing? Change, Values and Leadership in Turbulent Times*. Bristol: Policy Press.

Van Ewijk, A.R. (2011) 'Diversity within Police Forces in Europe: A Case for the Comprehensive View', *Policing* 6(1): 76–92.

Van Hulst, M. (2017) 'Backstage Storytelling and Leadership', *Policing: A Journal of Policy and Practice* 11(3): 356–68.

Van Maanen, J. (1974) 'Working the Street: A Development View of Police Behavior', in H. Jacob (ed) *The Potential for Reform of Crime Justice*. London: Sage, pp 88–130.

Van Maanen, J. (1975) 'Police Socialisation: A Longitudinal Examination of Job Attitudes in an Urban Police Department', *Administrative Science Quarterly* 20(2): 207–28.

Van Maanen, J. (1977) 'Experiencing Organisation: Notes on the Meaning of Careers and Socialisation', in J. Van Maanen (ed) *Organisational Careers: Some New Perspectives*. London: John Wiley & Sons, pp 15–45.

Van Maanen, J. (1978a) 'On Watching the Watchers', in P.K. Manning and J. Van Maanen (eds) *Policing: A View from the Street*. California, CA: Goodyear Publishing, pp 309–50.

Van Maanen, J. (1978b) 'Observations on the Making of Policemen', in P.K. Manning and J. Van Maanen (eds) *Policing: A View from the Street*. California, CA: Goodyear Publishing, pp 292–308.

Van Maanen, J. (1997) 'Making Rank: Becoming an American Police Sergeant', in R.G. Dunham and G.P. Alpert (eds) *Critical Issues in Policing: Contemporary Readings* (3rd edn). Illinois, IL: Waveland Press.

Van Rooy, D.L. and Viswesvaran, C. (2004) 'Emotional Intelligence: A Meta-Analytic Investigation of Predictive Validity and Nomological Net', *Journal of Vocational Behavior* 65(1): 71–95.

Villiers, P. (2003) 'Philosophy, Doctrine and Leadership: Some Core Beliefs', in R. Adlam and P. Villiers (eds) *Police Leadership in the Twenty-First Century*. Hampshire: Waterside Press, pp 15–33.

Villiers, P. and Adlam, R. (2003) 'Introduction', in R. Adlam and P. Villiers (eds) *Police Leadership in the Twenty-first Century*. Hampshire: Waterside Press, pp xi–14.

Violanti, J.M., Charles, L.E., McCanlies, E., Hartley, T.A., Baughman, M., Andrew, M.E., Fekedulegn, D., Ma, C.C., Mnatsakanova, A. and Burchfiel, C.M. (2017) 'Police Stressors and Health: A State-of-the-Art Review', *Policing: An International Journal of Police Strategies & Management* 40(4): 642–56.

Waddington, P.A.J. (1991) *The Strong Arm of the Law: Armed and Public Order Policing*. Oxford: Clarendon Press.

Waddington, P.A.J. (1999a) *Policing Citizens: Authority and Rights*. London: Routledge.

Waddington, P.A.J. (1999b) 'Police (Canteen) Sub-Culture: An Appreciation', *British Journal of Criminology* 39(2): 287–309.

Wall, D. (1994) 'The Ideology of Internal Recruitment: The Selection of Chief Constables and Changes within the Tripartite Arrangement', *British Journal of Criminology* 34(3): 322–38.

Wall, D. (1998) *The Chief Constables of England and Wales: The Socio-Legal History of a Criminal Justice Elite*. Aldershot: Ashgate.

Washbush, J.B. (2005) 'There Is No Such Thing as Leadership, Revisited', *Management Decision* 43(7/8): 1078–85.

Weick, K.E. (1995) *Sensemaking in Organizations*. Thousand Oaks, CA: Sage.

West, C. and Zimmerman, D.H. (1987) 'Doing Gender', *Gender & Society* 1(2): 125–51.

West, C., Fekedulegn, D., Andrew, M., Burchfiel, C.M., Harlow, S., Bingham, C.R., McCullagh, M., Park, S.K. and Violanti, J.M. (2017) 'On-Duty Nonfatal Injury that Lead to Work Absences Among Police Officers and Level of Perceived Stress', *Journal of Occupational and Environmental Medicine* 59(11): 1084–8.

Westmarland, L. (2002) *Gender and Policing: Sex, Power and Police Culture*. Abingdon: Routledge.

Westmarland, L. (2005) 'Police Ethics and Integrity: Breaking the Blue Code of Silence', *Policing and Society* 15(2): 145–65.

Westmarland, L. (2008) 'Police Cultures', in T. Newburn (ed) *Handbook of Policing* (2nd edn). Abingdon: Taylor & Francis, pp 253–80.

Westmarland, L. (2014) 'Ethics and Policing', in J. Brown (ed) *The Future of Policing*. London: Routledge, pp 463–92.

Westmarland, L. (2017) 'Putting their Bodies on the Line: Police Culture and Gendered Physicality', *Policing: A Journal of Policy and Practice* 11(3): 301–17.

Westmarland, L. and Rowe, M. (2018) 'Police Ethics and Integrity: Can a New Code Overturn the Blue Code?', *Policing and Society* 28(7): 854–70.

Whitchurch, C. (2008) 'Shifting Identities and Blurring Boundaries: The Emergence of Third Space Professionals in UK Higher Education', *Higher Education Quarterly* 62(4): 377–96.

White, D. (2006) 'A Conceptual Analysis of the Hidden Curriculum of Police Training in England and Wales', *Policing and Society* 16(4): 386–404.

White, D. and Heslop, R. (2012) 'Educating, Legitimising or Accessorising? Alternative Conceptions of Professional Training in UK Higher Education: A Comparative Study of Teacher, Nurse and Police Officer Educators', *Police Practice and Research* 13(4): 342–56.

Whitfield, K., Alison, L. and Crego, L. (2008) 'Command, Control and Support in Critical Incidents', in L. Alison and J. Crego (eds) *Policing Critical Incidents: Leadership and Critical Incident Management*. Devon: Willan Publishing, pp 81–94.

Willis, J.J. and Mastrofski, S.D. (2018) 'Improving Policing by Integrating Craft and Science: What Can Patrol Officers Teach Us about Good Police Work?', *Policing and Society* 28(1): 27–44.

Willis, J.J., Mastrofski, S.D. and Weisburd, D. (2007) 'Making Sense of COMPSTAT: A Theory-Based Analysis of Organizational Change in Three Police Departments', *Law & Society Review* 41(1): 147–88.

Wilson, J.Q. (1968) *Varieties of Police Behavior: The Management of Law and Order in Eight Communities*. Massachusetts, MA: Harvard University Press.

Winsor, T.P. (2011) *Independent Review of Police Officer and Staff Remuneration and Conditions: Part 1 Report* (The Winsor Review) London: The Stationery Office.

Winsor, T.P. (2012) *Independent Review of Police Officer and Staff Remuneration and Conditions: Part 2 Report* (The Winsor Review) London: The Stationery Office.

Wood, D. (2018) 'Embedding Learning and Assessment Within Police Practice: The Opportunities and Challenges Arising from the Introduction of the PEQF in England and Wales', *Policing: A Journal of Policy and Practice* (advance access).

Wood, D. and Bryant, R. (2016) 'Researching Professional Development', in M. Brunger, S. Tong and D. Martin (eds) *Introduction to Policing Research: Taking Lessons from Practice*. London: Routledge, pp 87–100.

Wood, M. and Ladkin, D. (2008) 'The Event's the Thing: Brief Encounters with the Leaderful Moment', in K.T. James and J. Collins (eds) *Leadership Perspectives: Knowledge into Action*. Hampshire: Palgrave Macmillan, pp 15–28.

Wood, D. and Tong, S. (2009) 'The Future of Initial Police Training: A University Perspective', *International Journal of Police Science & Management* 11(3): 294–305.

Wood, D., Cockcroft, T., Tong, S. and Bryant, R. (2017) 'The Importance of Context and Cognitive Agency in Developing Police Knowledge', *The Police Journal: Theory, Practice and Principles* 91(2): 173–87.

Wright, A., Alison, L. and Crego, J. (2008) 'The Current State of Police Leadership Research', in L. Alison and J. Crego (eds) *Policing Critical Incidents: Leadership and Critical Incident Management*. Devon: Willan, pp 54–80.

Wright-Mills, C. (1959) *The Sociological Imagination*. Oxford: Oxford University Press.

Young, M. (1991) *An Inside Job: Policing and Police Culture in Britain*. Oxford: Clarendon Press.

Young, M. (1993) *In the Sticks: Cultural Identity in a Rural Police Force*. Oxford: Clarendon Press.

Yukl, G. (1989) 'Managerial Leadership: A Review of Theory and Research', *Journal of Management* 15(2): 251–89.

Yukl, G. (2011) 'Contingency Theories of Effective Leadership' in A. Bryman, D. Collinson, K. Grint, B. Jackson and M. Uhl-Bien (eds) *The Sage Handbook of Leadership*. London: Sage, pp 286–98.

Yukl, G. (2013) *Leadership in Organizations* (8th edn). Essex: Pearson Education.

Zaccaro, S.J. and Horn, Z.N.J. (2003) 'Leadership Theory and Practice: Fostering an Effective Symbiosis', *The Leadership Quarterly* 14(6): 769–806.

Zaccaro, S.J., Kemp, C. and Bader, P. (2004) 'Leader Traits and Attributes', in J. Antonakis, A.T. Cianciolo and R.J. Sternberg (eds) *The Nature of Leadership*. Thousand Oaks, CA: Sage, pp 101–24.

Zaleznik, A. (1977) 'Managers and Leaders: Are They Different?', *Harvard Business Review* 82(1): 74–81.

Index